MAJAPAHIT

Herald van der Linde has travelled, lived and worked in Indonesia and Hong Kong since the 90s. Married to an Indonesian, he is passionate about the social and cultural history of Indonesia and is the author of *Jakarta: History of a Misunderstood City*. Fluent in Dutch, Indonesian and English, he enjoys delving into local Indonesian archives to unearth intriguing narratives from the archipelago's past.

Majapahit

Herald van der Linde

monsoon

monsoonbooks

First published in 2024
by Monsoon Books Ltd
www.monsoonbooks.co.uk

No.1 The Lodge, Burrough Court, Burrough on the Hill,
Melton Mowbray LE14 2QS, UK.

First edition.

ISBN (paperback): 9781915310286
ISBN (ebook): 9781915310293

Illustrations of medallions on title page and back cover by Sophie
Goldstone. Medallions were chiselled into Majapahit temple reliefs to
separate stories.

A Cataloguing-in-Publication data record is available from the British
Library.

Printed and bound in Great Britain by Clays Ltd, Elcograf S.p.A.
26 25 24   1 2 3

To David Pramoedja

Contents

Family Tree

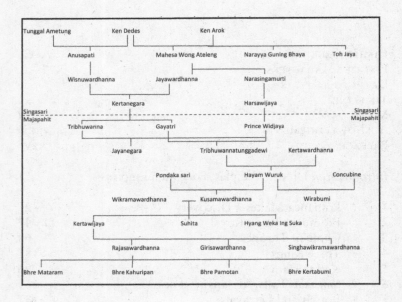

Simplified family tree of the Rajasa dynasty. For assumptions made, see endnotes in accompanying chapters. For detailed discussions on family relations, see Sidomulyo (2010), Noorduyn (1978).

Source: Sidomulyo (2010), Desawarnana, Pararaton, author's assumptions.

List of Characters

Airlangga	King who in 1042 divided his lands between his sons, setting up the division between Singasari and Kediri. Died in 1049.
Anepaken	Sundanese *patih* who confronts Gajah Mada prior to the 1357 Battle of Bubat
Antonio d'Abreu	Portuguese commander in the battle for Melaka in 1511
Antonio Pigafetta	Venetian explorer, last to mention Majapahit in 1522
Anusapati	Son of Ken Dedes and Tunggal Ametung who had Ken Arok assassinated
Aragani	Close friend and *patih* of Kertanegara
Ardaraja	Son of Jayakatwang, commander in Kertanegara's army
Arya Tadah	*Patih* before Gajah Mada was appointed *patih*
Bango Samparan	Gambling friend of Ken Arok
Bharada	Sage who divided the lands for Airlangga, but failed, opening the door for a reunion of the lands later under Ken Arok
Brahmaraja	Dharmadyaksa under King Widjaya
Brawijaya	Last king of Majapahit
Bujangga Manik	Sundanese prince/monk who wanders around Java around 1500
Candra Kirana	Princess in the Panji tales
Cayaraja of Bhaya	Rebels against Kertanegara in 1270
Citra Rashmi	Daughter of Sundanese King Wangi. She died in the Battle of Bubat in 1357
Damar Wulan	Imaginary character from a legend, husband of a queen
Dara Jingga & Dara Petak	Malay princess around 1290s

Domis, Hendrik	Resident for East Java in Surabaya, visits Majapahit ruins in 1831
Engelhard, Nicolaus	Dutch governor of north Java who in 1802 was one of the first Europeans to visit the Singasari ruins.
Enggon	*Patih* after Gajah Mada's death
Gajah Biru	"Blue elephant", ally of Sora
Gandring (Mpu)	Famed smith who made a keris that killed seven kings
Ganggadara	Prominent Majapahit priests in the 1470s
Gaoxing	Chinese admiral for Kublai Khan that led the invasion in 1295
Gayatri Rajapatni	Youngest daughter of Kertanegara, protector of Gajah Mada. She became the most powerful women in Majaphit and is a key character in the rise of the mandala empire.
Guning Bahaya	Grandson of Ken Arok, murdered by Toh Jaya
Ike Mese	Uyghur admiral for Kublai Khan that led the invasion in 1293
Janawidi	Head priest in the 1350s, presided over Gayatri's shraddu
Jayakatwang	King of Kediri. Attacked Singasari. Later defeated by Mongol invaders
Jayanegara	Son of King Widjaya, king of Majapahit
Jayawardhani	Mother of Kertanegara, granddaughter of Ken Arok and Ken Dedes and sister of Narasingamurti.
Jayeswari	Grand-old lady at the palace after her husband, King Kertawijaya, dies in 1451
Jorge Brito	Portuguese governor of Melaka after 1511
Juru Demung	Ally of Sora
Kebo Anabrang	Admiral that leads the expedition to Melayu/Sumatra

Kebo Hijo	"Green Buffalo", a close friend and chamberlain of Kertanegara
Kebo Marcuet	Balinese landlord in eastern Java in the Damar Wulan legend
Kebo Mundarang	General of the Kediri troops in the attack on Singasari in 1292
Kebo Tengah	Childhood friend and trusted advisor of Kertanegara
Kembar	Member of the royal family in the days of Hayam Wuruk. Opponent of Gajah Mada. His name means "twin"
Ken Arok	Robber and thief, reincarnated in 1182. He established the Rajasa dynasty in 1222.
Ken Dedes	An incredibly beautiful woman, wife of Ken Arok
Kertanegara	King of Singasari from 1254-1292. Unified the archipelago against Kublai Khan's threats
Kertawijaya	Half-brother of Suhita and ruled briefly after her death in 1447
Kublai Khan	Lived from 1215-1294. Head of the Mongol Yuan dysnasty that ruled China
Kusumawardhani	Daughter of Hayam Wuruk and Paduka Sori
Lawe	Friend of Prince Widjaya and his trusted advisor. Rebelled against Widjaya's son later
Lembu Ampal	Guard tasked by Toh Jaya to kill Wisnuwardhanna, but switches support and murders Toh Jaya instead
Linggapati	Rebels against Wisnuwhardanna with fatal consequences for him and his family
Loghawe	Brahmin, guardian and teacher of Ken Arok
Ma Huen	Translator in Zheng He's fleet who wandered in Majapahit in 1413

Mahapati	Rising power player in days of Jayanegara
Mahisa Rangkah	Rebels against Kertanegara a few years after 1270
Mahisa Wong Ateleng	Son of Ken Arok
Manguri	*Patih* after Gajah Mada and Enggon
Minak Jinggo	Warrior in the Damar Wulan legend. Name of temple in Majapahit
Nambi	Friend of Prince Widjaya and his trusted advisor
Narasingamurti	Deputy king in Singasari, son of Mahisa Wong Ateleng
Narendra	Father of Prapanca, a dharmadyaksa
Narendra Duhita	Third daughter of Kertanegara, caputed during the fall of Singasari and held captive in Kediri
Paduka Sori	Wife of Hayam Wuruk, daughter of his uncle Wengker
Pakararas	Imaginary character, friends and guide of Ma Huen
Panji	Prince looking for his beloved Candra Kirana in the Panji tales
Patah	Prince, founder of Demak
Patipati (son)	Life-long friend of Kertanengara and takes over his father's role as leading Shivaist priest
Patipati (the father)	Leading Shivaist priest in 1250s. Supporter of tantric Buddhism that Kertanegara adopted later
Prajnaparamita	Second daughter of Kertanegara, captured during the fall of Singasari and held capitive in Kediri
Pranaraja	*Patih* of Anusapati and Toh Jaya
Prince Elephant	"Raden Gajah", noble man who kills Wirabumi in 1406, marking the end of the Paregreg civil war

Prince Widjaya	Raden Widjaya or Kertarajasa Jayawardhana. Son of Narasingamurti, founder of Majapahit
Purwa (mpu)	Father of Ken Dedes
Raffles, Thomas Stanford	Lieutenant-Governor of the Dutch East Indies (1811-1816) and visitor to the Singasari and Majapahit ruins in 1815
Raganatha	*Patih* of Kertanegara
Ranangsa	Abbot of Darbaru monastery who rveals the history of kings to Prapanca
Ratna Sutawan	Assumed named by Kertanegara's youngest daughter Gayatri while in disguise in Kediri after the fall of Singasari
Santamurti	Religuous leader under Kertanegara. He became a hermit and crowned Widjaya to king
Shi-bi	Mongol admiral for Kublai Khan that led the invasion in 1294
Sodrakara	Servant of Gayatri who saves the princess in the attack of Singasari in 1292
Sora	Friend of Prince Widjaya and his trusted advisor
Tanakung	Late-Majapahit author of the "Siwartrikalpa"
Tantular	Author of the Sutasoma. Probably contemporary of Prapanca
Tapa Wangkeng	Famed sage who approved the reincarnation of Ken Arok
Toh Jaya	Son of Ken Arok
Tranggana	Ruler of Demak when it finished Majapahit in 1527
Tribhuwana	Oldest daughter of Kertanegara, a bit of a comedian. Escapes after the fall of Singasari. Married prince Widjaya and mother of Jayanegara

Tribhuwanatunggadewi	Daughter of Gayatri, mother of Hayam Wuruk. Queen after Jayanegara
Tunggul Ametung	Ruler of Tumapel, vassal of Kediri King Kertajaya
Wangi or Prabhu Wangi	"King Wangi", king of Pajajaran (Sunda) who was to wed his daughter to Hayam Wuruk in 1357
Wardenaar, Johannes	Surveyor who is tasked by Raffles to map Majapahit in 1815
Wengker	Region west of Majapahit. Uncle of Hayam Wuruk
Wikramawardhana	Husband of Kusumawardhani, son-in-law of Hayam Wuruk
Winotan	Minister of Jayakatwang in 1292
Wirabumi	Son of Hayam Wuruk by a concubine
Wiraraja	Governor of Madura adept in political games
Wisnuwardhanna	King in Singasari, son of Anusapari, father of King Kertanegara
Zhao Rugua	Habourmaster in Quanzhou, China, a major port
Zheng He	Ming dynasty Chinese admiral in 1413 who travelled to Java

Dates

BCE (Before Common Era) and CE (Common Era) are used in place of BC (Before Christ) and AD (*Anno Domini*).

Timeline

778	Start construction Borobudur in central Java
928	Eruption of Merapi in central Java. Population moves to east Java
990	Java attacks Srivijaya (in Sumatra)
1016	Srivijaya forces assassinates Javanese King Dharmawangsa. His son Airlangga escapes
1042	King Airlangga splits his kingdom into two
1049	Death of Airlangga
1122	Construction of Angkor Wat starts
1182	Reincarnation of Ken Arok
1214	Genghis Khan capures Peking
1222	Battle of Ganter. Ken Arok king in Tumapel (Singasari). Beginning of Rajasa dynasty
1227	Assassination of Ken Arok by Anusapati's servant, Balil.
1227	Genghis Khan dies
1236	Cordoba taken from the Moors
1248	Birth Kertanegara (assumed)
1250	Murder of Toh Jaya, Wisnuwhardanna becomes king. Narasingamurti as co-ruler
1250	Wisnuwhardanna fortifies Canggu, a trading centre
1254	Young Kertanegara appointed as king. Tumapel renamed as Singasari
1255	Jayakatwang mentioned as ruler of Wurawan
1257	Samala volcanic eruption in Lombok
1260	Kublai Khan proclaimed emperor in China
1268	Death of King Wisnuwhardanna.
1269	Death of Narasingamurti. Kertanegara becomes sole ruler of Singasari
1269	Sarwadharma ceremony, religious institutions are tax-exempt.
1270	Rebellion against kertanegara by Cayaraja of Bhaya and, later, Masiha Rangkah
1271	Marco Polo departs from Venice to China
1274	Kublai Khan attacks Champa in south Vietnam

1602	Dutch East Indies Company ("VOC") founded in Amsterdam
1613	Pararaton copied and finished in Bali
1619	Dutch conquest of Jayakarta (Jakatra), renamed Batavia.
1802	Engelhard visits Singasari and has some of its statues moved to his residence in Semarang
1807	Rama I in Thailand builds Wat Suthat with Majapahit Panji tales (Inao) on a murial
1811	British invade Java and take conrol
1815	Raffles visits Singasari (on Jun 8) and Majapahit ruins (in May that year)
1815	Wardenaar presents a map of Majapahit to Raffles.
1816	British leave Java and Netherlands ruled what is now called Dutch East-Indies.
1816	Publication of "History of Java" by Raffles
1818	Discovery Prajnaparamita statue in Singasari
1831	Hendrik Domis, resident for East Java in Surabaya, visits Majapahit ruins
1861	Alfred Wallace visits Majapahit
1883	Krakatao volcano in the Sunda Straits erupts
1894	Dutch attack Balinese palace in Lombok. Discovery of Prapanca's *Desawarnana* (*Negarakertagama*)
1914	Discovery Candi Tikus under a rat-infested hill
1940	Germany invades The Netherlands in World War II.
1941	Stutterheim finishes book on Majapahit's palace, but it is not published. He passes away a year later
1945	End of World War II. Indonesia declares independence
1948	Stutterheim's book is published
1970	The Netherlands returns Prapanca's *Desawarnana* (*Negarakertagama*) to Indonesia (actual shipment in 1972)
1978	Dutch government returned the Prajanaparamita statue to Indonesia
2008	Wardenaar's map rediscovered in the archives of the Britsh Museum
2023	Dutch government returned multiple Singasari statues to Indonesia

Maps

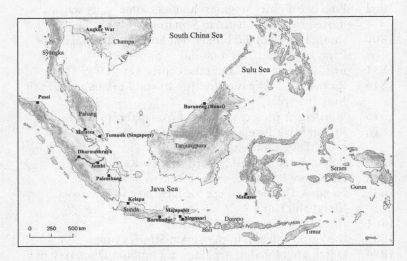

ABOVE Southeast Asia in the 14th century. [Illustration: HvdL]
BELOW Java in the 14th century. [Illustration: HvdL]

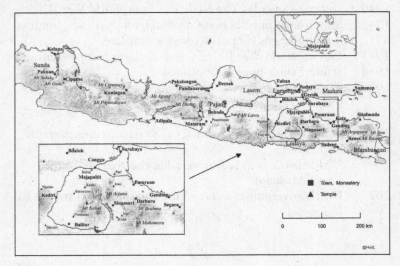

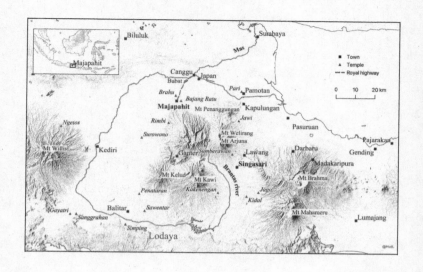

ABOVE
Two valleys
(Majapahit and
surroundings).
[Illustration: HvdL]

RIGHT
Majapahit, Bubat
and Canggu.
[Illustration: HvdL]

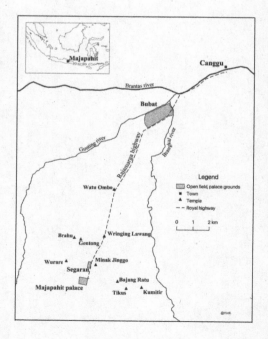

Acknowledgements

'Writing is the art of applying the arse to the seat.'

It is this comment, made after a Wednesday morning coffee by my colleague and friend Jon Marsh, that sparked the writing of this book.

The quote is actually not Jon's, but from Dorothy Parker, a New York poet and bon vivant, probably made in the 1920s or 1930s. But it was the best advice I got; if you want to write a book, sit down and start typing. For long I had been thinking about delving deeper into the history of Majapahit. After Jon's prodding, I started writing one Saturday morning.

However, it would be four years before the book was ready, during which time I completed another book on the history of Jakarta (a much-misunderstood city). The first two years were spent mostly on background reading and study. My father and my uncle Dinand in the Netherlands helped me to get quite a number of Dutch books to Asia, and when I was in Europe they joined me on trips to museums, libraries and small and sometimes obscure bookstores in Amsterdam and Leiden to find old Dutch papers or reports on Majapahit. Back in Hong Kong, my weekends were filled reading old texts (some in outdated Dutch), papers and books, and I happily lost myself in all manner of old maps.

During these first years of research, I came across Dr Lydia Kieven in Cologne, Germany, who had written extensively about art in East Java. She had all sorts of suggestions for additional reading material and put me in touch with Dr Adrian Vickers and Dr Jarrah Sastrawan in Sydney, two prominent Indonesian scholars who were always extremely helpful in pointing me in the right direction or coming up with suggestions and ideas. They also helped me access maps and texts. I am very grateful to them all.

After all the reading and research, it was time to embark on investigative trips to the land of Majapahit in East Java. There were three such trips in total and I walked battlefields, climbed mountains, visited old graves and temples, or just wandered around remnants of some old, decrepit building.

Accompanying me on these trips was local historian Pak Dwi Cahyono in Malang, Java. He proved to be an incredible resource on Majapahit and never tired of discussing all sorts of things I had come across in my research. This is also when I met Pak Hadi Sidomulyo, an equally incredible font of knowledge. No wonder, for while I had only been involved in it for a few years, he had been immersed in all things Majapahit since the 1970s.

I was never alone on these trips and was pleased to have friends and family join me on an endless string of visits to temples and ruins or to simply wander through open fields – Hidayah, Una, Laurence, David, Zahra, Via, Vandi, Vina, Joes, Harald, Ucu, Dini, my uncle Dinand and my wife, Teni. Regular visits to Blitar and Malang were made so much more pleasant by the attentive staff of Ibu Hartini at Sri Lestari Tugu Blitar and Pak Bagus's staff at the Tugu Malang hotel.

After the trips and the reading, it was time to start writing the story. That was mostly done in the evenings after work, and during weekends and on holidays. This took me almost two years and I am very grateful to a few people who gave me a helping hand. Jon Marsh – who years earlier had told me to apply my arse to my seat – was of great help in crafting the storyline and editing my work. We spent quite a few coffees debating my texts.

By the time I was sufficiently satisfied with a few chapters and thought they were ready for a fresh set of eyes, I emailed them to Dr Lesley Pullen in London, an art historian specializing in Singasari statues. She read them with a critical eye and I thoroughly enjoyed our Zoom sessions where she picked apart whole chapters and came up with hundreds of critical observations or showed me inconsistencies in the text. The discussions were both enlightening and good fun. I am very, very grateful for the hours of proofreading she put in.

My uncle Dinand, geographer by training, also checked the maps I created and pointed out more than a few geographical matters that I had overseen or got wrong. He also proofread the whole text, twice. I am very grateful to him for all those hours. And lastly, I had Mariska Adamson, James Brewis and Roland Haas read the text for style, flow and typos.

At the end of all the work, when the manuscript was in its final stages, I received great help from fellow author Philip Bowring, who introduced me to a few publishers. Pak Judo and Pak Yanuar at Periplus in Indonesia did the same. It was wonderful to get so much support from so many people.

But for all the other weekends and late evenings that I spent digesting books and papers or fixating on old maps, I thank my wife Teni for being so incredibly patient with me.

Preface

As diplomatic showdowns go, this summit was without parallel. In a grand pavilion in the magnificent grounds of the royal palace of Singasari in eastern Java, an envoy from Kublai Khan, probably the most powerful man in the world, sat down to convey a blunt message to King Kertanegara, without doubt the most powerful ruler in Southeast Asia. The year was 1290, the mood was tense, and the chances of everything going horribly wrong were increasing by the minute.

Much was at stake. Kublai Khan ruled a vast empire that had spread as far as the eastern fringes of Europe. King Kertanegara had united a sprawling archipelago – known today as Indonesia – for the first time in history and his power and influence was growing across Southeast Asia. Something had to give.

Meng Qi, the diplomat dispatched from the court of Kublai Khan in China, had been given clear instructions. Singasari was to become a vassal state and King Kertanegara must agree to pay annual tribute and send a member of his royal family to live in the court of the Great Khan at his capital in Dadu (now Beijing).

The king flew into a rage. He wasn't about to be lectured to by some lowly messenger and he had no intention of taking orders from Kublai Khan. Kertanegara feared nothing and no one. After all, he was a devotee of the dark art of magic and in his mind possessed supernatural powers. The king raised his voice for all to hear – Kublai Khan needed to be sent a strong message. On his signal, a guard took out a knife and cut off the unfortunate envoy's nose.

After the mutilated diplomat arrived back in China, an incensed Kublai Khan ordered a huge fleet to be built so his army could invade Java. Two years later the Mongols stepped once again onto Javanese soil, but this expedition also ended in total disaster. They found that King Kertanegara had been assassinated and the city of Singasari had been burned to the ground. The Mongol invaders soon became embroiled in a war with Kertanegara's usurper, which also ended badly. The retreat from Java was hasty and humiliating in equal measure.

It was in these tumultuous years that a new power centre, the city of Majapahit in eastern Java, emerged from the ruins of Singasari, ruled by Prince Widjaya, the nephew of King Kertanegara. At its peak, the Majapahit empire controlled a huge amount of territory, from present-day southern Thailand to Singapore, Java, Sumatra, Borneo, Bali, Lombok and beyond.

The aim of this book is to introduce the English-speaking world to Majapahit, the most powerful empire in Asia that most people have never heard of. While Angkor Wat, the centre of the Khmer empire that existed at the same time, has been visited by millions of tourists, Majapahit is known to few outside those familiar with Javanese history.

It is a story of ancient manuscripts saved from a burning royal palace, of wildly eccentric kings with equally eccentric notions about sex, of bloody royal family feuds, and of a tipsy court scribe who had the good sense to write down everything he saw.

Majapahit was a remarkably sophisticated society whose wealth and power were built on a combination of political cunning, huge rice harvests, and a navy so powerful that even the Portuguese, the European mariners extraordinaire, were impressed. The people of Majapahit liked to party, too, with palm wine the drink of choice.

Majapahit was a place of great artistic achievement, religious diversity and social tolerance. Kings worshipped Hindu and Buddhist divinities, and senior members of the priesthood were esteemed figures who held powerful positions at court. As did women. For context, in Europe, this was a time of religious crusades against Islam in the Middle East and constant strife between Catholics and Protestants.

Unlike Angkor Wat, little physical evidence of Majapahit remains and historical sources are both limited and of doubtful accuracy. I have delved deep into the few available primary sources as well as the work of Dutch, British and Indonesian academics and historians. Still, gaps remain, and events, dates and names vary, so I have had to make assumptions at various points in the narrative, which on balance I think are fair reflections of what was happening at the time.

With around 278 million people, Indonesia has the world's fourth largest population and is again becoming an economic powerhouse, just as it was in the days of the Majapahit kings and queens, and also an important player on the diplomatic stage. The old empire eventually worked out how to get along with the powerbrokers in China, so little has changed there, too.

In more recent history, Indonesian politicians have not

missed the opportunity to use the Majapahit legacy as a rallying cry for unity among Indonesia's myriad ethnicities, languages and geographies. The epic stories and legends have also been regularly retold in historical romances, martial arts epics, films, radio drama and even cartoons. I hope this book helps readers connect the dots between this great nation's glorious past, its tantalising present and a future packed with so much potential.

Two hundred years after the empire rose to power, Majapahit fell into rapid decline. Its cities were abandoned, and its palaces and temples were reclaimed by the jungle. That is until, almost three centuries later, a intrepid Englishman mounted an expedition into eastern Java and came face to face with the overgrown ruins of a long-lost treasure.

And that's where our story begins …

Introduction

Hidden Temples, Forgotten Empires

June 8, 1815. Lawang, 75 kilometres south of Surabaya,
northeastern Java.

At six o'clock on a cool, hazy morning, a dozen horsemen
assembled in front of a small fort, keen to avoid the sweltering
heat that would descend after the mist burned off. Aside from
the whinnying of the horses, all was quiet. The men awaited the
troop's leader: an Englishman in his mid-thirties with a confident
stride, a pointed nose, protruding lips and wavy hair. A few
moments later he emerged, said his goodbyes to his hosts – the
local regent and his wife – and stepped into the waiting carriage.
The company started to move, heading due south out of Lawang.

Even at that early hour, the small village of Lawang was
bustling with life. The horsemen passed barefoot labourers
accompanied by a pair of buffalos on their way to the paddy fields.
They overtook traders riding bullock carts filled with vegetables,
and boys carrying stacks of dry firewood on their heads. A couple
of stray dogs scavenged for scraps as children played on the
dusty street. As soon as the children spotted the horsemen, they
squealed with excitement and chased after them to beg for coins.

An old lady, her chest bare, her back bent from working the fields, emerged from a bamboo hut to see what all the fuss was about. As the strangers advanced from the village to the lush green paddy fields, a huddle of farmers commented on the unfamiliar goings-on while puffing on their corn husk cigarettes. You didn't see this sort of thing in Lawang every day.

The troop leader was none other than Thomas Stamford Raffles, Lieutenant-Governor of the Dutch East Indies. The young Englishman with the distinctive face was on a three-month tour across the verdant and alluring island of Java. He was accompanied by his private secretary, Mr Assey; his aides-de-camp, lieutenants Travers, Garnham, Watson, Dalgairns and Metvhen, all young officers in their twenties; two Dutch translators fluent in Javanese; a handful of English soldiers and a few Javanese servants.

The men shared a rising sense of anticipation, excitement even. If Raffles was right, more than halfway through a three-month expedition to explore the island, they would soon find evidence of the existence of a long-lost empire. Raffles had already made one remarkable discovery the previous year. After hacking through the jungles of central Java, Raffles became the first Englishman to set eyes on the vast Borobudur temple complex, one of the greatest Buddhist monuments in the world, which was constructed between about 778 CE and 850 CE and had been buried under volcanic ash since about 1000 CE. Now he was on the cusp of another great discovery – the palace of the lost Majapahit empire[1] that rose in the thirteenth century and thrived at the same time as the Khmer civilisation at Angkor in what is now Cambodia.

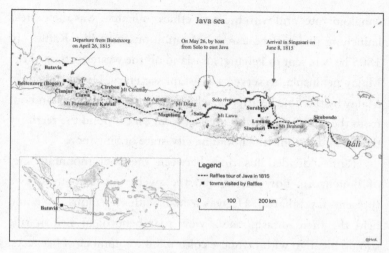

Raffles' journey across Java in 1815. [Illustration: HvdL]

Raffles had done his research. Java was studded with ancient temples and shrines and in 1812 he had commissioned a survey. The work was led by Captain Colin Mackenzie, a Scottish army officer in the British East India Company who was steeped in the study of antiquities and later became the first surveyor general of India. Based on conversations with a Dutch official he was friendly with, Raffles was convinced there was plenty of evidence, albeit rather sketchy, to suggest that another big find was within his grasp.

Raffles had come a long way in a very short time. Born on July 6, 1781, off the coast of Jamaica in the West Indies on board a ship commanded by his father, he had become a clerk in the office of the East India Company in London at the age of 14. The East India Company, perhaps the world's first multinational conglomerate, and with business ethics to match, was the perfect launching pad for the careers of ambitious men like Raffles. In 1805 he was sent to Penang, an island off the western coast of the Malay peninsula, to serve as assistant secretary. He was fluent in Malay by the time he arrived, which instantly made him stand out from the colonial crowd. Later, he went on to found the territory that would become the booming city-state of Singapore.

Raffles divided his time between the cool mountain city of Buitenzorg, now Bogor, and the sweltering heat of Batavia (present-day Jakarta). He was a man with enormous drive and held the then unfashionable view that benevolent British rule should blend in with Javanese culture. Like a number of his peers, he was a botanist and collected flora and fauna wherever he went. He also had an autocratic streak and once threw a man in jail for a month after he had the temerity to overtake his carriage, a privilege previously reserved for the highest-ranking Dutch official, the governor-general.

Then, suddenly, Raffles' world was in turmoil. His wife, Olivia, died in November 1814 at the age of forty-three. Three months later, news reached Raffles that his powerful friend and mentor Lord Minto had passed away in India. A grieving Raffles threw himself into his work and decided to tour Java.

Ironically, it was a bout of ill-health that had given him, years earlier, his chance to shine at such a young age. Having fallen sick in Penang, he was sent down the coast to Malacca to recover just at the time when the East India Company had to make a big decision: which was the better location in the region to throw its considerable resources behind, Penang or Malacca? Both were strategically placed to control the shipping lanes that linked India to China, the two markets where the East India Company generated most of its profits (think tea and opium). The consensus was titling towards Penang until Raffles, the man on the ground, prepared a report arguing that Malacca, on the mainland, would make the superior port.

The report came to the attention of Lord Minto, the governor-general of India. He summoned Raffles to Calcutta and was so impressed that he promoted him to an influential position: agent to the governor-general of the Malay States. Ever the opportunist, Raffles convinced Lord Minto that this would be a good time for the East India Company to annex Java, which was then in French hands. At the time, Britain and France were fighting the Napoleonic wars. The French had occupied Holland, so the Dutch colonies, including the Dutch East Indies, had fallen under the control of Napoleon. Raffles was quick to spot the opportunity to take control of Batavia[2], the main city on Java, along with the rest of the island.

In August 1811, a British fleet of some 100 ships with an expeditionary force of about 12,000 men arrived off Batavia. Following a short engagement, the poorly trained Dutch and French forces proved no match for the British. Java was in new hands. A few weeks after the invasion, Lord Minto appointed Raffles Lieutenant-Governor of Java. At the age of thirty he found himself in charge of a huge island populated by approximately six million people.

***

As the party advanced due south from Lawang, five majestic volcanoes – Kawi and Arjuna to the west, Bromo, Semeru and an unnamed peak in the east – slowly revealed themselves in the distance. Not long after they had left the village, the men entered a forest of teak and banyan trees, offering shelter from the sun that was starting to burn through the mist.

Raffles and his party had been on the road for weeks. Their journey had started on April 26, 1815, from his large palace in the cool mountain town of Buitenzorg on a fine day with 'the mountains perfectly clear and defined'.[3] They had initially travelled due east, following the Great Post Road, one of the main highways in Java built by the administration of the Dutch East Indies to connect the west and east coasts of the island. Here, the volcanoes huddled close together and the horses were soon struggling to pull the carriages up the mountains, so buffalos had to be brought in. When they finally made it to the town of Cianjur, Raffles and his weary men were welcomed by a troupe of performing musicians and a feast at the residence of the local government official where 'a beautiful board was spread in the European style and a plentiful supply of excellent wine crowned the banquet'.[4]

As the journey continued, they entered central Java, where the volcanoes were more dispersed, separated by wide river valleys and travel by horse and coach was easier. But the jungle was dense and the roads narrow, and at one point a tiger raced from the undergrowth and attacked one of the soldiers, tearing him to pieces before his companions could intervene.

Life on the road did have its more pleasant moments though.

They stopped in a town called Solo where they met the Javanese sultan, who had prepared a lavish banquet accompanied by a dance performed by young girls. Then came the highlight of the evening: a fight to the death between a buffalo and two tigers in a field in front of the king's palace, where a large, excited crowd gathered. The English soldiers probably missed the joke: the buffalo, slow but unbreakable, represented Java, while the savage tigers the English and Dutch. The buffalo always won.

From Solo, Raffles and his men pushed on into eastern Java towards the broad river valleys that accompany the Solo and Brantas rivers. On May 26, six weeks after their departure from Buitenzorg, the men boarded a boat on the Solo river that took them on a six-day voyage downstream to a village near the Java Sea on the north coast. From there they took carriages south and, like true British patriots, rode onwards to the major city of Surabaya in time to celebrate King George IV's birthday on June 4. They stayed for a few days, stocked up on provisions and continued their journey to the village of Lawang.

Lawang – which means door or gateway in Javanese – was aptly named. It gave access to an elevated valley near a chain of volcanoes that, counter to the usual pattern across Java, ran from north to south. The most northern was the smallest, the perfectly cone-shaped Penanggungan, surrounded by four smaller hills. Further south lay the taller and imposing Arjuna and Kawi mountains. The volcanoes separated two fertile valleys brimming with deep green rice paddies, fields of sugar cane, and dense teak forests.

The valley Raffles and his men were about to enter that day was the cradle of the mighty River Brantas, whose wide and shallow waterway and constant flow made it easy to navigate by boat. For centuries it was the main artery for local traders, or armies, moving around eastern Java. It started as small streams on the eastern slopes of the volcanoes near Lawang before converging as one and weaving its way around the mountains, first south, later north, to deposit its sediment in the Java Sea on the northern shore of the island. The river was wide enough for sea-faring ships to sail upstream for a considerable distance if the prevailing winds were right.

It is in the folds of this meandering river that the mighty Majapahit empire first rose in the thirteenth century in three towns: one west of the mountains, called Kediri, and one east, Tumapel – later renamed Singasari. After Singasari was destroyed during a civil war in 1292, a new capital was founded at Majapahit. Singasari was the destination of Raffles and his men that morning of June 8, 1815.

Singasari

After less than an hour's ride, Raffles and his company approached the village. This was his best guess in terms of where to start looking, based on what a Dutch official had told him about an earlier discovery. The men halted at the edge of a forest and dismounted. They tethered the horses to trees and instructed two men to stay behind and guard them while the rest took out their machetes and entered the dense jungle, hacking and slashing their way through the thick undergrowth of the teak forest. All of a sudden, one of the machetes came into contact with something hard. It was the moment they had all been waiting for – they had found the overgrown ruins of a temple, square at the base, tall and slender and about 10 metres high.

A short flight of steps led up to a narrow doorway in the tower-like temple, and the entrance was adorned with an enormous gorgon head with protruding eyes and sharp curved fangs. One of its eyes lacked detail, as if the stonemason had left his work unfinished. Two men climbed the steps and entered the dark void, the temple's cella. This inner sanctum was small, narrow and much cooler than the air outside. It also stank of bat shit.

When Raffles entered the temple it took some time for his eyes to adjust to the darkness. But slowly, a statue, lying flat on the earth, became apparent. It was, he reckoned, evidence of previous visitors who had disturbed the site.[5] After a few minutes he retraced his steps and walked around the outside of the temple. He ordered his men to make sketches and drawings of his discovery, in particular the head of the monster, and the relief carvings at the top of the tower. They then pushed deeper into the teak forest.

They soon stumbled across a number of Hindu statues, many of exquisite quality, 'more highly executed than seen previously on the island'.[6] One was of a seated bull, Nandi, with one of its horns broken off. Another was a large Brahma statue with four heads, face flat on the ground. A few minutes later they discovered a massive elephant-god Ganesha statue on a pedestal made of skulls, complete with skull earrings. Nearby was another of a chariot with a sun symbol, and depictions of horses galloping at full speed, tails extended.

Most of what they encountered that morning were overgrown ruins, piles of bricks and a few abandoned wells. Tree roots reached through crevices and cracks in the ramparts of what, centuries ago, was a palace. Ruins of buildings and temples appeared at irregular intervals across the forest floor. A bigger picture began to emerge. Taken as a whole, the crumbling walls and multitude of statues suggested that this was the remains of the royal residence of Singasari, abode of the famed King Kertanegara, assassinated inside these walls in 1292. It was exactly what Raffles had hoped to discover.

A few hours later, as exhaustion set in and the ecstasy that accompanied the discoveries started to fade, Raffles gave the signal to return to the main road. They mounted their horses and rode due south for a few kilometres to the local mayor's residence in the town of Malang. The sweat-drenched men watered the horses before enjoying the luxury of a much-needed bath. Raffles collected the drawings the men had made and stored them in one of his travel trunks.

In the late afternoon they visited a nearby fort, Kota Bedah[7], which revealed another faint trace of the Majapahit empire. Originally made of brick, little of its foundations remained. They rode around the fort and estimated it had a circumference of a little less than two miles, before making their way back to the residence of the local governor for a lavish dinner celebration washed down with copious amounts of sherry.

***

The next morning, Raffles visited two other temples, or *candi,* that he knew were located just outside Malang – Candi Kidal and Candi Jago. While he and his officers finished a hearty breakfast – a buffet of rice porridge with meat and vegetables, eggs, baked breads, sausages and local fruits – servants led the horses out of the stables and prepared the carriages. The troop then set off on the seven-mile ride to Candi Kidal. Unlike the long-lost temple in Singasari, this temple was regularly frequented by pilgrims, monks and local worshippers and was still intact and undamaged. Located in the skirts of a forest, the shrine was tall and slender with a spire-like roof and, as if to scare visitors off, adorned with an array of monsters, most impressively a *kala*, a fierce head with big, protruding eyes.

These temples were built to honour the Singasari kings who, like those who ruled in Angkor at that time, were considered '*devaraja*', god-kings. Candi Kidal was one of many monuments erected to proclaim the immortal, god-like nature of the kings. According to the local guardian of the temple, the king commemorated was a certain Anusapati. Upon his death, his ashes were placed in the foundation shaft and monks and pilgrims came from afar to worship. Raffles again ordered the men to take measurements and make sketches. After a short rest, they headed for Candi Jago.

To their surprise, Kidal and Jago, constructed only a few decades apart, could not be more different. Candi Kidal was slender and tall, while Jago was broad-based, a sort of truncated pyramid, resting on a wedge-shaped hill. The top of the candi was long gone and all that remained was a single stone doorway and parts of the surrounding walls. The reliefs at Jago were also very different. At Kidal they were raised, offering rounded three-dimensional forms but those at Jago were flat, two-dimensional, shallow and angular. One depicted a palm tree with lambs on either side, another a boar, presumably being led to sacrifice. There were depictions of wars, temples, hermitages in lush settings, and people praying or carrying fruit.

Nearby, one of the men discovered a Hindu statue with its head missing, and a farmer told them it had been carried off to Malang by a Dutchman some years earlier.

The son of the local regent suggested to Raffles that he should mentally reconstruct the temples in their original setting. They appeared black, grey or red but centuries ago they would have been full of colour – whites, yellows, reds and blues – with doors of carved wood; inside, oil lamps were lit during ceremonies with the statues bedecked in jewels[8]. In their prime, these temples were absolutely spectacular.

Raffles was particularly impressed by the incredibly detailed reliefs. These temples might be much smaller than at Borobudur in central Java, but they were just as exquisite and rich in detail. The reliefs showed how people dressed, their hairstyles, what they ate, how they lived and how they went to war – evidently feathers were popular headgear back then. Raffles' men completed their sketches and measurements before making their return to Malang, in time for another sumptuous dinner with local officials.

The resident of Malang had invited a few of his members of staff to dinner. One carried a gift for Raffles, a small square box with a golden lingam[9], discovered only a few weeks earlier by a local farmer while digging for stones to build a cooking stove. It, too, was intricately carved, showing great craftsmanship. The statue, just like the relief chiselled in stone that Raffles had seen earlier in the day, was perhaps Indian in origin but certainly Javanese in style. Raffles asked if they knew the Dutchman who had carried off the head of one of the statues at Jago, and the name Engelhard, the former Dutch governor of the Javanese north coast, was mentioned.[10]

Raffles knew this man very well.

Engelhard

Nicolaus Engelhard was a hard-nosed Dutchman, full of life, bustle and curiosity but short on patience and ethics. If his letters to Batavia are anything to go by, his basic Dutch grammar skills[11] were limited. He engineered a career, partially through marriage and with the help of his uncle, as a high official in the Dutch East Indies. At one point in the early 1800s he was even in the running for governor-general, the head of the Dutch government of the archipelago, but he had to settle for the powerful position of governor of Java's north coast, based in Semarang. During his assignment, he acquired an immense fortune. But his career came to an abrupt end when, in 1808, Herman Daendels, the new Dutch governor appointed by Napoleon, fired Engelhard for his pro-British sentiment.

Unusually for a Dutchman at the time – most arrived in Java with the single objective of making stupendous amounts of money in the spice trade – Engelhard had an interest in antiquities, curiosities, stones and old manuscripts.[12] From his letters to officials in Batavia, we know that he frequently displayed his collection of statues in the garden of his villa – named 'De Vrijheid' ('Freedom') – in Semarang to impress visitors.[13] He was no stranger to Raffles. Both were Freemasons and had joined a British and Dutch venture to buy plots of land in western Java. To Raffles, with only fifteen hundred English men at his disposal, mostly former Bengal army officers with few administration skills, Dutchmen such as Engelhard, with their intimate knowledge of Java and personal relationships with Dutch administrators across the island, were a vital resource.

In 1802, over a decade before Raffles arrived in Singasari, Engelhard was the first European to hack his way through the dense forest to see what was left of Candi Singasari.[14] He wasn't sure what he had found. When he asked local farmers who had built these temples in the jungle nobody knew for certain. His men's heavy-handed and clumsy treatment was the reason why many of the sculptures that Raffles came across were damaged.

Engelhard was also told that locals took bricks from these temples for religious purposes or simply to build houses. He decided that some of the best statues were better off in his garden in Semarang. In his letters written when he was governor, he tried to reassure others that his motivations were entirely noble. He had, so he suggested, to protect the statues as 'the locals might destroy them', a doubtful claim especially when he later informed the British that the previous government, of which he was the head of, had gifted them to him.[15]

During their visits, neither Engelhard nor Raffles stumbled over the exquisitely carved Prajnaparamita statue which local tradition links to the first queen of Singasari. Regarded as one of the most precious statues ever carved in Indonesia, if not the whole of Asia, it lay in the woods, overgrown with weeds and moss until it was discovered years later by the assistant resident of Malang.[16] It was later shipped to the Netherlands and was finally returned to Indonesia in 1978.

Pride of Java

In contrast to the days spent in Singasari and Malang, Raffles spent little time at the ruins of Majapahit, the last capital of the empire, some 100 kilometres from Singasari. Only a small image of a gate drawn during that brief encounter with Majapahit appeared in the first edition of his *History of Java*.[17] A comment on the same page tells us that it was difficult to discern what was left of this former 'pride of Java':

'The ruins of the palace and several gateways of burnt brick are to be seen; but the whole country for many miles is thickly covered with a stately teak forest, which appears to have been the growth of ages, so that it is difficult to trace the outline of this former capital. Ruins of temples, mostly executed in brick, are scattered about the country for many miles, and attest the extent and grandeur of this 'pride of Java.'[18]

Hoëvell's drawing of Majapahit ruins. [Van Hoëvell, 1849]

Clearly, little remained of this great ancient capital. The harsh tropical climate had left no trace of the wooden houses with palm fibre roofs that once filled the valley.

After his visit to the temples near Malang, Raffles continued the expedition further east, through the Bromo-Semeru mountain complex towards the neighbouring island of Bali. He eventually arrived back home in Bogor on August 1, 1815, just over three months after his departure. Raffles decided the next step was to create a map of the ruins of the city of Majapahit. Three weeks after he had returned home from his journey, on 22 August 1815, he summoned a thirty-year-old Dutch captain, Johannes Willem Bartholomeus Wardenaar, fluent in Javanese and trained at the Dutch navy's school in Semarang.

A few weeks later, in mid-October 1815, Wardenaar arrived

in Trowulan, a village in the midst of the Majapahit ruins. He was equipped with the latest military surveying equipment – an astrolabe to make astronomical measurements, a plane table with an alidade (a sighting device for measuring angles), a compass and a sextant. For weeks he diligently walked the fields, hacked his way through dense forests and climbed the overgrown ruins. He measured the length of the fields, the angle of the roads, the height of ruins and put it all down on paper.

By late 1815, Wardenaar's map was finished. He sent it with several drawings and a legend to Raffles in Batavia. But the lieutenant-governor, seeking evidence of a glorious Hindu-Buddhist-Javanese capital, was disappointed by the size of the city – only seven-and-a-half square kilometres, housing at best ten thousand people – hardly the major lost civilization he was hoping for.

With that, he filed Wardenaar's survey away with his papers and mentioned neither the man nor the map in his *History of Java*, published the following year in late 1816.

The map disappeared but was found nearly two hundred years later in a collection in the British Museum in 2008. It proved to be remarkably accurate.[19] Wardenaar passed away in 1869 and his own copy and three sheets of drawings were passed to the Batavian Society of Arts and Sciences[20] and were subsequently published by mining engineer, geologist, and pioneer of modern volcanology, Rogier Verbeek. Verbeek led an adventurous life. When Krakatoa, a volcanic island in the Sunda Strait between Java and Sumatra erupted in 1883 it was one of the biggest volcanic events in modern times. The entire region was devastated, and

Verbeek led a small team to assess the catastrophic scale of the damage; he submitted his report to the government of the Dutch East Indies in Batavia, which was published in 1885, marking the beginning of modern volcanology.

A year after Raffles had completed his journey, events in Europe intervened. In August 1816, the European theatre of war once again determined events in the East Indies and the British handed the archipelago back to the Dutch. Oddly, during the handover, there was no mention of Majapahit. Despite Wardenaar's surveys it was not listed among the prominent antiquities and archaeological sites which the returned Dutch rulers prioritized in the post-1816 period. It was as if Majapahit had never existed.

At the same time, Dutch merchants were eyeing the area surrounding the Majapahit ruins. It was suitable for growing sugar cane, so they cut down forests and removed stones and bricks to make way for plantations. Then it was discovered that the large octagonal-shaped bricks from the Majapahit era made splendid materials for building Dutch sugar factories. When those supplies began to run out they realised that the clay soil of Trowulan was perfect for baking bricks, digging up what was left of the ancient capital.[21] Large parts of Majapahit simply vanished.

But the ruins continued to attract visitors, such as Hendrik Domis, the resident for East Java in Surabaya appointed in 1831.[22] In his horse-drawn carriage he passed the remote villages that Raffles and his men had visited sixteen years earlier. He was impressed by the landscape of volcanoes and mountains but less so by the accommodation available. He stayed overnight in a small village named Japan (now Mojokerto) near the Majapahit ruins, where he was attacked by a small army of mosquitos in his hotel room, The next day he hacked his way through the forest, wary of lurking tigers spotted nearby, and stumbled on a colossal gate, Ratu Bajang, an entrance to a palace or temple.

In 1849, another Dutch traveller, Hoëvell, visited a different gate further north, the same one shown in Raffles' book. The area was still overgrown:

'The entire ruins were shrouded in a dark forest and covered with shrubs and trees. Majestic banyan trees have rooted their roots between the stones and pushed walls apart, raising their crowns high above the ruins. That is why nowadays the Javanese also call the place 'Warningin Lawang', banyan gate, while it used to bear the more splendid title of "gapuri gapi", royal gate.'[23]

And in 1861, one of the great men of science, Alfred Russel Wallace, paid a visit, noting that:

'Traces of buildings exist for many miles in every direction and almost every road and pathway shows a foundation of brickwork beneath it – the paved roads of the old city'[24]

While Charles Darwin is credited with developing the theory of evolution, Wallace made a significant contribution. Wallace proposed a theory of natural selection as a key part of evolution before Darwin published his own work. In 1854 Wallace travelled to Malaya and Java and, based on his observations of the variation of characteristics in species on different islands, he published *On the Law Which Has Regulated the Introduction of New Species*.

Majapahit was now just a pile of ruins, forgotten by all except for a few foreign adventurers and the local farmers who lived there. But all this changed two decades later, in November 1894, when a new manuscript, the *Nagarakertagama*, written at the height of Majapahit's power, was discovered. It was snatched to safety from a fire in a royal palace, and, with it, interest in Majapahit sparked back to life.

And this time everybody wanted a piece of the action.

A discovery

Cakranegara, on the island of Lombok, November 19, 1894.

The attack started at half past five in the morning, the time when General Segov expected the Balinese to be least on their guard, and the cool, dry weather suited his army. The previous evening Dutch reinforcements had arrived from the south of the island and had gathered on a small road near a forest. From a safe distance, they had quietly surrounded the royal city of Cakranegara, the heart of Lombok, on three sides.[25] By midnight, the troops had dug in.

General Segov and his three commanders, Colonel Swart, Lieutenant Colonel Scheuer and Major Williams, had assembled a formidable force – two battalions, three regiments, three artillery units, two special units in charge of lightweight mortars, and a unit of army engineers, supplemented by a large number of convicts and local men, most of them prisoners of war, who carried supplies and armaments.

The Balinese had been in control of the smaller, neighbouring island of Lombok since 1740 and the Sasak, the largest ethnic group, had suffered badly. Balinese rule was brutal and many Sasak were sold as slaves. The Dutch had not bothered to intervene and had bigger fish to fry elsewhere in the archipelago, such as a war in Aceh in northern Sumatra. Only after the Sumatran Muslim sultanate had been subdued, extending Dutch domination in the region, did their attention turn to the rice, coffee, tobacco and opium traded in the harbours of Lombok.[26]

Trouble had been brewing for some time. In 1891 the Balinese *raja* (king) of Lombok ordered his Sasak subjects to fight in Bali in a local conflict, but among the Sasak there was little enthusiasm for becoming cannon fodder on Balinese home soil. Instead, they rebelled against their Balinese overlords on Lombok.[27] It was the perfect excuse for the Dutch to intervene and support the Sasak. After all, there was plunder to be had.

The attack was over very quickly. The well-armed Dutch troops poured forward and used ladders to scale the four-metre-high walls. They entered a labyrinth of small alleyways, where all the defenders could do was pelt them with stones. It was a massacre. Men were hacked to death, women and children were shot, burned, or run through with bayonets. The Balinese mounted a '*puputan*', one final suicidal attack, children included, as a last act of defiance. Most were gunned down and many of the survivors were executed.

One of the soldiers was second lieutenant Hendrik Colijn, a future Dutch prime minister, and in a letter to his wife he tells of the attack. His men captured thirteen women and children who asked for mercy, and his men turned to him as commanding officer for a final decision. Colijn turned his back, lit a cigar and heard his soldiers open fire.[28] The Cakranegara bloodbath resulted in the death of 2,000 Balinese; only 66 on the Dutch side lost their lives. The Balinese king was captured and shipped off to Batavia where, a few months later, he died in prison.

At noon, Dutch troops entered the treasure chamber of the Balinese royal quarters. They were astounded by what they found as they were confronted 'with stacks of coins and gold 60 centimetres high'. They counted 230 kilograms of gold, 3,180 kg of silver coins and numerous paintings and pieces of jewellery.[29] What became known as 'the Lombok treasure' was loaded onto oxcarts and taken to the harbour to be shipped to Batavia. But the drama was not over. The royal compound was set ablaze by artillery fire and the flames shot across the dried palm rooftops. When the fire reached an arsenal full of gunpowder there was a huge explosion, which killed thirteen men and threw others into a pond.

One of the men there that day was Jan Laurens Andries Brandes, an expert in Sanskrit and old Javanese languages, who had rather different motives for joining the military campaign. He was eager to locate old manuscripts rumoured to be in the royal compound. Brandes entered the treasury just as the fire was spreading and while others filled their bags with gold, silver and Chinese coins, he hastily gathered all the manuscripts he could find, little more than bunches of dried leaves tied together with a string. What he managed to salvage was packed in a box and sent off to Batavia for further investigation.[30]

What Brandes had saved from the flames turned out to be a different type of treasure. One of the manuscripts was a book written in 1365 which was full of stories of kings, wars and intrigue, with detailed descriptions of both glorious ceremonies and humdrum daily live in fourteenth-century Java. It brought Majapahit – a kingdom that was feared and respected from Sumatra and southern Thailand in the west to the spice islands and Papua New Guinea in the east – to life. Brandes called his precious discovery *Nagarakertagama* (*The Complete Doctrine of the State*), based on the manuscript's colophon, the publisher's emblem or imprint. The original author was a man called Mpu Prapanca, his title indicating that he was a court poet. He called his work *Desawarnana* (*Depiction of Districts*), but Brandes' title prevailed and the book has been known as *Nagarakertagama* ever since.

Majapahit back on the map

Brandes had put Majapahit back on the map and now people wanted to see the ruins for themselves. A newly established Dutch East Indies antiquities department dispatched its best archaeologists to investigate the Majapahit site. But jealousy and infighting meant that information was not shared and new ideas were not followed up. The trail went cold for decades.

Then, fast forward to the early 1940s, Willem Stutterheim, a pipe-smoking chief archaeologist from the antiquities department with an intimate knowledge of Javanese and Balinese palace architecture, arrived to survey the area. He walked the site, looked at the overgrown ruins and then compared them with palaces in

Java and Bali, and started to see connections between what was left of audience halls, rooms and gates. From there, he worked out where the market was – just outside the palace – and where the religious leader lived – to the south of the palace walls. For the first time, he could start to see the city in his head. Excited, he returned to Batavia and wrote 'De Kraton van Majapahit', *The Palace of Majapahit*[31], a book he finished in July 1941.

But his timing could hardly have been worse. In the early 1940s, the Second World War was coming to the Dutch East Indies. The Japanese arrived on Java's shores, the Dutch struggled to defend their colony and nationalist movements in Indonesia gathered momentum, led by charismatic leaders such as Sukarno, who went on to become the country's president after the Dutch left. To them, Majapahit became a new symbol of identity for the Indonesians, evidence of past glory well before the European colonisers had arrived. So potent was Majapahit's image that Stutterheim, possibly under pressure from local Dutch officials, had to delay the publication of his book. The last thing the colonials wanted at the time was their chief archaeologist writing about the glory of ancient Majapahit.

Stutterheim never saw his book published as in 1942 he fell sick and died. It was published posthumously in 1948 but when the book eventually appeared in bookshops in Batavia, readers were puzzled. In the opening pages, Stutterheim warned them *not* to draw the conclusion that he had discovered the Majapahit palace and told readers that he could not discuss the palace's location:

'*We repeatedly find such imprecisely formulated descriptions;*

they could easily set us on the wrong track if we were to accept them literally and transfer them onto a map.' [32]

So, after centuries of mystery, Stutterheim was the first to discover where the place was and what Majapahit really looked like, only to mysteriously choose to hide it again. Modern historians suspect Dutch politics was at play – the colonists saw no reason to publicise and eulogise a symbol of Javan supremacy at such a sensitive time. Later, archaeologists and engineers, with satellites and advanced mapping technologies at their disposal, found that Stutterheim's descriptions of the 14th-century Majapahit royal palace were incredibly accurate.[33]

1
Prapanca Makes a Discovery
(1359 CE)

*Prapanca goes on an epic journey across Java
and makes a dramatic discovery*

November 1359 (456 years before Raffles). Near Singasari.

Prapanca – the author of the book saved from the fire in Lombok
in 1894 which gave the modern world its first detailed description
of the Majapahit world in the fourteenth century – was, if truth be
told, a bit of an oddball. He was a slight, delicate, bookish figure
with a shaven pate and dark brown eyes. From his ears dangled
large bronze earrings, regularly exchanged for red emerald
studs; on his hand he wore an oversized oval ring topped with a
purple stone. His friends regarded him as scholarly and slightly
disorganized, but also curious, observant and not easily influenced
by others, something that his teachers thought was evidence of his
stubbornness. Despite this, Prapanca was generally thought to be
honest, virtuous, and forthright.[34] And he did like a drink.

As a young boy of six or seven, he played every day at the
Majapahit royal court where his father Nadendra held an exalted
position as one of the two *dharmadhyaksa*, or bishops. One was

Buddhist – his father – and the other a Shivaist who worshipped the Indian god Shiva. They were in charge of religious matters in the realm, acted as supreme justices at court, and chaired the *dharmopapati,* a religious council that dealt with the preparations for religious ceremonies. The job required daily court attendance and regular interactions with the portly and feared vizir, or *patih,* Gajah Mada, the most powerful man at court aside from the king himself.

Prapanca lived just a few steps from the palace, his room and courtyard adjacent to the southern wall, in a residence reserved for the two dharmadhyaksa. In the early morning, often before dawn, young Prapanca joined his father on his way to the palace. As soon as they entered the northern gate, Prapanca would run off to see his friends, including Prince Hayam Wuruk, who was to become the ruler of the Majapahit kingdom. In the mornings they played near the elephant stables and in the late afternoon the boys rushed to the second, inner courtyard and watched in fascination as men gambled on fighting cocks which clashed feet-first in mid-air flurries of squawks and feathers. No wonder that Hayam Wuruk translates as 'scholar rooster', and as a little boy he was nicknamed 'Tetep', or cockerel. Afterwards, to cool off, the boys sucked on sticks of sugarcane under the banyan trees that lined the road along the northern palace walls near the stables for the elephants and horses.

To them, this was the centre of the universe. Estimates put the number of people in the city of Majapahit at around 25,000.[35] To put that into context, the population of Kublai Khan's capital Dadu (Peking) by the middle of the fourteenth century was estimated to be 95,000.[36] For European context, London's population probably reached 50,000 around that time, but at least a third died when the Black Death struck in 1348-49. Majapahit was largely a rural kingdom and the vast majority of the two to three million people in Java at the time lived in small hamlets and villages dotted throughout the island. But the king's power extended much further. The Majapahit 'mandala'[37] empire controlled a huge swathe of territory, running from what is now southern Thailand, Malaysia and Singapore, all the way through to the islands of Sumatra, Java, Bali, Lombok and further east. It left a powerful legacy and future kings and even ambitious politicians in modern-day Indonesia have basked in the reflected glory of the Majapahit empire and the days when it was feared and respected across Southeast Asia.

Later, when he was older, Prapanca assisted with the preparations for ceremonies and rituals, sitting quietly and cross-legged behind his father. There were regular deliberations on religious matters and recitals of texts from old manuscripts. He was allowed to strike large ceremonial bronze bells set up on tripods in the courtyard and carry bowls full of burning incense into the audience halls. Prapanca was nearly twenty when he was put in charge of preserving the palace collection of old and fragile documents and manuscripts telling of past glories. These ancient texts were written on *rontal* (*lontar* in modern Indonesian), the dried leaves of palmyra trees which had been used as writing materials in Southeast Asia for centuries. As an avid collector of books, he took his work very seriously, taking care to keep hungry white ants away from his precious charges.

By the time they were teenagers, Hayam Wuruk and Prapanca had drifted apart. The prince loved hunting and gambling on cockfights and was a talented singer and dancer. He adored parties and performing on stage. Prapanca was the opposite. More of a loner, he took pleasure in reading old scriptures and preferred long drinking sessions to hunting, song and dance. In religion, too, the two men grew distant. While Hayam Wuruk's mother was a devout Buddhist queen, when she stepped aside and the prince was crowned king, he assigned Shivaist priests to the dharmopapati council and installed officials to oversee some of holy places of the *rshi*, the Shivaist seers.[38] The young king showed more interest in some of the more demonic Shivaist rites than observing the solemn Buddhist ceremonies Prapanca's father presided over. Although the two boyhood friends lost touch, there was never any animosity or hard feelings between them.

The limited evidence available suggests that one thing is clear: Prapanca did not have much luck with the ladies. One of his first amorous advances ended in abject failure when the young woman of his desires walked off telling him that he was off-putting, humourless, withdrawn and utterly unromantic. He was later described rather bluntly by one of his contemporaries as 'refusing to go to bed and having erections'. He turned to poetry (and drink) for solace. But while Prapanca was allowed to use the title *Mpu*, an honorific that distinguished Majapahit court poets, he had little confidence in his own ability and remained in awe of the great poets who visited the royal court. His work received scant attention and he was jealous of his friend and fellow Buddhist poet, Mpu Tantular, the author of the *Sutasoma*,[39] who had the support of none other than one of the princes at court, Ranamanggala.[40] The work is considered unique in Javanese literature because it is Buddhist rather than Hindu in nature and also the origin of Indonesia's national motto, '*Bhinneka Tunggal Ika*', or 'Unity in Diversity'.

A journey

When it came to writing poetry, Prapanca's problem was that he didn't follow the rules. His teachers instructed him that, just like prayers and religious rites, poems must be regulated by strict conventions. A truly epic story needed demons, gods, wars, delicate princesses and handsome heroes. There had to be blood-soaked battles, steamy scenes to arouse the senses and a smattering of contemplations and deep thoughts. Instead, Prapanca preferred to observe everyday life.

Then fate lent a helping hand. A royal expedition was proposed.

Early one early morning, as a gaggle of female servants swept the courtyards and pavilions, Prapanca was summoned to an audience with Hayam Wuruk, who by now was the king. As Prapanca sat down to wait his turn, the king looked up and, with a brief nod, acknowledged his old friend. An assistant to the royal master of ceremonies approached Prapanca and explained what was needed of him. Prapanca's father, now eighty-two, was too feeble to accompany the royal family on a three-month tour through eastern Java to inspect the realm. The king wanted

Prapanca to take his place.

In the weeks that followed, Prapanca was busy preparing for his trip. He recruited two servant boys to carry his luggage: a small box for betelnut, scriptures for religious recitals, umbrellas for shade, a selection of Javanese *keris* – daggers that were both weapons and spiritual objects considered to possess magical powers – and sashes of different colours for rites and ceremonies. He also needed a special jacket to protect him from the magical powers that were unleashed during these sacred rituals. Other ceremonial essentials – copper bells, bowls, and sticks of incense – were to be carried on separate bullock carts.

He had joined similar trips in the past but this time he had to take care of his father's duties. They included inspecting monasteries to check on the allegiance of local abbots to his father and, if required, offer advice about how to defend their ecclesiastical domains against grasping local landowners eager to get their hands on these valuable properties. But this journey was on a much grander scale.

The itinerary involved a 900-kilometre loop around eastern Java, with a stop scheduled in Singasari, where the royal family planned to stay in the abandoned city, the former abode of Hayam Wuruk's great grandfather, the famed King Kertanegara. Ceremonies were planned to honour the spirit of his acclaimed ancestor, who had been assassinated in his Singasari palace in 1292. After the city was burned down by his murderers, its inhabitants fled and many moved to establish a new city, Majapahit. While a few court officials suggested rebuilding the royal palace, Hayam Wuruk believed the place could never become a centre of power again; cities, when captured by enemies, simply lost all their majesty and magical powers forever.

A few days before departure, his father came to Prapanca with a small request. Could he visit an old friend, Ranangsa, the old abbot in far-off Darbaru? It would require only a small detour from the king's planned route and, after the visit, he could rejoin the royal caravan at Singasari.

Ranangsa in Darbaru

With great pomp and ceremony, King Hayam Wuruk and his impressive entourage of carriages, horsemen, court officials, servants and countless oxcarts set off on his royal tour. Prapanca could barely suppress his excitement as this was the opportunity he had been waiting for. They would visit more than two hundred villages and small towns and, with the blessing of the king, he could write about his glorious rule, the history and terrain of the Majapahit realm, as well as the day-to-day life of the people.

A few years later, in 1365, he published his epic work based on the journey with the king and his entourage, *The Depiction of the Districts*, or *Nagarakertagama*, as it came to be known. The court critics gave it the thumbs down, saying it was devoid of the magic, heroism and philosophical musings required.[41] That was a setback for Prapanca. He lost face and became a source of gossip around town.

So be it, he thought, it was best to simply accept this fate. But history eventually proved him right. The descriptions of everyday life across Java that his contemporaries thought dull and stodgy were the main reason that, years later, Balinese copyists eager to link their own traditions to that of Majapahit culture, thought that the book was worth reproducing. Modern scholars regard the work as a primary source for studying the period.

Nearly three months after departure, the caravan reached the penultimate leg of the tour before Singasari, the site of the old palace of King Kertanegara. Tents were pitched, horses watered, guards collected food from surrounding villages, and the court servants prepared the king's luxurious quarters. It was an opportunity for the armourers to sharpen swords and tighten bowstrings and for doctors to tend those with blisters, cuts and bruises from the long journey.

The camp was a hive of activity as chickens and goats were slaughtered for the pot, dried meats were unloaded from the oxcarts, and priests prepared bronze bells, colourful banners, incense and drums for the evening ceremony. As dusk fell, the moon bathed the vast caravan in a milky light, fires and torches were lit, and the whole of the royal camp dazzled against the night sky.

The next morning Prapanca woke early to prepare for his journey to Darbaru to visit his father's friend, Abbot Ranangsa. He stretched his tired limbs, shivered in the cool air, and performed a perfunctory inspection for the fleas that had feasted on his flesh during the night. It was still dark and the cocks were starting to crow in response to the croaking bullfrogs in a nearby ravine. The scent of the ocean was in the air as he washed himself in cold river water. After a simple breakfast – steamed rice and vegetables wrapped in banana leaves – he was ready to go. He was travelling light but the two servant boys were instructed to take extra care of his ceremonial jacket and red silk sash. The Darbaru monastery near the village of Hujung was due south in the direction of Mount Bromo,[42] an active volcano. It was a good day's march and Prapanca wanted to be at the foot of the hills before the sun became too hot.

They followed a bumpy path through flat, wide fields that ran towards the sea shore. In the distance were large ponds where men harvested salt from shallow basins to sell in nearby markets. Gradually, the path rose and the flat meadows were replaced by a verdant forest of teak, sandalwood and coconut trees. They walked to the accompaniment of a cacophony of birdsong and Prapanca identified the yellow-crested cockatoo, the white-flanked sunbird, bulbuls, and the calls of white-breasted babblers, parrots, myna birds, and those still yet to be named.

His servant boys did not like the dark forests. They feared the spirits that they sensed were all around. Back home, spirits resided in the dark recesses of houses and hidden gardens, as well as in their minds, of course. They were used to that. But the dark and unfamiliar woods were clearly full of them – in branches, roots, the tree tops. Everywhere. That was not all. There were also tales of ferocious creatures that roamed the woods.

Prapanca detected their unease. 'City boys,' he sighed to himself before reassuring them with a clever piece of reverse psychology. 'It is true that these forests are full of spirits as well as spiders bigger than tigers and giant snakes that can swallow a whole goat,' he said as he pointed to his necklace. 'But do not worry. This magic amulet will keep us safe.' And on they went.

On the narrow forest road they encountered a small caravan of travelling merchants on their way to peddle their wares in the villages or *dapurs* – clusters of dwellings that often specialised in a particular trade – that were scattered across the countryside. They were accompanied by young boys who hunted for game or fish and helped with menial tasks like collecting firewood.[43] Better travel together, the merchants told Prapanca, as the forests were home to gangs of robbers, the scourge of the Javanese countryside.

Curious as ever, Prapanca asked what the merchants were selling. They included clay ceramic pots wrapped in a thick layer of dried leaves to avoid damage, blue and red cloth, preserved meats or *dendeng*, and salted fish, blocks of salt, pieces of Chinese porcelain and a selection of knives and axes. Some traders carried two woven baskets suspended from a *pikulan,* or carrying pole, balanced across their shoulders, full of dried indigo leaves, sappan wood and roots to be ground into powder and sold as dye to village weavers.[44] Prapanca took detailed notes.

Later, Prapanca and the traders emerged from the woods and the path opened to emerald green rice paddy fields, dotted with white herons, scarecrows and small canals.[45] Long bamboo water pipes diverted the plentiful rainfall from the low mountain ranges to the paddies. Farmers with buffalos were busy tilling, preparing the fields for the next growing season. They were entering Hujung, the hamlet or *desa* not far from the monastery.[46] Some local farmers approached, spitting red juice from betelnuts as they walked, and asked what they had for sale. From nearby homes came the regular 'tock-tock' sound as women weaved *ikat* cloth, known for its distinctive patterns. On a wooden rack outside, buffalo meat was being cured to prepare *dendeng,* the thinly sliced dried meat that was part of the region's cuisine.[47] Prapanca's eyes lit up when he saw a woman selling palm wine but then thought better of having a drink, given his destination.

The villagers offered Prapanca a betelnut wrapped in leaves and asked him where he was heading. Darbaru was further up the hills, he was told, and the men chatted about new river ferry services on the Brantas river that were attracting more merchants to the village.[48] When the conversation turned to religion, it was with some dismay Prapanca learned that in these parts local deities or Siva were preferred to the teachings of Buddha.[49] Again, he took notes; all this was useful material for his book, the *Description of the Districts,* or *Desawarnana.*

It was time for Prapanca and his servant boys to press on by themselves. They soon passed the estate of a squire, an *anden,* and, later, smaller manors of landowners, *akuwu.* Prapanca knew from his father that years ago the king's mother had granted some of these *akuwus* land after they assisted the royal family in a war by supplying soldiers.[50] Prapanca steered clear of these *akuwu* landowners as many behaved like petty kings and often surrounded themselves with armed men who were short on patience.[51]

The landlords' fields were tended by bondsmen, who were essentially little more than slaves.[52] At court he had witnessed how some men who had committed minor offences were fined well in excess of what they could pay. Instead, they paid with their freedom, often their wives and children too. Landowners were always in need of labour and these bondsmen could be used to work the land and construct houses or shrines. There were other advantages – they could be sold for cash or used as collateral to secure a loan.

The path rose as they entered the hills and the sun started to burn, so they took refuge under a banyan tree at the edge of a small forest. As they sat down and drank water from a *kendi*, a ceramic pot, three strange-looking women passed by. They told him they had withdrawn from village life to spend their days as hermits and live in caves and huts high in the hills with a few dozen other men, women and children. Most were recluses and mythical seers, the *rshi*, easily identifiable by their dreadlocks or matted hair, and being dressed in nothing but bark. They filled their days in meditation or uttering mantras to find spiritual release. In the early mornings, these rshi walked to the villages in the valley to collect rice, betelnuts and vegetables the villagers shared with them because, after all, the spiritual welfare of the whole valley depended on these devout worshippers.

They continued through forests of lush foliage that protected them from the beating sun. Later, when the sun lost its strength, Prapanca and his two servants followed a narrow, steep path into the hills. They were getting close.

***

The monastery at Darbaru was at the top of a broad hill, with views over the surrounding fields. Standing near the entrance gate, he could see the Arjuna volcano on the other side of the valley and the flat lands that led to the sea. He felt an overwhelming sense of spiritual calm.

A low surrounding wall featured a small *bentar* gate, a split gateway commonly found at the entrance of religious compounds or palaces in Java. It led to a courtyard with pavilions grouped around a lotus pond. At the edge of the water, a fragrant pandanus tree stood in full bloom. The cries of a peacock muffled the sound of the ceremonial bells. Beyond the pond, a steep rock face sheltered a Buddhist shrine. Next to it were some small wooden huts and a kitchen with a large fireplace and a steaming cauldron.

Two young monks greeted Prapanca and then ran off to inform the old abbot about this unexpected guest. It created a stir in the quiet sanctuary, and men and women emerged from huts to see the new visitor, a rarity in these remote parts. Prapanca approached the shrine, pressed his palms together, knelt down and prayed to the bodhisattva inside. Afterwards, the monks greeted him and took him to bathe in a rocky pool adjacent to the monastery, where, to his surprise, water spurted from the breasts of two female statues. Refreshed, he donned a clean loin cloth and sat bare-chested in a pavilion in the shade of a banyan tree.

By now, the colour of the sky had turned a deep orange and the sun was already sinking towards the horizon. Two women – one the wife of the abbot, he was told later – emerged from a kitchen with fresh water and, to Prapanca's delight, some *kilan* sugarcane wine. But there was no time to drink as he was summoned to see Abbot Ranangsa.[53] Said to be older than a thousand months, the venerable elder was resting in a bamboo-roofed hut on the opposite side of the lotus pond.

A diminutive figure, the abbot stood up, straightened the faded yellow sash on his waist and smiled, revealing brown and broken teeth. He greeted Prapanca with the respect due a bishop or dharmadhyaksa (this was an honour as Prapanca would only later inherit the position from his father). Prapanca said it was a privilege to be in the abbot's presence and passed on greetings from his father, the abbot's old friend, adding that his journey had been uneventful and King Hayam Wuruk was in good health. The abbot, as you would expect, spoke at length about the rewards of monastic life, both spiritual and dietary; the yam season had been good, the papayas were plentiful, and millet planting had started.

Prapanca asked about the lands owned by the monastery and the people who lived in the surrounding area. But he confessed he was also interested in the history of the kingdom and understood that the abbot knew a great deal about long-gone kings and royal families. *'Hail to Gerindra!'* the abbot said excitedly, looking up to the god of the mountains. Prapanca, he continued, should read the old manuscripts the monastery held in safe keeping. Better still, he would arrange a reading the next day. But now it was late in the afternoon and time for the abbot to rest, the old man said. Prapanca exchanged a final few kind words and walked back into the inner courtyard.

By now, the senior monks knew of Prapanca's arrival and walked over to invite him to an evening meal. At the pavilion, torches were lit and servants prepared an assortment of dishes on banana leaves – steamed tubers, wild mushrooms, bitter karavila gourd, *petai* beans (Prapanca enjoyed these but the beans had an unusual effect on the aroma of his urine the day after) and papaya leaves cooked in the cauldrons he had seen earlier. Even better, palm wine was decanted from bamboo tubes. A lively dinner followed as old tales were told, monastery gossip was shared, and songs were sung.[54] Much later, the moon was shining brightly as he stumbled to one of the bamboo huts to rest.

The next day, Prapanca woke up to the sound of clucking hens and the mallets of bark-beaters. He washed his face and contemplated his peaceful surroundings. The quiet of Darbaru was something he savoured, a reminder of the unhurried monastic life that might offer solace to an aspiring recluse such as himself. Life at the monastery seemed completely at odds with the bustle of the Majapahit court.

But it was time to see the abbot. Prapanca walked to the pavilion in the central courtyard where his host sat, straight-backed, cross-legged and bare-chested. The old man seemed full of energy in the morning sun and the weariness of the previous evening was gone. In front of him was a stack of lontar leaves, neatly arranged. This was the monastery's most cherished possession, he said, a version of the famed 'Chronicle of Kings', also known as the Pararaton,[55] that told the history of the kings of Singasari and Majapahit in eastern Java. The fragile leaves required careful attention and were copied every few decades to save them from the humidity and the ants; Prapanca, something of an expert on old manuscripts, judged them to be perfectly preserved. The abbot said they contained stories of the kings that founded the Rajasa dynasty, the bloodline of King Hayam Wuruk.[56]

By now it was clear Abbot Ranangsa was going to give a

reading. Monks, women and children all gathered round. The abbot relished the attention and knew how to tell a story, especially in front of such a captive audience. First, he said, some historical context was required.

Recreation of a temple relief at Candi Penataran near Blitar, East Java, depicting a teacher reading to students. [Illustration: Ilyasza]

Ranangsa sets the stage

Long before the monastery existed and kings ruled the lands, Hinduism and Buddhism had arrived in Java. There was no great Hindu conquest with armies rampaging through the archipelago or a massive influx of Buddhist immigrants. Instead, religious ideas seeped slowly across the island chain as around the seventh century sailors, merchants and traders began to arrive from India on the monsoon winds.

Most were in search of riches – it was long believed that there were cities in the archipelago made of silver and gold. Having overcome their disappointment after reaching Sumatra or Java, they had to make do with the more humdrum business that merchants indulge in while waiting for the monsoon winds to change so they could return home with full cargoes.

Some decided to stay to source more goods, particularly valuable spices. Others, claiming to be learned Brahmins or sages, wandered the islands narrating stories of Shiva, Brahma and Vishnu or the enlightenment of the Buddha in small towns and villages. It was said that the arrival of one of them, Aji Saka, a saint-merchant (what a great job title), marked the adoption of the Saka calendar that starts from AD 78. Saka dates adorn many Javanese temples[57] and the calendar is still used in Java and Bali among Indonesian Hindus, as well as in parts of India.

As more local people adopted these new religious ideas and rituals, temples began to appear across the land, usually on high ground or close to sacred springs where villagers had previously venerated ancestors or gods. Over the centuries, the scattering of villages coalesced into fiefdoms, and fiefdoms into royal realms. Among the first was Srivijaya on the island of Sumatra.

Srivijaya, located near today's city of Palembang in southern Sumatra, commanded control over the sea lanes between the island and the Malay peninsula. It was a trading empire and a centre of Buddhist learning. Famed Chinese monk-traveller I-Tsing recommended Srivijaya as a suitable stopover for Buddhist students on their way to India.[58]

Chinese emperors ordered their navies to sail all the way to these 'southern barbarians' in Sumatra to acquire camphor, pine resin, and the precious 'unicorn desiccate' or dragon's blood which it was said 'worked on the five viscera and on the evil air inside the body. It relieves pain and breaks up accumulations of blood, works on ulcers, and creates flesh.'[59] Others recommended the blood for vitality and it was said to have the added benefit of warding off wretched evildoers. Many believed it to be dried blood from dragons and elephants that had lost their lives in battle, but it was often just the powder of dried berries from a tall climbing rattan plant[60] and the east coast of Sumatra was a major supplier.

Cannibals were supposed to live beyond the Srivijaya capital in Sumatra. Buzurg Ibn Shahriyar was a tenth-century sailor from the Persian Gulf who wrote a number of texts that tended to confuse real-life events with the legends he heard from other sailors. He wrote: *'The same man told me that he had heard from a sailor that in Louloubilenk, which is a bay of the sea, there are people who eat men. These cannibals have tails. They live between the land of Fansour and the land of Lâmeri.'*[61]

Centuries later, Marco Polo took measures to protect himself from such tailed maneaters.[62] The picture emerged that cannibals were everywhere on Sumatra although such tales were probably deliberately spread by clever locals to keep foreigners away.

At the time, Java was less powerful than Sumatra, with smaller, fractured fiefdoms competing with each other. But by the ninth century this had changed, leading to the construction of the majestic Buddhist Borobudur and Hindu Prambanan temple complexes in central Java. But just as power in Java was becoming more centralised, the island was thrown into turmoil.

There was a quick succession of kings, accompanied by a liberal sprinkling of assassinations. Then, in the year 928, the mighty Merapi volcano erupted, flooding the valleys with scorching molten lava. To the people this was a clear sign that the gods were angry and many packed up and settled further east in the flat, fertile valley where the Brantas river flowed.[63] New towns such as Kahuripan, Janggala, Kediri and Tumapel – later renamed Singasari – appeared and the valleys were soon dotted with temples.

Over time, a new centre of power emerged in eastern Java. King Dharmawangsa, a patron of the arts, was also a warrior and he conquered several neighbouring territories, including Bali. Then, in 990, he overreached himself, launching a naval invasion against the Srivijaya fiefdom on Sumatra in an attempt to capture the city of Palembang in the south of the island. It failed. The Srivijayans bided their time and retaliated in 1016, killing Dharmawangsa and most of his family during the wedding of his daughter. His son, a sixteen-year-old boy named Airlangga, narrowly escaped the massacre and took refuge in the jungle.

Several years later, a king from Tamil Nadu in southern India fell out with Srivijaya and his armies ransacked the capital city, Palembang. The timing was perfect for Airlangga, who had just emerged from his jungle retreat to stake his claim as king of Java. He established his own kingdom in Kahuripan, just south of Surabaya and only a day's walk from the Darbaru monastery. It must have been a prosperous place because Chinese traveller Zhou Qufe wrote in 1178 that the kingdom was richer than Srivijaya – whatever was left of it – and second only to the Arab countries.[64]

When King Airlangga's wife died, he gave up the throne and returned to the forest sanctuary of his youth. But the king then made a fateful decision that came to haunt eastern Java for centuries – he divided his realm into two, one part for each of his sons.

To establish the demarcation line, he called upon the services of a sage, Mpu Bharada. It did not go well. The plan was to take a mystical flight over the kingdom and pour holy water on the spot that would form the border. Sadly, as the tale goes, his loin cloth became ensnared in a gigantic tamarind tree, bringing him back down to earth with a bump. He promptly cursed the tree and a border was never established.

The poor old sage wasn't much good at curses either. Legend has it that the offending tamarind tree was revered for centuries and later became the site of the city of Majapahit.[65] It was two hundred years before the realm was united again, leading to endless conflicts and disputes between the two parts of the kingdom that were ruled by Singasari in the east and Kediri in the west. As will be revealed, it was Singasari that eventually emerged as the leading power in the land.

And, with that, the abbot said it was time to read *Chronicle of Kings,* the legend of Ken Arok.

2

From Robber to Royal

(1220s and 1359 CE)

Prapanca reads the Ken Arok legend

Prapanca was deeply impressed by both the abbot's knowledge of history and his story-telling skills. To most people, himself included, the history of the Rajasa dynasty, the forefathers of his lord and boyhood friend, King Hayam Wuruk, was a bit of a mystery. But there he was, in the year 1359, sitting in a remote Buddhist monastery about to hear the story of what had happened way back in 1182. He was joined by a small group of monks, a handful of local children, and the abbot's wife and her servant, who were not going to miss the chance to listen to the reading, a rare break to daily routine in this remote outpost. The abbot straightened his back, picked up the first lontar palm leaves, cleared his throat and, in a low voice, started to read from the old Kawi text of 'Chronicle of Kings'.[66]

Abbot Ranangsa began by dropping a bombshell. Yes, Ken Arok was the first ruler of Singasari and considered to be the founder of the Rajasa dynasty of the Singasari and Majapahit line of monarchs. He was also, according to legend, the son of a

Hindu god. But he was neither a saint nor the son of a nobleman nor a refined prince. He was a brutal robber, a liar, a cheat, a rapist and a murderer.[67] The audience gasped and wanted more.

***

In 1182,[68] deep in the forests near the small town of Jiput in the southern part of eastern Java, in the shadow of Mount Kawi,[69] the sound of axes filled the air, punctuated by the thud of falling trees. The men, most of them hermits, were building simple dwellings thatched with palm leaves so they could worship Shiva in a quiet and peaceful setting. The man in charge was a sage called Tapa-Wangkeng.

Tapa-Wangkeng organised a modest gathering to mark the completion of this forest retreat; a few prayers, a communal meal, and an offering to the spirits that would protect them. That was important because every grove of trees and every stream had its own spirits and their permission was required to cut and build in the forest. If the spirits were upset or angry, they would not be able to remain here for long. They made their supplications to the assorted spirits present and by the time they had finished, a light rain began to fall. 'That is,' sage Tapa-Wangkeng said, 'the blessing we need.'

Among those present was a troubled youth who had come to seek the guidance of the sage. The young man made a bold statement – he proposed sacrificing his life for the guardian spirit of the hermitage on the condition that he was given a new beginning, a re-incarnation, on the opposite side of Mount

Kawi.[70] The sage consulted Brahma, the Hindu god of creation, and upon the deity's approval the young man from Jiput was reborn. To get things going, Brahma then impregnated a farmer's wife named Ken Endok in the village of Pangkur[71] and told her: 'Do not allow your husband to make love with you again because if he does it will be his death and my son will not be pure. And I want you to name him Ken Arok, as he will be a boy.'

Ken Endok was excited and rushed to the paddy field to tell her husband. After all, it wasn't every day that you got to sleep with a deity. Not surprisingly, in her flustered state, the story she told was a jumble of outrageous claims that made little sense to her bewildered husband. Things went from bad to worse when that night he wanted to make love to his wife but she gave him the cold shoulder, citing the divine warning. The couple argued and then agreed to separate.[72] And just as Brahma had foretold, the farmer died a few days later, presumably for wanting to have sex with his wife. Tough crowd, these gods.

All this had not gone unnoticed by the elders, the *buyut*, in the village of Pangkur. One morning they gathered to discuss the matter. They were alarmed. One warned that Ken Arok had caused the death of a farmer even before he was born, so imagine the danger the villagers would face when the child was born. It was clearly a warning. The others agreed that the unborn child was a threat to their community and it was decided that when the baby was born he would be left in a cemetery on the edge of the village. It was a place of ill omen, suitable only for blood-soaked sacrifices, incantations and witchcraft.[73]

This particular graveyard was frequented by a notorious local robber and highwayman called Lembong. Late one evening he heard a disturbance among the graves and, on further investigation, found the baby boy and took him home. When Ken Endok heard about this she visited Lembong in his small shack to warn him that that boy was nothing less than a son of a deity. Lembong and his wife were not convinced and, despite the warnings, decided to raise the child at their own peril. It was a decision they would live to regret.

A few years later, Lembong introduced Ken Arok to the art of thieving. The young boy proved to be an eager student and over the years became a criminal with a soft spot for gambling on cockfights. One day, he lost a lot of money. A group of angry men turned up at Lembong's shack to demand the repayment of Ken Arok's debts. Lembong offered the men two buffaloes, his only possessions, but that was not enough. Better give us the boy as a slave, they said. But the Lembongs had grown fond of Ken Arok and did not want to lose him, even at the risk of becoming bondsmen, *bhertya*, and having to work for the men for the rest of their lives. The village elders gathered again to discuss the matter. Too bad, they said, and the Lembongs had to pay with their freedom.

When Ken Arok heard what had happened, he immediately fled deep into the woods. In the years that followed he had a series of adventures that you would expect of a man of divine origins. There was plenty of gambling that came with some god-like luck, an encounter with a magician who claimed he knew how to make gold, and a visit to a magical school deep in the forest where bats flew out of Ken Arok's head. He eventually settled on the outskirts of a village and made a living as a highwayman and, over time, added cattle rustling to his repertoire of crime; he also grew increasingly violent and once raped the daughter of the village palm wine brewer. Soon, the name Ken Arok struck fear into the hearts of the people who lived in the valley east of Mount Kawi.

At the time, this valley was ruled from Singasari – still called Tumapel in those days – by a powerful landlord called Tunggul Ametung, who paid tribute to King Kertajaya who lived in Kediri on the other side of the mountains. One day, messengers arrived to tell Tunggul Ametung about Ken Arok's misdeeds and he ordered his commander to track this scoundrel down. When he heard that he was a wanted man, Ken Arok went on the run again. After several days, his pursuers were closing in near a fast-flowing river which was impossible to ford. He climbed a tall tree in the hope they would not spot him, but to no avail; the soldiers started to hack the tree down.

At that moment, it looked like it was all over. He was a dead man. But having a deity as a father has its advantages. Suddenly, a voice from the skies instructed Ken Arok to pick large leaves from the tree, tie them to his arms and fly over to the other side of the river. To the astonishment of the soldiers, Ken Arok paraglided over the river and landed safely on the opposite bank. And so, he was free again to wander the forests and valleys.

But Ken Arok could never stay out of trouble for long. One day he walked into a village and got into a fight with a group of men following an argument. He was taking a terrible beating when suddenly a voice came from the skies. It was his old friend Brahma again. 'Do not kill this man as he is my son and he still has some unfinished business on earth.' In awe, the men stopped beating up the troublesome intruder and let him go. By now a crowd had gathered and people were whispering that the scoundrel Ken Arok had been spotted and a few of them ran off to ask Tunggal Ametung to send soldiers.

Yet again, Ken Arok ran off to hide in the jungle. There he met a wise old woman who told him that the gods were about to assemble for an important meeting at the top of the mountain.[74] As he was well acquainted with the benefits deities had to offer, he climbed to the peak, took cover behind a large rock and waited. Thunder and lightning filled the air, followed by strong gusts of winds and a massive downpour, all signs that the gods had arrived. The lead item on the agenda was the dismal state of affairs on the island of Java. It was a divided place with kings or powerful *akuwu* landlords at war with each other. 'Who should be the king of Java?' asked one. And Brahma (who else) answered: 'Know that I have a son, born as a human out of Ken Endok, a woman of Pangkur, who can make the land of Java united and strong.'

Ken Arok knew that this was the moment to reveal himself. He appeared from behind the rock and after a brief introduction the gods agreed that Brahma's plan to make Ken Arok the king was a good one.[75] Before making a move, he first needed a guide and father figure. The job was given to a man named Loghawe, a skinny high-caste brahmin with dreadlocks who had been a pupil of none other than Vishnu, the god of preservation. Ken Arok and Loghawe lived in the forest until news arrived that local lord Tunggal Ametung wanted to meet all the religious leaders in the valley to the east of Mount Kawi. Loghawe knew this was the opportunity they had been waiting for, so the two set off for Singasari.

From robber to royal

Several months earlier, Mpu Purwa, a Buddhist priest, was living happily with his beautiful daughter in a small hamlet in a valley not far from Tumapel. Her name was Ken Dedes and everyone believed that there was no woman east of Mount Kawi who came anywhere close to matching her beauty. Tunggul Ametung, the local ruling landlord, heard about her beauty and decided to see her for himself. On the day he arrived, he found Ken Dedes alone at home. He was immediately smitten, abducted her and took the young woman back to his palace in Singasari. Landlords had a lot of rights in those days.

Her father returned to find his home empty. When he heard what had happened, Mpu Purwa flew into a rage and cursed Tunggul Ametung: 'May the kidnapper not enjoy my daughter to the fullest and be killed by a keris.' And for good measure, he cursed his neighbours for letting it happen: 'May the wells of the village turn dry because my neighbours have failed to warn me when my daughter was in danger'.[76]

Back in Singasari, Tunggul Ametung was a very happy man. He had married the local beauty Ken Dedes and, by the time Ken Arok and Loghawe arrived in town for the gathering of religious leaders, she was pregnant. Then fate intervened again. Ken Dedes was visiting some local gardens just when Ken Arok was passing by. As she descended from her carriage, her skirts parted momentarily to reveal her calves and a lot more besides. Ken Arok, upon catching a glimpse of what he described as her 'flaming mystery', fell hopelessly in love.

Later that evening he asked Loghawe: 'What woman has flames coming from her loins?' Loghawe told him that Ken Dedes must be a *nareswara*, a master female, and whoever married her would become a king of kings and rule over the whole of Java. Ken Arok was thrilled. 'The woman I saw is the wife of *akuwu* Tunggal Ametung, the lord of Singasari,' he said. 'I will kill him, if you don't object.' Loghawe hedged his bets, saying: 'Tunggal Ametung will be killed by you but as for the matter of murder I cannot give nor deny your permission because that is not what we brahmins do.'

Ken Arok turned to an old gambling friend, Bango Samparan, for help. What was needed for the planned assassination was a magical curved Javan keris. This made sense to Ken Arok as everyone knew that blacksmiths, through the power of the flames and their anvils, had the ability to forge magical tools.[77] Not surprisingly, a blade embodied with magical powers was a prized personal possession.[78] And Bango Samparan knew just the man, a blacksmith called Mpu Gandring, who lived in a nearby town called Lulumbang. 'He can make a keris that even the strongest of men cannot withstand.'[79]

Ken Arok immediately placed his order, telling the blacksmith he needed the dagger in five months. Like tradesmen the world over faced with a difficult task and a tight deadline, Mpu Gandring threw up his hands and said it could not be done. It would take up to a year to make such a special weapon. Ken Arok, not known for his patience, told the blacksmith to get on with it.

Five months later he returned to pick up his keris. When he was told it was not ready, Ken Arok, never big on anger management, exploded. He snatched the half-finished dagger, stabbed the hapless blacksmith, and destroyed his smithy. In his last moments, Mpu Gandring cursed Ken Arok: 'This keris will kill you too as it will kill your children and grandchildren. Seven kings will be killed by this keris.' Shaken, Ken Arok tried to make amends, telling the dying man: 'When I am a great man, I will allow your descendants to receive my gratitude.'[80]

Ken Arok then concocted a plan worthy of the truly devious man he was. He showed off his new dagger to a friend, Kebo Hijo – 'Green Buffalo', presumably because of his hefty build and dim brain – who was immediately impressed. Ken Arok generously offered to lend the dagger to his friend, who wasted no time in showing it off to his friends, neighbours, and young women he wanted to impress. Soon, the whole town knew Kebo Hijo possessed a magical keris.

A few nights later Ken Arok broke into the house of Kebo Hijo, grabbed the dagger and made his way to the house where chief Tunggal Ametung was asleep next to Ken Dedes. After stabbing him in the heart, Ken Arok left the dagger in the motionless body and returned home. The curse made by the father of Ken Dedes – 'May the kidnapper not enjoy my daughter to the fullest and be killed by a keris' – had come to pass. The devious plan worked to perfection. In the morning, the whole city was in uproar and everybody knew the dagger belonged to Kebo Hijo. Tunggul

Ametung's family didn't need any more evidence and the poor dupe was stabbed to death before he could protest his innocence.

King Rajasa

The assassination of Tunggul Ametung opened an unlikely path for Ken Arok to become the ruler of the city. And for someone with the morals of a man who had lived almost his whole life on the wrong side of the law, he was blessed with the one quality that is beyond measure – luck. Somehow, no one seems to know why or how, the murderer, rapist and highwayman managed to catch the eye of his fantasy woman, Ken Dedes, shortly after murdering her husband. And, just like that, they were married and Ken Arok became the most powerful man in the land east of Mount Kawi and vassal to King Kertajaya of Kediri on the other side of the mountains.

But before Ken Dedes agreed to marry Ken Arok, she had made several demands. Ken Arok had to accept her son with Tunggal Ametung as his own, and the boy, Anusapati, would be heir to the throne. It was agreed and Anusapati grew up believing he was the son of Ken Arok. And, to the astonishment of those who knew about his dark past, once he became ruler Ken Arok had some sort of moral epiphany. He helped people he had abused, decreed that the fatherless children of the blacksmith Mpu Gandring would be free from paying taxes, and also looked after the son of the hapless Kebo Hijo.

But Ken Arok, ever the opportunist, was not satisfied with

ruling Singasari. He had to pay tribute to King Kertajaya in Kediri[81] on the other side of the mountains. The king was unpopular, arrogant and cruel. He said he wanted to be worshiped as a god and showed off his supernatural powers in surely the unlikeliest of ways, by sitting cross-legged on the tip a sharp spear.[82] His demands were resisted by the Hindu and Buddhist priests but he persisted and asked them to bow to him, an act of respect reserved for the gods. They had had enough and took refuge with Ken Arok in Singasari. Grateful and impressed by his generous hospitality, they crowned him King Rajasa.[83]

Ken Arok basked in the glory of the moment, celebrating yet another metamorphosis in his charmed life. From cowherd to king, with a lot of robbing in between. Nice work.

By now, things were getting heated. King Kertajaya[84] vowed to punish the disobedient ruler of Singasari and the disloyal priests who had abandoned him. Ken Arok sensed the danger and immediately put his kingdom on a war footing by raising an army. Soon, news arrived that King Kertajaya's troops had left Kediri.

Ken Arok's army went out to meet the enemy in the mountains that divided the two valleys, just north of a town called Ganter. It must have been a spectacular sight, the hills filled with thousands of men with feathers on their heads carrying slingshots, bamboo spears, discs, lances, arrows and rattan shields, accompanied by chariots and nobles on horseback. Royalty, like the new King Rajasa, rode on war elephants adorned with large bells. The thundering of war drums, conch shells and trumpets reverberated through the mountains.[85]

The Battle of Ganter was a brutal, blood-soaked business as

thousands of men engaged in hand-to-hand combat. The turning point came when some of King Kertajaya's top commanders were killed and the Kediri army simply disintegrated. Stories about the fate of King Kertajaya differ. Some sources say that, seeing defeat was imminent, he ordered a handful of devotees to follow him into the woods where he hanged himself.[86] Others say he became a hermit, or used his supernatural powers befitting a god to rise to the heavens. Whatever the story, he was the last ever king of Kediri. In 1222 the kingdom, the valleys east and west of mount Kawi, divided after Airlangga, was united again after two hundred years. Singasari ruled. The robber-turned-royal, Ken Arok, was now the all-powerful King Rajasa.[87]

* * *

It was quiet in the hermitage when Abbot Ranangsa decided that it was time for a short break. Prapanca was excited. He had just discovered that King Hayam Wuruk's royal lineage went all the way back to Ken Arok, a son of a god no less, and clear evidence that King Hayam Wuruk, a Rajasa, was of divine origins. He needed to tell the king about these ancient texts that very few people knew existed. The abbot agreed.

As the heat of the day rose, the small crowd dispersed, abuzz with excitement about the extraordinary stories they had been told. Prapanca ate a light vegetarian lunch and spent the afternoon contemplating the enormity of what he had just heard. He wanted to know more. As the sun started to set, the abbot reappeared and called Prapanca back to the pavilion. It was time to finish the *Chronicle of Kings*.[88] Curious monks gathered as a resident peacock strutted through the yard. The abbot knew he had the audience in his hands. 'Now,' he said, 'Ken Arok, the founder of the Rajasa dynasty, is going to die.'

Ken Arok murdered. Ken Dedes burned.

After the Battle of Ganter, the newly crowned King Rajasa, perhaps an early candidate for the world's luckiest man, was living a life of joy and fulfilment with his beautiful wife Ken Dedes. He had nine children – seven boys and two girls – including a son named Toh Jaya he fathered with a concubine.[89] As agreed, they had kept the first-born son, Anusapati, in the dark about who his real father was and all the children grew up as one big happy family in Singasari.

Before long, the next generation started to appear. Anusapati had a boy named Wisnuwardhana, the first grandson, and Ken Arok's own firstborn son with Ken Dedes, Mahisa Wong Ateleng, also had a son, Narasingamurti. The two boys grew up together, playing hide and seek in the palace courtyards, sitting as young princes with their parents at ceremonies, and being tutored in religion by a wise guru. Ken Dedes adored playing the part of devoted grandmother, keeping an eye on what the boys ate, teaching them how to address different people at court, and administering punishments when necessary.

But behind this picture of domestic bliss, trouble was brewing. Ken Dedes started to have regrets about her early life. After all, she had been kidnapped from her father's house and forced to marry Tunggal Ametung. Later, she married a murderer and had to lie to her son Anusapati about who his real father was.

The bigger problem was that the king did not conceal his preference for his own first-born, Mahisa Wong Ateleng, or the son he had with a concubine, Toh Jaya. Anusapati felt rejected and wondered why his father treated him so differently. One day in 1227[90] he decided to confront his mother.

The long streak of luck enjoyed by reformed-bad-boy Ken Arok was about to run out. His wife was finally going to tell the truth. Her answers to her son's questions set the stage for a series of events which brought bloodshed to Singasari. She told Anusapti that Tunggal Ametung was his real father. Anusapati then asked who had killed his father. It was Ken Arok, she said.[91]

Anusapati was a hot-headed young man at the best of times. For years he had been lied to, people had gossiped behind his back that he was a bastard, and his father had long favoured his other brothers. Now he had the truth and he wanted revenge. Anusapati asked his mother for the magical keris used to kill his father, the one made by the blacksmith Mpu Gandring who was murdered by Ken Arok. Ken Dedes could not calm her raging son and gave way. She handed the dagger to him in full knowledge that the keris was cursed and would kill seven kings. Anusapati then called his most loyal servant, Batil, and ordered him to kill the king.

Just after sunset,[92] Ken Arok strode up the stairs of a pavilion to sit down for his evening meal. The torches were lit and food was about to be served. He saw Batil, his son's most trusted servant, walk towards the pavilion but paid little attention to the man – he was a familiar presence and probably had an important message. Seizing his opportunity, Batil took out the dagger and stabbed the unsuspecting king in the back and ran to tell his master. Anusapati then took the dagger from Batil and stabbed him to death too. Now the king was dead, Anusapati had taken his revenge and, so he thought, was free of suspicion.[93] Within minutes, the whole city of Singasari was in uproar and for days rumours swirled around the court and streets about who had murdered the king.[94]

A royal funeral on a grand scale followed. Ken Arok's body was bathed with holy water, and his hair was oiled and scented. The royal family placed gifts next to the body, which was then wrapped in a white cloth and placed in a wooden sarcophagus. Musicians played the music of mourning, while brahmins recited prayers and splashed the body with holy water. An auspicious day was selected and the night prior to the burning ceremony[95] men beat large wooden drums to signal that it was time to assemble at the court and say farewell to the monarch.

The next day at two in the afternoon, with the sun beating down, the body was carried to the cemetery outside the city as people thronged the streets to catch a last glimpse of their beloved king, the famed unifier of the lands. At the cremation ground, just outside the city near a river, a flock of cawing crows hovered above, eyeing lunch.

In the middle of the cemetery, a large pyre was prepared in a wide, open pit and priests performed rites to dispel any lurking demons. When the body arrived, the cloth cover was cut open to reveal the face of Ken Arok. Holy water in ceramic vessels was splashed over the body and when the vessels were empty, priests shattered them on the ground.

It was time for the devious eldest son, Anusapati, to light the funeral pyre. As the flames rose to engulf the body of the king, another drama was about to unfold. Queen Ken Dedes, dressed in white with garlands of flowers around her neck and on her head, stepped forward from the crowd while saying a prayer.

Silence descended on the huge crowd of mourners. The only sounds were the faint rustling of the palm trees in the evening breeze and the crackling of the fire. The queen held a keris in her hand and stared at the furnace in front of her. She walked up to the rim, paused for a moment, finished her prayer, and stabbed herself in her stomach. She then threw the dagger into the fire, smeared her head with the blood gushing from her wound, and walked into the fire pit. Her white gown was the first to catch fire and the air was soon full of the smell of charred flesh as her body fed the flames. The queen had done her final royal duty.[96]

After the cremation, the bone fragments were taken from the ashes, ground into a paste, stored in a special ceramic container and carried in a clockwise direction around a series of religious offerings. Some of Ken Arok's ashes were scattered in the Brantas River, while the rest were used for a ceremony that took place at his commemorative shrine on a hill in Kagenengan, just south of Singasari.[97] Ken Arok, King Rajasa, was forty-five when he died in 1227.

* * *

The abbot put down the old manuscripts and smiled at Prapanca. The reading had come to an end. The sun was fading, the threat of an afternoon thunderstorm had passed, and the two men walked together to join the monks for dinner. Prapanca was distracted. Even for someone who had read the ancient scripts at the palace and was well informed about the history of the royal family, this was an amazing discovery. It changed everything.

According to the official history that Prapanca had learned as a child, the founder of the Rajasa dynasty was a man called King Wisnuwardhana. He was the father of King Kertanegara, who died in Singasari in 1292, sixty-five years after the death of Ken Arok. It was King Kertanegara who was the first Javan ruler to cross swords with Kublai Khan,[98] the grandson of Genghis Khan. In 1289 Kublai Khan sent ambassadors to Java, demanding tribute and submission to the Yuan dynasty. Kertanegara arrested the envoys, branded their faces, cut off their ears and sent them back to China. As will be revealed later, what happened next had profound consequences for the Majapahit empire.

To Prapanca, this was a day he would never forget. He had now learned the true origin of the Rajasa dynasty. Perhaps later, when he was old and tired, he would return to the sanctuary of the Darbaru monastery, the place that had finally given his life meaning and purpose.

3

Game of Thrones

(1220–1250 CE)

Ken Arok's sons go after one another

The next morning, Prapanca told his two young servants it was time to leave the monastery and then bade the abbot a fond farewell. He was keen to share his remarkable news with the king, Hayam Wuruk, who was completing his grand tour of the kingdom. They walked down the hill, through the village of Hujung and entered the forest on the flat land near the sea. They then turned south across the dykes, the farms and the fields, arriving back at Singasari in the early evening. Prapanca was immediately struck by the stark contrast with the quiet and calm of the monastery. The huge royal camp was a blaze of campfires and torches, and the aroma of a hundred grilled chickens filled his nostrils. He washed, devoured some of the delicious roasted meat and, exhausted from the long walk, fell into a deep sleep.

The following morning Prapanca rose early, keen to talk to his old friend and master. Inquiries at the royal household revealed that the king was holding a flower ceremony in honour of his ancestor, King Kertanegara, in the ruins of a holy site nearby, the seductively named Abode of the Heavenly Nymphs.[99] King Kertanegara was a revered figure. It was he who, back in 1289, had refused to pay tribute to the Chinese empire of Kublai Khan, perhaps the most powerful man in the world at the time; as a result the royal house of Java had flourished. The ceremony was a grand affair – first a celestial bath for the sovereign, followed by the recital of ancient verses, incense burning, the ringing of bells and finally offerings of baskets full of fresh flowers to the former king.

As soon as the ceremony was over and the large crowd had drifted away, Prapanca approached the king, who was sitting in an elevated wooden pavilion. Prapanca bowed as he entered the royal presence, sat down cross-legged, took a deep breath to calm himself and told his story. He spoke of the tranquillity of the monastery, the wisdom of the old abbot, the recital of the *Chronicle of Kings*, and the remarkable tale of Ken Arok and how the old scripture proved that the king – and of course the whole dynasty – was of divine origin. 'Not that I ever thought otherwise,' Prapanca added quickly.

King Hayam Wuruk, already delighted by the success of the royal tour, was thrilled by Prapanca's revelations. He immediately called for his most senior royal advisors, led by the feared and respected vizir, Patih Gajah Mada. The *patih* probed Prapanca, checking and double checking his story to confirm that this was indeed clear evidence of the king's divine status. A huge celebration was in order and he proposed a *puspa*, or flower offering, at Ken Arok's burial ground in Kagenengan, a hill a few hours walk south of Singasari where they were camped. The king approved, geomancers were instructed to select an auspicious day, and plans for the grand puspa were put in place. Prapanca would of course attend as an honoured guest.

A few days later, the royal family, court officials, Buddhist and Hindu priests, and hundreds of servants left the camp and made their way to Kagenengan. In the early afternoon, the royal procession ascended the hill and approached the shrine of Ken Arok, the newly revealed founder of the dynasty. It was a spectacular sight, worthy of the occasion. A large crowd of excited onlookers gathered as teams of flag bearers walked ahead of the mounted imperial guard, led by Gajah Mada on a magnificent stallion, accompanied by musicians, religious chants and the beating of a hundred drums.

Finally, the members of the royal family made a grand entrance, descending from their carriages and thanking the officiating priest before entering the shrine to make offerings to the beautiful bouquets of flowers – large sums of money, exotic foods, and items of clothing spun from the finest cloth. Prapanca admired the scene. Surrounded by trees and a wide terraced garden, the temple looked fit for a king of divine origins. Small pavilions allowed people to rest and soak up the atmosphere. After the king had offered a prayer to his ancestor and burned incense in honour of the gods, the day finished with a large *selamatan,* a communal feast.

The next morning the royal entourage made its way slowly down the hill to return to the Singasari camp and a day or two later journeyed back to the royal palace in Majapahit. All was well. It was the year 1359, Hayam Wuruk's inspection of his kingdom was complete and he had returned to his capital a god king, or close enough.

The port of Quangzhou in China

In 1222, around the time Ken Arok was smitten by his future wife Ken Dedes after catching his first glimpse of her flaming loins, thousands of kilometres further north in the prosperous port city of Quanzhou on the south-eastern coast of China, a man named Zhao Rugua held the esteemed position of inspector of maritime trade. Zhao was a man of significant standing as his family had links with the Song dynasty emperors going back eight generations. But he went down in history for an entirely different reason: his fascination with what lay beyond China. Every day he saw ships arrive in the harbour from different parts of Asia and he became intrigued by the tales of distant lands which are now Indonesia, Vietnam, the Philippines and India.

This made Zhao a very unusual man. The history of China, the art, poetry and philosophy of the classical, Confucian, Buddhist and Taoist schools of thought were studied with a passion worthy of a period which many called the age of renaissance in China. Few were interested in people who lived in other countries – they were barbarians, after all. But the nature of Zhao's job made it impossible for him to ignore them.

Every day, the harbour master patrolled the port, conversing with captains and sailors about their voyages, the countries they visited, the goods they traded, and the towns they lived in back home. He wanted to know everything. How good were their maps? How sophisticated were the ships they encountered in other places? What marvels had they seen in distant lands? And why did oceans not overflow when water from rivers continuously flowed into them? His appetite for knowledge was insatiable. And so, in 1225, Zhao wrote *A Description of Barbarous Peoples*[100], a detailed account of the countries, islands and cities with which Chinese merchants traded, including Sumatra, Java, Malabar on India's western coast, Cairo and Baghdad.

In those days, Tuban, on the north coast of Java, not far from Surabaya, was the port where Chinese seamen, arriving on the monsoon winds, first mingled with Arab, Indian and Malay traders. The journey to Java came with considerable risk and Zhao heard that many foreign ships were plundered by pirates and reports of captured foreign merchants fetching high prices as slaves or hostages were common. But Tuban was an important port in the Majapahit era and became an international trading hub. Many merchants stayed on and set up businesses to acquire spices, pepper and cloth.

The traders from China soon started to explore the villages and towns that dotted the hinterland, and a few made their way to Singasari, still named Tumapel at that time. It was only a three-day journey on foot and after Ken Arok had unified the rival kingdoms of Kediri and Singasari in 1222 following his victory at the Battle of Ganter, a flourishing city had developed.[101] The arrival of the Kediri spiritual leaders who had grown weary of the haughty, sore-bummed, spear-sitting King Kertajaya, had attracted craftspeople who made bells, drums and fabrics for religious ceremonies. Local geomancers were kept busy too, finding the best locations for new shrines and residences for these immigrant spiritual leaders, creating demand for skilled masons.[102]

Ken Arok – by now the mighty King Rajasa – was keen to strengthen his grip on power. He summoned the men who had distinguished themselves in battle and awarded them lands, made them nobles, and instructed them to grow rice and vegetables and raise chickens, pigs, boars and buffalos to feed the growing city. He also ordered the construction of roads and bridges across the valleys, built temples and strengthened his army. And to safeguard against any invisible, evil forces hostile to his rule, two enormous club-wielding giant statues, *darwapalas*, were consecrated and positioned at the entrance to the city.

Two *darwapalas* from the Singasari period, still standing today in East Java, the largest being 3.7 metres tall. [Illustrations: Ilyasza]

Of course, all this needed money. He sent tax collectors to the towns, villages and hamlets in the two valleys where they also collected rice and other goods from local merchants peddling their wares at markets. Back in Quanzhou, Zhao Rugua had heard about this as sailors had told him that these Javanese traders paid a tenth of their produce in tax. Charters written on copper plates discovered later showed that there were lower rates for small traders who often lived in the villages, and higher rates for the professional merchants who travelled from town to town to market their wares.[103]

The city was growing rich and, with more and more people coming to town to pay their respects to Ken Arok, the king did what so many strongmen do the world over – he gave his royal palace a big makeover. There was no shortage of bling. Lotus pools adorned with moonstones were dug and lavish audience halls and pavilions were constructed. It was said that the quarters of the king's women were adorned with gold ornaments, doors were studded with rubies, and pathways and trees were decorated with precious stones to reflect the light of torches that were lit in the late afternoon.[104]

The traders from China were impressed. They saw a vibrant city with streets thronged with men and women going about their daily lives, many bare-chested, others with a simple cloth wrapped around the waist down to the knees; men let their hair down and women wore their hair in buns.[105] They watched farmers and traders arrive from the countryside with bullock carts carrying everything from vegetables, rice, millet, salt and dried meats, to fish, parrots and fermented beverages, to be sold in stalls set up along the sides of the streets.[106]

At busy road crossings, Ganesha statues were raised to protect against accidents and evil spirits. The whole city was filled with the smell of burnt wood and the delightful, sweet fragrance of the jungle. Understandably, a lot of sailors decided to skip the risky return journey to their deprived homes in China and stayed in Java.

The houses were of a grand scale and decorated with gold and jade; some were raised above the ground on timber poles and a few privileged nobles had their own private temples in their gardens.[107] Visiting merchants were housed in special guesthouses, the local diet was judged to be rich, and it was noted that the Javanese were attentive to cleanliness.[108] On one occasion, a merchant from China saw the king and his huge entourage pass by on the street; it's unclear who it was but it was quite possibly Ken Arok:

The king of this country ties his hair in a mallet-shaped topknot and wears golden bells on his head. He wears a brocade robe and leather shoes and sits on a square-shaped throne. His officials report to him daily and prostrate three times before leaving. When he leaves his palace, he rides an elephant or a litter, attended by five to seven hundred armed warriors. The people of this country sit down when they see the king and stand up only after he has passed.[109]

These traders were in search of exotic merchandise that would fetch high prices back in Quanzhou. Silk weaved in Java was in demand and they were amazed at the quality available in markets: *They have various coloured brocaded silks, cotton and damasked cotton gauzes.*'[110] The traders were also surprised at the variety of fruits and spices: lychees that cured bowel disturbances, jackfruits the size of a well-fed tummy, bananas a foot long, sugarcane ten foot tall – its juice, with some mushrooms added, was brewed into a tasty beverage. Pepper was abundant although the Chinese traders complained about killer headaches after inhaling the acrid fumes. And they looked on in amazement at how female Javanese barbarians applied cinnabar to their fingernails and silk clothes, giving them a vibrant red hue.[111]

The social life was pretty good, too. The merchants placed bets on afternoon cock fights and gambled at wild boar fighting contests while getting drunk on fermented juice from coconut and sago palm trees. They were especially intrigued by what they called *'xia nau dan'*, a popular drink that these seasoned voyagers had not consumed anywhere else. It was excellent stuff. And they told the harbourmaster in China that throughout the year there was no shortage of entertainment as the Javanese were a lively bunch:

'In the fifth month, they go on boating excursions. In the tenth month, they go on excursions into the mountains either on hill ponies or on cloth hammock litters. Their musical instruments include transverse flutes, drums, and clappers, and they are also skilled dancers.'[112]

But a few things baffled them. There was no tea in Java, people had no family names, the people were quick tempered *'and when they are sick, they take no medicines, but simply pray to their local gods or the Buddha.'*[113]

This picture paints Singasari as a prosperous, peaceful place around the year 1222. Its citizens had widely different backgrounds and spoke many languages and dialects, but the streets were safe and most people had money to spend, and, despite his shady past, the king was wildly popular. But, of course, this couldn't last and it was not long before treason, murder, court intrigue and social upheaval would arrive in town.

Game of Thrones, Java style

When the old abbot at Darbaru had finished his epic reading of the *Chronicle of Kings*, he signalled to Prapanca to stay a little longer. He wanted to have a conversation in private. The abbot had a confession to make – he had left out the gruesome tale of Ken Arok's blood-filled legacy. After he died, his sons started, one after the other, to kill each other. It was bad enough that the king had been murdered on the orders of his stepson, Anusapati, who had flown into a fury when he finally discovered who his real father was. But once he had assumed the throne, the plotting, murders and general mayhem continued.

Prapanca listened in horror as the abbot told him a story of fratricide on a grand scale. He confirmed that he had omitted this part of the royal history because he feared the king would probably not want to hear it; bad omens, cursed daggers and all that. What did he think? Prapanca agreed, it was better to erase this serious blemish on the king's legacy from history.

As Prapanca had just heard, everything started to go horribly wrong in Singasari once Anusapati was crowned king. After years of prosperity and contentment under Ken Arok, the mood soon changed. The atmosphere in the palace became hostile and the city's streets and taverns were filled with conspiracy theories. The gossip was that Anusapati must have had something to do with the murder of Ken Arok. After all, it was Anusapati's servant, Balil, who had done the deed and then, rather conveniently, had been killed before any questions could be asked. Surely, as day follows night, the king's legitimate sons, Mahisa Wong Ateleng and Toh Jaya, would want to take their revenge. Many thought it wasn't a case of when Anusapati would be gone, but rather how it would happen.

Anusapati, perhaps with good reason, grew increasingly paranoid. He saw conspiracies and plots against his life everywhere – during ceremonies, at dinner at his grand pavilion, in council with ministers, or while he slept. For added protection Anusapati ordered a large fish pond to be dug around his residence, and only trusted guards were allowed in his presence. He avoided crowds and did not dare to venture into the city.

This did not stop Anusapati's young son Wisnuwardhana and nephew Narasingamurti enjoying innocent, if somewhat pampered, childhoods. They played hide-and-seek in the courtyards, received religious instruction from the palace priests, and, when they were older, learned how to use lances, knives and daggers.[114] Little did they know at the time but, in a family such as this, these survival skills would later play an important role in keeping them alive.

Anusapati's paranoia soon extended to the spiritual world.

He knew that after death a soul could go up to the heavens or be dragged down into the underworld. The gods took their time before making a final decision so souls spent a period in spiritual limbo, a sort of purgatory, for twelve years to be exact. This was when Anusapati feared his soul was most vulnerable and prone to attacks from evil stepbrothers using magic or performing dark ceremonies.[115] He was clearly in need of proper protection in the afterlife. Anusapati called in stonemasons and architects and ordered that, upon his death, his commemorative shrine in Kidal was to be adorned with powerful, ferocious monster-headed *kalas* to protect his soul.[116]

It turned out to be a wise move.

As the plots thickened, Anusapati's deepening fears about his own demise became a self-fulfilling prophecy. Distracted by a high-stakes cockfight one afternoon, the king for once lowered his guard. His stepbrother Mahisa Wong Ateleng saw his opportunity and stabbed him in the back with the very same dagger that had been used by Anusapati's servant to kill Ken Arok. A ferocious power struggle ensued as the sons of Ken Arok went after each other.

First, Mahisa Wong Ateleng, the newly crowned king, was murdered by his younger brother Guning Bahaya. He didn't last long. Toh Jaya, the son of Ken Arok by a concubine, then stabbed Guning Bahaya, his stepbrother.[117] Again, that magical dagger – truly a family heirloom to be feared – was used in both killings.

Toh Jaya's coronation was a lavish affair, designed to send a signal that, after so much bloodshed, he was the undisputed leader of the realm. All the region's power brokers attended, including district leaders and wealthy landowners, the *akuwu* who had travelled for days from distant cities. He sat on a raised platform in a richly decorated pavilion, with his trusted advisor, the vizir Pranaraja at his side.

Ruins of Candi Kidal in Rejokidal village, Tumpang, near Malang, East Java. It was constructed in memory of Anusapati and has a large *kala* head. [Illustration: Ilyasza]

In front of them lay large silver plates laden with turmeric-coloured rice, grilled chicken, cooked beef, vegetables, crackers, and his favourite fruit: jackfruit, mangosteen and rambutan. His close family – a definition that was a something of stretch given the circumstances – sat nearby, including Wisnuwardhana, the son of Anusapati, and Narasingamurti, the son of the recently departed Mahisa Wong Ateleng; both cousins were fatherless and had been raised at court.

Priests chanted, prayers were recited, gongs were beaten, and an abundance of gifts offered by the assembled courtiers and nobles, keen to keep on the right side of a king with blood on his hands. The celebration continued with a large communal feast, a selamatan, for the hundreds of people in attendance. Toh Jaya looked at the scene with satisfaction and commented rather smugly to his vizir, Pranaraja, that his family members looked happy and content. The wise vizir, turned to him, grinned, showed off his chipped teeth and responded. *'Yes, they all look good, but compare them with a boil, they will eventually be the cause of death.'*[118]

The words sent chills down the new king's spine. Pranaraja was right. What a fool he had been – the only person he was kidding was himself. The next generation of the Rajasa dynasty, especially Wisnuwardhana and Narasingamurti, who were now adults, was clearly a threat. The king called his most trusted guard, Lembu Ampal, and ordered him to get rid of his two young nephews. To make his point clear, he told Lembu Ampal to act quickly or the guard's own head would be on the chopping block.

But in a royal court of many informers and very few secrets, someone[119] warned the two young men and they fled into the jungle before Lembu Ampal could get to them. An influential priest, Sang Apanji Patipati, offered the princes protection at a remote hermitage. Lembu Ampal and his men looked everywhere – deep in the forests, on remote mountain tops and in far-off villages – but the two young men were nowhere to be found.

The guard panicked when he realised that he could not fulfil his master's orders and, fearing for his life, also decided to leave town. By sheer chance, he sought shelter with the same influential priest who was protecting the two princes. Lembu Ampal trusted the man and liked the two cousins – he knew them well from court. And he was tired of all the killing. So instead of arresting them and condemning them to certain death back in Singasari, he proposed a plan that would keep everyone safe (including himself, of course).

Lembu Ampal knew that the years of intrigue and fratricide had caused a rift among the guards at the palace. There were two factions, those loyal to Toh Jaya and others who supported the two young men, the sons of Anusapati and Mahisa Wong Ateleng. This could be turned to their advantage, he argued. With that in mind, he returned to the city under the cover of night and killed two members of the palace guard, one from each faction.[120]

The plan worked. Amid the increasingly poisonous atmosphere of the royal court, the divided guards started accusing each other of murdering their comrades. When King Toh Jaya heard about all the trouble within the ranks, he ordered two more guards, again one from each faction, to be put to death. Problem solved? Hardly. The mood darkened and the split widened. Lembu Ampal then approached the guards loyal to the two young men. They were still alive, he said, and ready to take over from Toh Jaya.

Lembu Ampang was both a trusted soldier and a convincing orator. A group of loyal and heavily armed guards soon marched to the residence of Toh Jaya, where they tried to break into the room where he was sleeping. A scuffle broke out as the faction loyal to the king rushed to protect him. Toh Jaya was wounded but was able to flee the palace with a handful of followers and head north through the forests towards the sea, in a desperate bid to get off the island.[121]

But the coast was far from Singasari and progress in the royal sedan was slow, especially at night, when the forest was illuminated by only a silvery moon. Hours later, in the morning, by the time the bedraggled party arrived in the small town of Katang Lumbang,[122] soldiers sent in pursuit from the palace were closing in fast. The guards raced to prepare the sedan for a hasty departure but, so the story goes, history's first serious wardrobe malfunction intervened with deadly consequences.

One exhausted guard was slow to return to his post and, as he fumbled to wrap his loincloth around his waist, in his panic he inadvertently exposed his buttocks to the king, causing further confusion. Those buttocks were probably the last thing Toh Jaya ever saw. The pursuers attacked the sedan and, after a short scuffle, Toh Jaya was stabbed to death.

The year was 1250 and with this murder, the curse of Mpu

Gandring, the magical smith, was fulfilled: seven men had been killed by the dagger – the smith himself, Tunggual Ametung, Kebo Hijo, Ken Arok, Balil the servant, Anusapati and Toh Jaya.

4

Three Kings

(1250–1280 CE)

*Wisnuwardhana unifies the lands
and puts his son on the throne*

1250 CE (a few days after the assassination of Toh Jaya), Singasari.
A group of elderly men hastened over the large *alun-alun,* the
open square in front of the royal palace in Singasari. There was
urgent business to attend to. They were members of the city's
elite – ministers at court, senior advisors and spiritual leaders –
and were gathering to deliberate the sorry state of affairs in the
city and the future of the kingdom. With the citizenry on edge,
mace bearers had to keep an excitable crowd of onlookers under
control.

Once inside the palace grounds, the men walked through the
central courtyard to the large pavilion, opposite the lotus pond.
They were soon joined by members of the royal family, including
Prince Wisnuwardhana and Prince Narasingamurti, Patih
Pranaraja, and the widely respected Sang Apanji Patipati, the
priest who had protected the two princes from their murderous
uncle, the late King Toh Jaya. Security was tight and only a

handful of trusted palace guards and servants were allowed in the presence of the most powerful people in the land.

Sang Apanji Patipati sat down and started to talk.[123] For two decades now, he said, the city had been in turmoil, with the sons of kings assassinating their fathers, princes killing rival princes, and uncles trying to murder their royal nephews. The most recent casualty was of course King Toh Jaya, stabbed to death a few days earlier while running for his life. The centre of power in Singasari was weak. The people had lost respect for the royal family, taxes were going unpaid, the commanders of the palace guard were unsure whose orders to follow, and there were rumblings that in districts beyond the mountains powerful landowners were plotting to break away. The whole realm was about to shatter like a ceramic vase.

The revered priest took a few moments before he continued as he knew what he was about to say was controversial. The most crucial matter to be decided following the death of Toh Jaya was the issue of royal succession. A new king was needed to restore stability to the kingdom and it was a decision that, after so much bloodshed, they could not afford to get wrong.

Then he shared his plan. The man most befitting this important task, he said, was Prince Wisnuwardhana, the son of Anusapati. There were gasps of surprise. It was Anusapati who had set in motion the cycle of royal bloodletting by ordering his servant to kill King Ken Arok over twenty years ago. Anusapati, who had flown into a rage when he discovered that Ken Arok was not his real father, had in turn been murdered by his stepbrother Mahisa Wong Ateleng. The men sitting in the pavilion knew very well that this appointment would carry with it serious risks for the simple reason that Prince Wisnuwardhana was a bastard and not a direct descendant of Ken Arok.

But Sang Apanji Patipati had not finished. There was more to the plan. To restore the bloodline of the Rajasa dynasty, he proposed that Prince Wisnuwardhana should marry Jayawardhani, the granddaughter of Ken Arok and Ken Dedes and the sister of Prince Narasingamurti. And to avoid a continuation of the endless plots and bloodletting, they should appoint Prince Narasingamurti as deputy king, a newly created position. After a brief discussion, the elders saw the wisdom of the priest's idea- a child from Wisnuwardhana would be from both the bloodline of Ken Arok and Ken Dedes.

They also had a proposal of their own. To ensure a propitious start to the new reign, religious shrines should be built to honour the gods (and please the priests, of course). And with that, they all adjourned for a feast to celebrate finding such a clever solution to the knotty problem of the royal succession[124]. Long into the night they raised toast after toast to peace and prosperity returning to the kingdom.

The two new rulers, King Wisnuwardhana with Prince Narasingamurti as his deputy,[125] had a lot in common. Both were young boys at the court of King Ken Arok, both enjoyed a pampered childhood in the confines of the palace, both were witnesses to bitter royal feuds, and both their fathers had been killed. The time they spent hiding in the forest from their uncle Toh Jaya had brought the two young men close together and that is why the council of elders thought they would rule together in harmony, like 'two snakes in one hole' or 'like Vishnu and Indra',[126] two Hindu gods who were also the best of friends.

Wisnuwardhana stood at the centre of the ritual, dressed in an abundance of jewellery, an elaborate crown, his long locks falling over his shoulders with silver dripping from his neck, upper arms, waist and ankles. He had a long cloth belt around his waist covered with special motifs, the royal *sinjang* and *kawung*.[127]

A few weeks later a magnificent double coronation and a royal wedding took place in Singasari. Immediately after the elaborate ceremonies, the new king presided over a special assembly at which members of the royal family were given authority to rule the various regions under Singasari control.[128] He gave Wengker, a territory east of Kediri, to his daughter Turuk Bali and her husband Jayakatwang, who we will meet again later.[129]

The king also wanted to reward those who had remained loyal to him when he was in great peril. The family of Lembu Ampang, the guard who had played a role in keeping the two princes safe, was granted land,[130] as was vizir Patih Pranaraja,[131] whom the king referred to as his 'hands and feet'. The gossip in the palace courtyards was that the gift was evidence that it was the *patih* who had spirited the two young princes out of the royal court and into the woods before their uncle could kill them.

Following his inauguration, King Wisnuwardhana heeded the council's advice and ordered the construction of religious monuments around the city to honour his ancestors and restore the dynasty's weakened prestige. Keen to be accepted as the leader of all his people, he instructed his masons to build both Buddhist and Hindu temples, much to the delight of all the spiritual leaders who immediately acclaimed the new king as a truly glorious leader.

More good news followed. Queen Jayawardhani became pregnant, and she gave birth to a boy, Kertanegara. The boy had the blood of Ken Arok in his veins and the continuation of the royal bloodline was now secured, just as the council had hoped. But behind closed doors, some affluent landowners scorned the new 'bastard' king and trouble was soon to follow.

Kertanegara as a boy

In 1260, when Kertanegara was just a young boy, completely unknown to him a momentous event took place far north of Java. Kublai Khan, a Mongolian general who was the grandson of Genghis Khan, was proclaimed emperor and by 1279 he had completed the conquest of China begun by his grandfather. He was the first ruler of all of China. One of his first acts was to move his capital to Peking, which was called Ta-tu by the Mongols, the same city that his grandfather, Genghis Khan, had razed to the ground. Kublai Khan turned to a classical text of Chinese literature, the *I Ching*, the *Book of Changes*, for an auspicious name for his dynasty which he modestly called 'Yuan' or 'Origin of the Universe'.

The Mongol empire had emerged from the unification of nomadic tribes under the leadership of Genghis Khan to become the largest land empire in history. At its peak it stretched from the Pacific Ocean and parts of the Indian subcontinent to the River Danube in Europe and the shores of the Persian Gulf. By the time

Kublai Khan became emperor his armies were ready to attack the Dai Viet monarchy centred around what is today the city of Hanoi in northern Vietnam and the coastal kingdom of Champa further south. First, he tried a diplomatic approach, sending the Dai Viet leader, King Tran Thai Tong, a letter requesting his presence in Peking. The king suspected a trap but keen to avoid angering the new emperor, wrote back explaining that he was frail and sick, so perhaps his nephew could travel in his stead. A series of sporadic attacks followed but the Dai Viet proved a very tough nut to crack.

It was an interesting time. In 1271 Nicollo and Maffeo Polo, two brothers from Venice, set out on a journey along the Silk Road through central Asia,[132] accompanied by Nicollo's son, Marco. In 1275, they arrived in Peking, where Marco Polo would serve as an advisor at Kublai Khan's court for seventeen years. In the same year envoys from China were sent to Bagan in modern-day Myanmar to ask for tribute. No tribute was forthcoming and not one of the envoys returned.[133]

In 1283, Kublai Khan gave up on diplomacy and dispatched ten new envoys, this time accompanied by a thousand cavalrymen. They rode into the city and entered the palace, ignoring demands from guards to take off their shoes. Manuscripts from the time tell us that the Burmese were neither impressed nor intimidated and: 'Not only did they refuse to kowtow to the Burmese king, but also talked on a high chair, being conceited and extremely arrogant.' After the envoys ordered King Narathihapade to provide one thousand white elephants in tribute to the Great Khan, the king promptly had them executed.

When the news reached Peking, Kublai Khan launched a full-scale invasion of the Irrawaddy Delta. In 1287, his army crossed the treacherous mountains in the southwest of China, losing seven thousand men along the way, and then besieged Bagan, chasing King Narathihapade out of town.[134] This was all part of a wider expansion into Southeast Asia. Back in 1281, Kublai Khan's navy had attacked Champa, seized the capital Vijaya, and forced King Indravarman V to flee into the mountains. But while the Khan controlled Bagan and Champa, defeating the Dai Viet took years.[135]

This victory allowed Kublai Khan to exert further pressure on the stubborn Dai Viet.[136] Eventually, after years of attacks, the Dai Viet finally surrendered and by late 1288 the kingdom was a vassal of the Yuan dynasty. The neighbouring Khmer empire, where the magnificent Angkor Wat temple complex was built between 1122 to 1150, was also threatened but avoided war by paying annual tribute to Peking, starting in 1285.

But it was only a matter of time before Kublai Khan would look further south and turn his attention to Java.

Securing the throne

Far removed from the turbulence further north, village life in the valleys of eastern Java was peaceful and uneventful. Farmers planted and harvested the paddy fields, women weaved cloth, and traders sold their wares on market days. The only real changes to the rhythms of daily life were observed at Tuban, a small port on the north coast of the island. When the winds were favourable, more and more foreign merchants started to arrive and the town prospered. Some then ventured inland, following the Mas River upstream to dock on the banks of the small settlement of Canggu, just a day's walk from Singasari.

In a short period of time, what had been little more than a village turned into a booming town. Men unloaded cargo from ships, goods changed hands in the bustling market, and wholesalers loaded caravans of bullock carts destined for Singasari and the surrounding area. King Wisnuwardhana was pleased to see Canggu become a major trading gateway for Singasari, so much so that he ordered defensive walls and forts to be built.

But behind this veil of peace and prosperity, trouble was brewing. There were persistent rumours that groups of powerful landowners were plotting to rebel against the king. One of the main threats came from a man called Linggapati who lived in Mahibit, not far from the recently fortified market town of Canggu. An attack could cut Singasari off from its main source of food and basic necessities.

Instead of waiting for the insurgents to strike, King Wisnuwardhana moved first, and fast. His soldiers slaughtered the rebellious landowner, his wife, children and, for good measure, the whole extended family. He also confiscated all their lands. The king was sending a stern message that the days of division and disloyalty were over and disrespecting the king came at a very high price.[137] No one dared question King Wisnuwardhana's authority again.

But the king knew the troubled history of the dynasty all too well. If his upbringing in the tumultuous years of the rule of his father, Anusapati, had taught him anything, it was that peace can be an illusion. He was aware that any sign of weakness in the royal family would be taken advantage of and his legitimacy as ruler challenged. In 1254 he assembled his ministers and spiritual leaders at the royal palace and made a remarkable announcement. His son, Prince Kertanegara, who was still a young boy, would be crowned king and he would rule in his name for the time being.[138] It was a clever move and established a clear bloodline going back to King Ken Arok, making his son the legitimate heir and ruler. And after the annihilation of the Linggapati clan, nobody was going to take issue with the king.

Kertanegara would become one of the most powerful and longest-reigning kings the empire would ever see.[139] Rulers from across the realm arrived to pay their respects to the young boy.[140] At the coronation ceremony, his father proclaimed in honour of the new king that the capital city, Tumapel, as it was known then, was to be renamed Singasari – 'The Essence of a Lion' – a name befitting the most powerful city in Java.[141]

The boy king had an idyllic childhood. While his father and Patih Pranaraja took care of the affairs of the state, Kertanegara grew up in the palace in a large walled compound with open courtyards, fountains, ornamental ponds and intricately decorated pavilions shaded by banyan trees. Opposite the palace was the central square, the *alun-alun*, guarded by giant *dwarapala* statues to keep out evil spirits. Nearby stood a row of temples, set amongst patches of tropical forest, and the compounds that housed the large community of priests.

Spirituality played an important role in the young king's life from an early age. He saw and felt its presence everywhere. He would venture out of the palace to see a scraggly-haired sage who lived under an expansive banyan tree that had aerial roots down to the ground. People arrived from afar to listen to his teachings and soak up his mystic energy. In return, they left plates of mangoes and guava and pots of cooked rice with beans, lentils and water spinach, treats that did not go unnoticed by a band of black monkeys.

With two young female students holding an umbrella to protect the wild-haired guru from the sun, he adopted the lotus position and remained still, with his eyes closed, for hours. Crowds gathered, hoping he would speak. When he did, it was in riddles: 'Pain is inevitable. Suffering is optional' or 'To understand everything is to forgive everything'. The longer his silence, the larger the crowd. Eventually, he would look up and utter a few words: 'What you think, you become. What you feel, you attract. What you imagine, you create.' Such were his revelations. With that, he would close his eyes again and silence returned.

The sage was revered as a man of immense wisdom. Many, Kertanegara included, were left in awe. The holy man was seen as a paragon of spiritual strength, a jewel of the city, and an asset to the kingdom. The young boy king never forgot what he saw and the power the old man held over people.

Kertanegara prepares for royal duty

Kertanegara and the sons of nobles of similar age, some from distant parts of the kingdom, were all tutored at the royal court. Trusted officers trained the boys in how to handle *keris*, lances, maces, spears and clubs and initiated them in the art of hand-to-hand combat and how to ride horses and elephants. Religious teachers introduced them to spiritual rituals and in the afternoon tutors taught the boys dance and music.

The young king's closest friend was Pati-Pati, the son of the Sang Apanji Patipati, the priest who had given his father sanctuary in the forest all those years ago when King Toh Jaya was growing increasingly paranoid and wanted him dead[142]. Years later, Pati-Pati[143] had a copper plate inscription made to commemorate their longstanding bond: '*As for the one who bore the court-name panji Pati-Pati, he was clearly the beloved page of Lord Sri Kertanegara; from childhood never separated from his Kertanegara's footstool, gradually rising in the court ranking-system, finally holding the function of demung at the death of Lord Sri Kertanegara*'[144]. Pati-Pati went on to inherit his father's position of 'Master of Divine Weapons' and became proficient in magic spells that forced enemies to surrender at his will. Kertanegara, his friend and now master, was intrigued and retained a great fascination for the dark arts.

As he grew older, Kertanegara started to attend official meetings chaired by his father and Patih Raganatha. This gave him an early introduction to the petty bickering and squabbles that were part of life at court.[145] Tax was a regular grumble (some things never change).

One day, some priests from out of town complained about the amount of taxes being imposed on their religious establishments. Every year, they had to send the king substantial amounts of rice, fruit, vegetables, dried meat and cloth. Surely, they argued, their high volume of prayers constituted an important spiritual contribution to the realm and thus should be exempt from taxes. After giving it some thought – it was always wise to keep priests happy – Wisnuwardhana agreed and the priests returned home in good cheer. But they forgot the first rule of dealing with bureaucracy – get it in writing. They never received the order inscribed on an official copper plate and had to keep paying tax. The grumbling continued and some wondered if they should change their approach and raise the issue directly with King Kertanegara.

In 1268, when Kertanegara was around twenty-two years old,[146] his elderly father fell seriously ill. He rushed to his bedside where his mother, Prince Narasingamurti, and leading ministers and the religious leaders had gathered. The old king looked up and gave his son a last piece of advice – beware of rebellious landlords and nobles, especially in Kediri.[147] The city on the other side of the mountains had played second fiddle to Singasari for decades and, while its rulers dutifully paid tribute to the Rajasa dynasty, suspicions about their loyalty remained.

The dying monarch also had two last requests. Prince Narasingamurti, his friend and deputy king, had a baby grandson called Widjaya. He wanted Kertanegara to consider the young prince as his own son in order to strengthen the bloodline. And he also asked for a grand monument, to be known as the Jago temple, with views of Mount Arjuna and Mount Welirang across the valley, to be built in his honour.

When Wisnuwardhana passed away after reigning for twenty-two years[148] he became the first Rajasa monarch to die from natural causes since the rise of the dynasty. A huge crowd gathered for his funeral and his dutiful wife Jayawardhani followed him into the funeral pyre, as dictated by tradition.[149] and their ashes were scattered in the River Brantas. He was judged by all to be a great king, for he had brought peace and prosperity to the land; an inscription made decades later, in 1289, still praised Wisnuwardhana for unifying the kingdom.[150]

After all the rituals were complete, King Kertanegara summoned masons to the palace and ordered the construction of Candi Jago.[151] He wanted to create something truly extraordinary to set it apart from the shrines of other forefathers. The design featured layers of receding terraces that led up to a high roof, with stone reliefs recording legends that appealed to both Hindu and Buddhists, and with a full view of Singasari and two mountains, Arjuna and Welirang.[152] He selected his most talented craftsmen to erect a special statue to commemorate his father as a multi-armed Buddhist deity with infallible powers of salvation.[153]

After his influential uncle Narasingamurti, the deputy king, passed away a year later in 1269,[154] King Kertanegara became the sole ruler of Singasari and Kediri.[155]

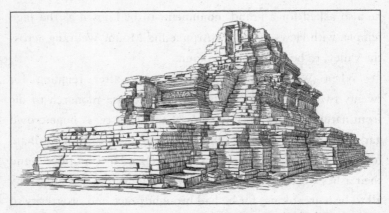

Remains of the 13th-century Candi Jago that overlooked Singasari
still stand today near Malang, East Java. [Illustration: Ilyasza]

Kertanegara as the only ruler

It soon became clear that King Kertanegara was going to face a
completely different set of challenges to those of his predecessors.
For the first time, the major threat would come not from domestic
politics but from overseas. Sailors and merchants were arriving
in the trading town of Canggu with worrying tales about the
growing regional ambitions of Kublai Khan, the Mongol ruler
in distant Peking. Bagan, the Dai Viet, Champa and the Khmer
empire were now under his control and the imperial navy was an
increasingly menacing presence.

This had not gone unnoticed in peaceful Singasari. Priests
started to warn that the time when the world would turn
violent and chaos would reign was drawing near. Signs of the

coming apocalypse were everywhere; traders from previously unknown lands had arrived on Java's shores, Islamic preachers were spreading dangerous new religious ideas, and there were reports that Buddhist and Hindu communities were clashing in the spiritual homeland of Buddhism, the Indian subcontinent.[156]

The tone had been set a decade before by the massive Samalas volcanic eruption on the island of Lombok in 1257, which darkened the skies and precipitated a period of much cooler weather.[157]

At the same time, Kublai Khan's forces were pushing ever southward and were now in the Malay peninsula, close to Java. It was clear that King Kertanegara would have to look beyond the local quarrels between land-grabbing overlords. For the kingdom to be protected against a totally new threat, he had to immerse himself in what today would be called the rising geopolitical tensions in the region, and, in more contemporary terms, the domain of magic.

5

Kertanegara

(1270–1292 CE)

Magical powers, sex in the cemetery
and the wrath of Kublai Khan

An auspicious night in 1269, Singasari.

King Kertanegara was a slender man with bright, round eyes, a small mouth with full, prominent lips, a square, flat nose and long fingers.[158] He was shrewd and determined, intelligent with a scholarly interest in ancient scriptures and rituals and a special inclination towards all things spiritual. While on rare occasions rash and impetuous, he was generally perceived to be a man who weighed his options carefully.

After the death of his father and uncle, he was the sole ruler of the realm and no one could accuse the king of taking his royal duties lightly. He was willing to do anything within his power to protect the kingdom. Yes, it was important to be seen as a strong, just ruler and to keep the peace throughout the land. For that he needed good judgement, a firm hand, and a loyal, well-trained army. But this was not enough. He wanted to harness the power of the magical forces introduced to him by Pati-Pati, his childhood friend.

Pati-Pati was the son of the Sang Apanji Patipati, the priest who had given his father, Wisnuwardhana, sanctuary when his life was in danger during the long period of royal bloodletting. Pati-Pati had inherited his own father's position of Master of Divine Weapons and soon became exceedingly proficient in the dark arts. And that is what brought the king, Pati-Pati and his new advisors Kebo Hijo and Aragani, accompanied by a small group of hand-picked followers, to the cemetery outside the palace grounds on a particularly auspicious night.

A young Kertanegara,
Hermitage, St Petersberg.
[Photo: Lesley Pullen]

The four young men were a fearsome sight, illuminated only by a bright moon that bathed them in a silky glow. They entered the crematorium grounds wearing crowns and ornaments made from bone and skull earrings as musicians played haunting tunes on ancient musical instruments – skull drums, thighbone trumpets and conch horns. A tantric priest raised a large bowl of red powder and walked in a circle, allowing the grains to fall from his hands to mark the sacred ground for the night. He signalled to the men to be seated. Bowls of rice, meat and fish were passed around the circle to be shared. The priest then filled a skull cup with palm wine and everyone drank their fill. He started to chant prayers and men danced to the rhythm of the drums and trumpets, falling into a trance-like state, while singing and reciting incantations.[159]

As the singing and chanting grew louder, the priest led a naked young woman into the sacred circle, laid her down and signalled for the king to perform the *maithuna*, a Sanskrit term for ritual sex, in order to release *sakti* or spiritual energy.[160] The ritualistic coupling was the spiritual climax of the ritual in every sense of the word, but the drinking and dancing continued deep into the night.

For King Kertanegara, these regular night-time, alcohol-fuelled, sexual unions were of great importance as they reinforced his spiritual powers. Hey, the dark arts could be fun too. He displayed his supremacy over the forces of evil by placing a Bhairava, a demonic form of the god Shiva, both the destroyer and creator of all things, in the centre of the royal palace at Singasari for all to see. It was a grisly, four-armed sculpture carved in stone, portraying a fearsome figure standing on a circle of skulls, holding a skull to drink blood, with bulging eyes, sharp fangs and a prominently displayed penis.[161]

Bhairava. [Leiden University KILTV A314]

A cabinet reshuffle

It was just a few weeks after the funeral of Wisnuwardhana that Patih Raganata had the first inkling that his position as the king's eyes and ears was under threat. Raganata was a perceptive and intuitive man, a master of dealing with three royals at the same time: King Wisnuwardhana, his young son Kertanegara, and the king's deputy, Narasingamurti. Many considered him trustworthy, ruthless and pragmatic, with razor-sharp political instincts. The *patih* had a web of acquaintances and sources across the land providing him with information. If anyone knew what was going on anywhere in the kingdom, it was Raganata. Despite criticism from the younger men at court for his reluctance to embrace new ideas, he was held in high esteem for his expertise in old scriptures, ceremonial procedures, tax payments, road maintenance and magic. One day, a group of eminent but disgruntled priests had arrived in Singasari to request an audience with King Kertanegara. A guard at the palace gate caught Raganata's attention and asked where he should send them. He agreed to hear their grievances in a nearby pavilion and had just seated himself on a raised dais when, to his surprise, the king arrived.

The priests had come to discuss the prickly matter of taxes, normally paid in the form of rice and other staples. Religious establishments clearly provided spiritual support and benefits to the king, they argued, and should therefore be exempt from other, more material contributions to the royal court. A brief silence followed. Slightly unnerved, the religious leaders hastily added that they meant no disrespect but had in fact raised the same matter with his late father, King Wisnuwardhana. He had agreed to exempt them from paying taxes but, unfortunately, no doubt due to some minor bureaucratic oversight by a palace underling, this was never ratified. As such, nothing had changed.

Raganata thought it unwise to change the status quo; the large religious community was a major source of income for the royal family. He was ready to make the point when the king raised his voice and agreed to the demands, with some conditions. Important *candi* such as Kidal and Jago, where his forefathers were commemorated as deities, would remain under firm royal control.[162] And while spiritual establishments were now free from paying taxes they would still have to pay *pamuja*, a contribution to the court at the annual religious festival held in the city.[163] The king ordered his proclamation to be engraved on copper plates and said the landmark ruling would be made known to all at a ceremony to be held at Sarwadharma, the religious compound in Lokeshwara outside Singasari. While Raganata agreed the matter had been deftly handled, what troubled him was that the king had not sought his opinion on the matter.

A few weeks later, in November 1269, King Kertanegara arrived in Sarwadharma for the grand ceremony mounted on a stallion decorated with bells and ribbons.[164] He was accompanied by priests, guards, court scribes, close friends and, of course, Patih Raganata. The engraved copper plates were unveiled and the king proclaimed that the lands overseen by the religious leaders were now exempt from tax. Keen to cement the bond, he threw in some other sweeteners. The people living in Sarwadharma were free to wear certain ornaments and types of clothing previously reserved for officials. They could also beat bondsmen charged with mischief into submission 'until blood flows, being overwhelmed and brushed with rasps' and were allowed to 'live with their bondswomen', and eat delicacies reserved for royals, such as turtle, boar and deer.[165] Lastly, their lands were to be separated from those of the royal family.

In return, the religious community was to honour the king and his relatives with ceremonies befitting a great leader. Anybody who dared to disobey this royal order would go to hell or risked reincarnation as a leper, a brain dead or an idiot.[166] The priests got the message and immediately proclaimed the king a reincarnation of both Shiva and Buddha (you could never be too careful in these matters). Church and state were now a united, powerful force, just as Kertanegara wanted.

But no sooner had he forged this important bond, the young king was faced with the first real challenge to his authority. Less than a year after the death of his uncle, King Narasingamurti, powerful landlords who regarded him as inexperienced and weak started to plot a rebellion. Taking a page from his father's book, he acted quickly and decisively against the rebels.

The 'odious scoundrel' Cayaraja of Bhaya was no match for the royal forces and was wiped out in 1270.[167] A few years later he was challenged by 'the very wicked' Mahisa Rangkah,[168] who received similar treatment, along with his wife, children and extended family. King Kertanegara was now a force to be reckoned with and also a man not afraid to lead his men into battle. An inscription described one battle he fought with his magician friend Pati-Pati in the most glowing terms:

The one who bears the court-name Pati-Pati was not left behind. When they reached the place of the enemy, the divine nature of the king manifested itself: completely subdued and shivering with fear, the enemies were seized by terror, unable to make even a single hair of the king's men fall. They found themselves completely overpowered: their military troops were crushed, the kings taken captive; their children and wives were led away as slaves, the royal property was confiscated.[169]

Given the unrest in the kingdom, Patih Raganata remained convinced that the inexperienced monarch would need his guidance. But his hopes were dashed when the king convened a meeting of his counsellors and religious leaders. There were going to be changes at court. The new royal privy council would comprise three members of the royal family. They would receive his orders, which would in turn be passed on to Raganata to implement. This was a clear demotion. The king also appointed his close friend Aragani as *demung,* or chamberlain. Aragani 'always provided the king with good food',[170] and Kebo Tengah, another childhood friend, was promoted to trusted advisor.[171] Pati-Pati was elevated to a new role, *dharmadyaksa* for Shivaist affairs, a role worthy of such a spiritual man, and there was a similar position created for Buddhist affairs.[172]

While this brought new energy to the royal palace, Raganata was left with no direct access to the king. He was now outranked by much younger advisors who had strong personal bonds with Kertanegara and delighted in joining him in the regular tantric sex rituals. Raganata, the older statesman, had been completely outflanked.

An expedition to Sumatra

In 1274,[173] four years after the political reshuffle at the royal court, news arrived that the Mongols were on the march and Kublai Khan was about to attack the Buddhist kingdom of Champa, on the coast of what is now Vietnam. This would put them close enough to the narrow Strait of Malacca that lay between the island of Sumatra and the Malay peninsula, the sea route used by traders on their way to Java. The danger was clear. If the Mongols weren't stopped, they could control the sea lanes to Java and threaten the kingdom. There were also whispers that an influential Tibetan monk, Chogyal Phagpa, had elevated the Great Khan to the status of being an enlightened being, which Kertanegara was only too well aware would give his adversary enormous spiritual power.[174]

The king called his ministers together. He sat in a small pavilion under a large flame tree as the ministers arrived and seated themselves on the ground in front of him.

He told them that the best strategy was to take military control of the state of Srivijaya in the southern part of Sumatra. Srivijaya, a long-time adversary of the Javanese, had once been a powerful empire but was now a shadow of its former self.[175] Raganata was still of sufficient seniority to attend the meeting and saw his chance. True to his conservative instincts, he warned the king not to rush into such a complex military expedition. There were not sufficient numbers of large ships available, Singasari's commanders did not have the necessary naval experience to mount such an expedition, and when the fleet reached Sumatra, the troops would still have to march inland to subdue the local rulers. It would be too risky[176] and also leave Singasari largely undefended. The king was surely aware of fresh rumours of rebellious leaders inside the kingdom looking to take advantage of any sign of weakness.[177]

The views of the experienced *patih* were immediately countered by the new men of the moment, Aragani and Kebo Tengah. In their opinion, there was no time to be lost. They should assemble a fleet, sail to Sumatra and assert the king's authority in the region. And then they played their ace. It was not sufficient to prepare the military. The king also had to think of his spiritual might. They proposed that a ceremony should be held to elevate the king to a spiritual status akin to Kublai Khan. Not surprisingly, Kertanegara agreed and immediately ordered his commanders to make preparations for a naval expedition which he called the 'Pamalayu',[178] loosely translated as 'the move west'.[179]

With this final humiliation, Raganata knew that he was yesterday's man. He informed the king he was unable to continue to serve him in the capacity of *patih* and resigned.[180] He knew it was risky, particularly if the king regarded this act as a reproach or even a betrayal. Heads had been severed for less. But Kertanegara was a wise man and recognised the huge contribution Raganata had made to the kingdom over many years. He made him a *dharmadyaksa*, a religious leader and judge in Singasari, replacing the chief of religious affairs, Santasmerti, who wished to live the rest of his life as a hermit on Mount Semeru.[181]

The king called in Aragani and told him that he was grateful for Raganata's sound advice and counsel and wished for the rebirth of his spirit in an even more bountiful incarnation. 'But now,' Kertanegara told him, 'You will be my *patih* because you are too ignorant and bigoted to advise on matters of religion. That is now the job of Raganata, the new *dharmadyaksa*.' And so Aragani became the new *patih*.[182]

The following year, Pati-Pati, Kebo Hijo and Patih Aragani completed the lavish preparations for the ceremony at which King Kertanegara would become an enlightened being, the spiritual defender of the realm. Priests led the king inside a temple, where he was given a holy bath and donned a special hip cloth of red, blue and gold motifs of interlocking circles, the powerful '*sinjang kawung*', a royal cloth to protect the world.[183] He then followed the priests to a small pavilion where they worshipped a specially made statue – known later as the Joko Dolog, 'the plump lad' – and sprinkled it with holy water while chanting incantations. A priest recited ancient scriptures and made offerings of food to the effigy of Bhairava and his dogs, the animals that traditionally accompany the frightening spirit.

King Kertanegara now possessed the same spiritual powers as Kublai Khan and was ready to defend his kingdom against the most powerful empire in the world.

* * *

Despite his new powers, Kertanegara knew that a military campaign of this scale, overseas in Sumatra, merited his full attention and he promptly banned the drinking of alcohol at the palace and shunned night-time rituals.[184] He consulted his trusted confidants. Pati-Pati, Patih Aragani, Kebo Tengah, and the commander-in-chief of his forces. The commander had a plan. The first problem they faced was a possible attack from the rear by hostile elements on the nearby island of Madura off the north-eastern coast of Java opposite the strategically important port of Tuban. Only a narrow, shallow channel separated the island from the mainland.

Take control of Madura first, the commander argued, and then use it as a base from which to launch the larger campaign in Sumatra.[185] And he knew just the man to run the troublesome island once it had been subdued. Wiraraja was an official with a good reputation who had climbed through the ranks quickly, rising from village head to a position at court in just a few years. Madura fell with little resistance and Wiraraja was duly appointed governor. At the time, he saw this 'promotion' rather differently as it removed him from the centre of influence in Singasari. Years later, Wiraraja was to play a pivotal role in establishing a new city in Java, Majapahit, which would become the power in the land.

The next task was to strengthen the navy. Carpenters, smiths, rattan weavers and sail makers descended on the Tuban seafront. The port turned into one vast shipyard, with thousands of men hammering, sawing, and splitting wood on the beaches. The population mushroomed. Cooks arrived in numbers to feed the shipbuilders, weavers to make ropes from the bark of sugar palm trees, doctors to treat injuries, and priests to render the ships sacred. Palm wine sales soared, and local innkeepers toasted the king every day as the money rolled in.

The ambition of the military campaign reflected the wealth

of the Singasari kingdom as well as the seafaring heritage of the people of Java. Merchant vessels, fishing boats and warships had been built on these beaches for centuries. But this was on a wholly different scale. It was an enormous operation and the ships – *jongs* – were colossal, measuring more than fifty metres in length with the capacity to carry hundreds of crew and soldiers, as well as horses and several elephants.

A very distinctive technique was used. Highly skilled carpenters worked with teak brought in from Kalimantan and each ship was constructed from the outside in. The outer shell was made from multiple layers of planks to make the vessel watertight, with the hull pointed at both ends. Then the inner frame was assembled with great precision – no nails were used, only wooden pegs which were inserted into the hull.[186] The ships were equipped with two rudders, huge sails, and between two and four masts.[187]

An auspicious day was chosen by royal geomancers for the grand departure. Admiral Kebo 'The Crosser' Anabrang was appointed head of the largest fleet to ever set sail from Tuban. As his name implies, he was an experienced navigator. But they had more than military might on their side. On board Anabrang's flagship lay a four-and-a-half-metre-tall stone Mahakala statue imbued with Kertanegara's god-like spiritual powers.[188] The statue was to be a gift to the conquered people of Sumatra and provide them with his protection, an extension of the king's spiritual aura.[189]

As the monsoon winds shifted westward and the rains stopped, it was time to set off. Anabrang hoisted anchor and the fleet set sail westward towards Sumatra, charting a course along the northern shore of Java. A few weeks earlier he had ordered a small number of ships to cross the Java Sea and set up two forward bases – Bakulapura in Kalimantan on the island of what is now Borneo, and Pahang on the Malay peninsula.[190] From there, Anabrang planned the final assault on Srivijaya, targeting the strongholds of Jambi Melayu in southern Sumatra. These precautions showed what an astute admiral he was. The base in Kalimantan allowed him to control the narrow strait between Borneo and Sumatra, which provided access to the whole archipelago.

Back in Singasari, all they could do was wait. The cycle of rituals and ceremonies continued and King Kertanegara frequently checked on the progress of a new statue he had commissioned from the best stone cutters in town. This was the intricate *Prajanaparamita,* a goddess of wisdom seated in a perfect lotus position, the *vajrasana,* her hands out in front with the fingertips almost touching each other.[191] He said that the carving was the most stunning he had ever set eyes on.

Then, several months later, two of Anabrang's ships were spotted approaching the Tuban harbour. A messenger rode straight to the palace in Singasari with the news everyone at court was waiting for. The expedition had been a complete success and, perhaps not surprisingly, the defeated Sumatrans had accepted the giant statue of Kertanegara with as much enthusiasm as they could muster in the circumstances.[192] The messenger also reported that the king of Sumatra was offering a 'gift' in order to acknowledge his submission to his new master in Singasari. Two princesses of the Jambi royal family, Dara Jingga and Dara Petak,[193] were available to become wives of King Kertanegara.

History does not record their views on this arrangement.

The commander's strategy was clearly working. Kertanegara now had a vassal state in south Sumatra, a powerful navy, and a highly effective army led by commanders who knew how to fight in different conditions. He also had control over the immensely lucrative trading routes across the sprawling archipelago. Singasari was now strong enough to face a Mongol attack, or at least possibly prevent one.

In 1279, five years after word had first reached the palace that the Mongols were on the march in Southeast Asia, Kublai Khan, perhaps aware of recent strategic developments in the region, played a diplomatic card. He sent envoys to Singasari to establish the first official contact between King Kertanegara and the Great Khan. The tone was cordial, and the envoys were invited to meet the king in the royal compound; both sides expressed a desire for trade to flourish between the two nations.

With the diplomatic niceties over, the real message was delivered – Singasari was required to pay tribute to Dadu (Peking). Kertanegara was non-committal but replied that, out of respect, it was appropriate to present the Great Khan with a valuable collection of precious stones, exotic birds and other wildlife. After a banquet and a performance by the court's leading dancers and magicians, the Chinese sailed back home. Back in Dadu (Peking) the diplomats reported that Singasari's *inhabitants were ugly and strange and their nature and speech are not understood by the Chinese*.[194] They then showed the Khan the jewels, strange birds and beasts that Kertanegara had sent as gifts, sheepishly admitting to being great admirers of 'the wondrous skill of

Javanese magicians'.[195]

Two years later, in 1280, more diplomats from China arrived to deliver fresh demands about paying tribute. Again, Kertanegara played for time and sent them on their way with an array of gifts as an expression of goodwill. There was no reply. In 1282, Kertanegara felt the time was right to send his own diplomatic mission to China. To show his respect, a shrine made of pure gold would be presented to the Khan. Then, as fate would have it, after the ships set sail, the Khan ordered his envoys to visit Java again and the two diplomatic missions crossed at sea.

As negotiations with Dadu (Peking) were at a standstill, Kertanegara turned his attention to matters closer to home. With southern Sumatra subdued, he wanted to expand his influence by taking control of the island of Bali in 1284.[196] The navy set off along the northern coast of Java and, on arrival, the troops met little resistance. The Balinese queen was captured and imprisoned in Singasari. The city rejoiced at the news of another victory[197] by their mighty king. In just a few years, large parts of the archipelago had been unified for the very first time. It was the start of the geographical and political concept of Indonesia as a single entity, and that required a proper celebration.

The unification ceremony

Wurare, three days north of Singasari, 1289
The location where the ceremony was held was highly symbolic. More than two hundred years ago, Wurare was the place identified

as marking where the ancient realm of King Airlangga would be divided between his sons (a reckless act, so it proved). The wise sage tasked with the division of the lands got thrown off his game when he got tangled up in a tamarind tree. Still, for the time being, it had essentially created two centres of power, Singasari in the east and Kediri in the west. The lands were first unified under Ken Arok and now, another celebration was in place, as the whole archipelago was united; Singasari had long since been the ruling power in the land, but its influence now stretched far beyond Java.

And so, on the morning of 21 November 1289, the royal family, court officials, noblemen, priests and palace musicians made the three-day journey north from Singasari to the cemetery at Wurare, the kingdom's most sacred ground, not far from the port of Tuban. It was quite a spectacle. The music of drums and flutes accompanied the procession as elephants decked in bells and vibrantly coloured cloth carried members of the royal family, including Kertanegara's daughters, 'the four princesses of Singasari', Prince Widjaya, and, of course, the king himself. Ornate howdahs protected them from the heat of the sun. The line of carriages, horses and oxcarts stretched into the distance and mace bearers had to prevent curious villagers from getting too close to the most powerful people in the land.

Another centre of attention was a massive stone statue carried by a cart drawn by four oxen. This was the same Joko Dolog statue that had been imbued with Kertanegara's powers during the ceremony in Singasari in 1275, when the king was first anointed as the spiritual protector of the realm. A lengthy

Sanskrit inscription carved around the base praised the reign of King Wisnuwardhana, Kertanegara's father, who had reunited the two parts of the kingdom. Now the statue was being given a place of honour in the cemetery at Wurare where Kertanegara's far greater military triumphs were being celebrated.[198]

Singasari now controlled not only the whole of Java but also Bali, most of southern and eastern Sumatra, Bakulapura in Kalimantan on the island of Borneo, and Pahang on the Malay peninsula, and had also formed an alliance with the state of Champa in what is now Vietnam. It is also assumed by some historians that at the height of his power the king had sent expeditions to Sunda on the tip of western Java with access to the narrow and highly strategic Sunda Strait between Java and Sumatra that linked the Java Sea and the Pacific Ocean with the Indian Ocean, and the Maluku islands far to the east.

The king dismounted from his elephant and accompanied the most senior religious leaders into a temple. There he was bathed in holy water, dressed in special royal cloth brocade with red, blue and gold motifs of interlocking circles, the auspicious 'sinjang kawung'.[199] Then, once again, the king was revered by the religious leaders as an enlightened being, a protector of the land. That evening, he was once again raised to the exalted status of an enlightened being.

A diplomat without a nose

Later that year, a few weeks after the Wurare ceremony, a diplomat from China, Meng Qi, arrived at the port of Tuban and made his way to Kertanegara's palace in Singasari.[200] Kublai Khan was growing impatient with Singasari, which he regarded as an inferior kingdom that needed to be brought under his control. The diplomat had received clear instructions – King Kertanegara must agree to be a vassal of the Yuan dynasty and send a member of the royal family to Dadu (Peking) to live in the court of the Great Khan.

Over the years, palace life had widened Kertanegara's waist and denuded his scalp. Other qualities, too, were diminished. Patience, for example. Although deeply resentful of the increasingly aggressive demands received over the years, when he heard the Chinese envoy had arrived in town, he agreed to grant Meng Qi an audience.

When the envoy entered the courtyard, Kertanegara sat on an elevated pavilion. In attendance were the royal council, his four daughters, Prince Widjaya, his *patih* and his senior advisors. He made a point of introducing the daughters to the visitor from China. Tribhuwana, the eldest, was playful and a bit of a comedian, he said, Prajnaparamita was the queen's favourite, Narendra Duhita was the most obedient, and Gayatri, the youngest, was the brightest and the king's pet.[201]

The envoy, who remained standing, nodded politely and greeted the king and his family. After a brief summary of his journey from China – rather uneventful, bar an encounter with some pirates – he went on to say that he was pleased to see Singasari flourishing and was delighted to report that Kublai Khan was in excellent health. Then he got to the point. He had been instructed by the Khan to return to Dadu (Peking) with a member of the royal family and Singasari must also become a vassal state.

Kertanegara, who normally weighed his options carefully, lost his temper. He told the diplomat that he was arrogant, and he had no intention of sending any members of his family anywhere. The king ordered his guards to seize the envoy and raised his voice for all to hear that Kublai Khan needed to be sent a strong message. On his signal, a guard then took out a knife and cut off the unfortunate envoy's nose.[202] The bleeding diplomat was put on a cart and sent back to China.

A few months later, in late 1290, the mutilated diplomat walked through the halls of the palace in Dadu and presented himself to Kublai Khan, who was outraged by the mistreatment of his envoy. By then, he had received reports that Kertanegara had secured southern Sumatra and also sent a young princess, Tapasi, to Champa, to marry a local prince.[203] The Khan was also made aware that Champa had sent seedlings of the kingdom's renowned high-yielding rice to Java.

And that was not all. He was equally unimpressed by the loss of domestic tax revenue – and Chinese currency – as a result of the huge volumes of Chinese goods being traded in and around Singasari. Kertanegara was clearly becoming a force to be reckoned with.[204] The Khan summoned his commanders and ordered them to assemble a huge fleet, sail south to Java, and teach Kertanegara a lesson.

It took two years to build the ships but by February 1292, three admirals – Shi-bi, Ike Mese and Gao Xing – had twenty thousand soldiers and one thousand ships at their disposal, backed by a year's supply of provisions and forty thousand silver ingots.[205] Kertanegara was about to face the wrath of Kublai Khan.

War was coming to Java, in more ways than one.

6

Singasari Falls, Majapahit Rises

(1292 CE)

Internal fights and the destruction of a city

One sunny day in 1268, when Prince Widjaya was a little boy,[206] he was playing happily with his friends in the palace at Singasari, just as he always did. Suddenly, a gaggle of flustered ladies from the court appeared and rushed him to a large, darkened room where King Wisnuwardhana was lying on a bed surrounded by a sombre group of adults. His own father, Narasingamurti, the deputy king, was there, as was the ever present Patih Raganata, as well as various religious leaders who he didn't recognise. He acknowledged Prince Kertanegara, the king's son and heir, with a polite nod of his head. The little prince did not really know what was happening, but the king did not look well and he sensed something sad but of lasting importance was about to take place.

In a voice that was barely above a whisper, the king asked Kertanegara to look after the young Widjaya, 'just as an elder brother care for his younger brother'. He knew how important this was as the dying king and Narasingamurti had been like brothers all their lives. Kertanegara, a young man at the time, looked at the prince and smiled. The king then passed away and a year later so did Widjaya's father.

While Widjaya grew up without his father, the ladies at court ensured that he enjoyed a pampered childhood at the palace. As he grew older, he received religious instruction and military training with the children of noblemen and court officials. He made three lifelong friends – the raw and restless Lawe, the powerfully built Nambi, and the insightful and clever Sora. Of course, given his exalted position, Prince Widjaya was the centre of attention. He was handsome and considered by all to be kind and caring, and a very good listener, a quality that was often in short supply in a court riven by different factions. His ability to straddle a political divide or two when needed was a skill that proved to be very useful later in life. Most importantly, he was a Rajasa, a descendent of the legendary King Ken Arok, and a future king of the realm.

King Kertanegara treated him not just as a younger brother but also as his successor. As the years passed and Kertanegara's wife delivered not a son but four daughters, it became increasingly clear that the prince would marry Kertanegara's eldest daughter, the playful and mischievous Tribhuwana.

Young Prince Widjaya soon became immersed in matters of state. He saw off Admiral Anabrang at a farewell ceremony before the expedition to Sumatra, and he was in attendance when the first envoys from China arrived. By the time Kertanegara ordered the invasion of Bali, the prince was an ambitious young man in his early twenties. He witnessed the grand procession and sacred rituals at the Wurare cemetery to celebrate the unification of the archipelago and sat close to the king when a guard cut off the nose of Ming Qi, the unfortunate Chinese diplomat.

Wiraraja's revenge

The prince might have been popular at the Singasari court but, as he and the royal family knew all too well, trouble was never far away. On the far side of the mountains lay the city of Kediri, which had been the dominant force in eastern Java until 1222, when Ken Arok triumphed at the Battle of Ganter. Playing second fiddle for decades had never gone down well with the Kediri nobles and landlords, especially after Singasari grew increasingly powerful.

It wasn't just a matter of territory – King Kertanegara now controlled the whole of Java, parts of Sumatra, Bali, Madura, Bakulapura in Kalimantan on the island of Borneo, and Pahang on the Malay peninsula, and had an alliance with the state of Champa. It was also about wealth. The large numbers of merchants flooding into Canggu, the fortified trading town on the River Brantas and Mas River, not far from Singasari, meant that trade, money and luxury goods flowed freely on one side of the mountains. In truth, Kediri had become a bit of a backwater. As such, it was no surprise that the disgruntled noblemen kept a close eye on Prince Widjaya, the successor to the throne.

The governor of Kediri was a nobleman called Jayakatwang, who was, in theory, a loyal servant to the king. Kertanegara, mindful of the festering disquiet in Kediri, as a sign of respect, appointed Jayakatwang's son, Ardaraja, as the commander of his army. There were even plans for Ardaraja to marry one of the king's daughters. On the surface, the gesture of goodwill had the desired effect. Every year, Kediri noblemen would journey to Singasari to honour Kertanegara and participate in rituals and festivities. But behind closed doors they were waiting for the right opportunity to restore Kediri to its former glory.

That opportunity[207] arrived in 1292 as a consequence of another long-standing grudge. Before Kertanegara's army had set sail to subdue strategic parts of Sumatra in response to the Mongol advances, the commander in charge of the campaign had taken measures to prevent an attack from the rear. He was concerned about potentially hostile elements on the nearby island of Madura, opposite the strategically important port of Tuban. After Madura surrendered, the ambitious court official, Wiraraja, was appointed governor.[208] The problem was that he saw this 'promotion' as an insult, a way to remove him from the centre of power in Singasari. He was an embittered man.

As the fleet set off for Sumatra under admiral Kebo 'The Crosser' Anabrang, Kertanegara was not worried that a relatively small number of soldiers were left to defend Singasari. Madura was secure and Kediri was an ally, he thought, so there was nothing to fear. It was a mistake that would cost him his life. Jayakatwang, the governor of Kediri, ever the opportunist, was mulling his options when a messenger arrived with a letter from Wiraraja in Madura. The letter contained a cryptic message:

'Master, if you want to go hunting, this is the time. There are

no alligators, tigers, wild buffalos or snakes or thorns. There is a tiger, but he is toothless.'[209]

Jayakatwang knew exactly what Wiraraja meant. Kertanegara's soldiers – the alligators and buffalos – were in Sumatra, while the toothless tiger was the politically astute Raganata, the *patih* who had been side-lined several years earlier. Wiraraja, still angry about missing out on a powerful position at the royal court,[210] was telling him this was the moment to attack Singasari.

Jayakatwang called his advisors together. His *patih* had a cunning plan. They would split the Kediri army into two and attack Singasari from the north and the south. One group would take the northern route to act as a decoy. The troops would make no attempt to hide their presence and would raise Kediri's trademark red-and-white banners to the accompaniment of drums and trumpets. At the same time, a far larger army of ten thousand of the Kediri's best soldiers would approach from the south under the cover of night to avoid detection. General Kebo Mundarang – 'The Buffalo', presumably because of his girth and strength – was put in charge of that main force. It was a risky strategy as the general's men would have to navigate a series of ravines and valleys around Mount Kelud and Mount Kawi, the two mountains that separated the rival states.

The precise day of the attack was agreed before the two armies left Kediri. It would be on an auspicious day when Kertanegara was intoxicated with palm wine[211] while he attended a night-time tantric sex ritual. To inspire his troops, Jayakatwang vowed to lead a life of austerity, abstaining from all worldly pleasures for the duration of the military operation.

Meanwhile, back at his palace, Kertanegara was surprised when Raganata, his former right-hand man, shared some disturbing news. A village head had seen a group of Kediri soldiers nearby[212] and dispatched a messenger to inform Raganata about these strange troop movements.[213] Despite being shifted to a religious role, the old *patih* had maintained his network of contacts across the kingdom and remained totally devoted to the king. But Kertanegara brushed the warning aside. Jayakatwang was his brother-in-law, his son was a commander in the king's military, and every year he drank and ate with the Kediri nobles. The village head must have been mistaken. But shortly afterwards, another messenger arrived. There were confirmed reports of skirmishes between Kertanegara's guards and the Kediris with their trademark red-and-white banners, just north of Singasari.

Recreation of a relief on Candi Ceto, Mount Lawu, Java, depicting a soldier carrying a banner. [Illustration: Ilyasza]

Kertanegara, realising he had been betrayed, flew into a rage. He summoned his two leading commanders and told Prince Widjaya and Ardaraja, the son of Jayakatwang, to each take a thousand men and put down the revolt. The counter attack was an immediate success, with Prince Widjaya pushing the Kediri troops back to a place called Kedung Peluk[214] near the ocean. The revolt seemed to have been quelled well before the Kediri troops had gotten anywhere near the city.

But Kertanegara was walking straight into a trap.

Kertanegara's assassination

At the time Prince Widjaya was pushing the Kediri troops back to the sea, several local stonemasons were perched high up on scaffolding on a new temple being constructed just south of Singasari, a stone's throw from the two giant stone *darwapala* statues that acted as spiritual guardians to the city.[215] The *candi* was nearly finished but the reliefs and inscriptions – mostly heads of monsters, tales of heroic battles, and the king's good deeds – still had to be carved on the walls. It was the same tower that, centuries later, would be rediscovered deep in the jungle by Sir Stamford Raffles in 1815.

The chatter among the men early that fine morning was all about the treasonous Kediri, how they had shamelessly attacked Singasari, how prince Widjaya had saved the day, and how the detestable Jayakatwang deserved to be wiped off the face of the earth. The stonemasons had an excellent view over the surrounding paddy fields and forests surrounding Singasari. One of them noticed something glinting in the distance. He squinted to take a closer look and saw large numbers of armed men making their way through fields. They carried no banners but they were clearly not local soldiers as most of them were away fighting in Sumatra. It was the start of another Kediri attack, this time from the south.

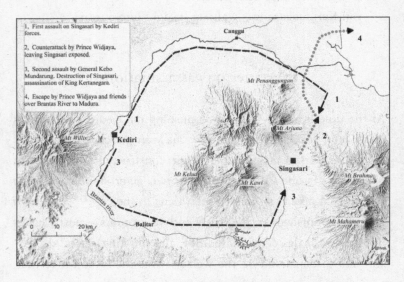

Kediri assault on Singasari, 1292. [Illustration: HvdL]

The men raised the alarm and the news of a second attack spread quickly across the thinly defended city. The streets were soon jammed with terror-stricken people trying to flee to safety. But it was too late. The Kediri army indiscriminately slaughtered men, women and children, shops were set on fire and houses plundered, but the main prize was the palace.

King Kertanegara remained a true believer in his spiritual powers right to the end. Hopelessly outnumbered, with the city ablaze and the rebel forces closing in, he summoned priests to create a sacred space. Incantations were chanted, and palm wine was passed between the members of the king's inner circle. Kertanegara, a skull cup filled with wine in hand, summoned all his powers to release *sakti*, the spiritual energy that would protect his palace. Alas, the gods deserted him in his hour of need.

The soldiers stormed through the palace gates and across the central square. They pushed the priests aside, stabbed the king to death, and proceeded to kill everyone in the room. Patih Kebo Tengah tried to fight them off but was cut down.[216] After nearly forty years on the throne, King Kertanegara, and the men who had been closest to him throughout his life, including his childhood friend Pati-Pati, lay dead on the ground, soaked in blood.

The palace was in chaos. Three of the king's daughters were seized and held as hostages.[217] The youngest, Princess Gayatri, managed to hide her identity. Her quick-witted servant, Sodrakara, dressed the princess in a simple smock and told the Kediri soldiers she was the daughter of a minor official. They were taken with the other commoners to Kediri, where the princess posed as a servant in the rather modest (or so she thought) royal palace.

Prince Widjaya and his men were returning from the north of the city when the news of Kertanegara's death and the capture of the princesses reached them.[218] Morale sank even further when it became clear that Jayakatwang's son, Ardaraja, had sided with his father's forces.[219] For a moment the prince wanted to return to Singasari to salvage what was left of the city but he soon realised that all was lost. He fled into the forests with his closest friends, Lawe, Nambi and Sora, as well as a handful of loyal soldiers.

General Kebo Mundarang, well aware that Widjaya was officially the next in line for the throne, wanted the prince's head. He took some of his men and tracked the fugitives down to an old paddy field. There they battled it out in hand-to-hand combat which left bodies strewn across the muddy field. The general, spear in hand, was about to impale Prince Widjaya when, flailing around on the ground, he found a shard of metal from an old plough and slashed the general across the eyes. In the confusion that followed, the prince and his men escaped into the forests.

Dusk had fallen and the Kediri soldiers set up camp in preparation for continuing their search the next day. Prince Widjaya, happy to be alive but bent on revenge, was planning his next move when his friend Sora suggested that this was the perfect time to launch a surprise attack under the cover of darkness. Guided by moonlight, the small band of men emerged from the forest, crossed the paddy field, entered the camp, and killed a large number of Kediri soldiers as they slept.

Amid the blood and the screams, the prince's men beat a hasty retreat into the woods. As they stumbled through the darkness, to their amazement they came across Princess Tribhuwana, the eldest daughter of Kertanegara, sitting near a campfire[220] with hardly a guard in sight. Her rescue was completed in seconds. It transpired that she was to be taken to Kediri, where two of her sisters were already being held hostage. The unexpected reunion lifted the prince's spirits. He wanted to stage another attack in the hope of finding the other princesses. But Sora persuaded him against it. The plan was too dangerous, they had few men, and the element of surprise was gone.[221] The prince decided to withdraw into the forest, lick his wounds, and rest up.

Escape to Madura

Prince Widjaya knew they could not survive in the open for very long. The half-blinded General Kebo Mundarang, enraged at letting the heir to the throne slip through his fingers, was bound to be sending out search parties. They needed a safe refuge and the prince knew where to go. The bedraggled group, some wounded, trekked across valleys and ravines to the slopes of Mount Semeru, living off coconuts and fruit collected along the way. Santamurti, the former religious advisor to Kertanegara, had retreated there in order to live out his life as an ascetic.[222] Santamurti's successor was Raganata, the king's former right-hand man shunted aside by younger advisors, who had first alerted the king to the impending attack on Singasari.

They were in good, loyal hands. Santamurti offered them food, shelter, and the opportunity to recover from their ordeal. He was shocked by what had happened and would do everything in his power to help the royal family. As the prince regained his strength, Santamurti offered him a piece of advice. He should escape to Madura and seek sanctuary in Wiraraja's palace.[223] Neither, of course, knew the devious hand the governor of this relatively insignificant island had played in the king's downfall. As far as they knew, Wiraraja was a man on whom they could rely.

The next day, the prince and the princess led their followers north towards the River Brantas. From there they hoped to reach the coast and make the short sea crossing to Madura. But they were soon spotted by Kediri soldiers and had to make a run for it. Their only chance of escape was to cross the fast-flowing river, providing target practice for the Kediri archers. Some men were dragged downstream by the strong current and drowned and only twelve, including the prince and princess, Sora, Nambi and Lawe, made it to the other side.[224]

The small band wandered through fields and forests and eventually stumbled, exhausted, on the tiny settlement of Kudadu. The head of the village knew he was risking his life by offering them food, water and shelter. He had loved the old king and despised the rebels so agreed to hide his unexpected guests just before the Kediri troops arrived. Asked if he had seen the prince, the village head sent the soldiers off in the wrong direction. The next day, forever in their debt, the prince bade farewell to the villagers; the twelve survivors reached the coast, made the short crossing to Madura and, from there, made their way to Wiraraja's palace.

Their arrival created quite a stir. Nobody expected a prince and a princess to turn up unannounced, especially Wiraraja. Did they know that he had encouraged Jayakatwang to attack Singasari? Were they here to take revenge? He calmed down once it became clear that the prince was completely in the dark. He welcomed his visitors with open arms while he plotted his next move. Surely, the treacherous Jayakatwang was going to reward him for his timely advice and frankly he had quite enough of being just about the only fish in the very small pond that was Madura.

Prince Widjaya was pleasantly surprised by Wiraraja's generous hospitality. He spent a lot of time with him, dining at his high table and enjoying the best food and palm wine Madura had to offer. The prince had plenty of time to tell him what had happened, from the treacherous attack on Singasari to the assassination of King Kertanegara, the capture of the princesses, and the series of narrow escapes from the Kediri soldiers.

While Wiraraja feigned shock and outrage he was happy to finally know the whole story. Reliable information took a long time to reach Madura. The prince warmed to his host and one night, after perhaps a few too many cups of wine, made a very bold statement. Should he ever rule Java, he would divide his realm with Wiraraja.[225] It was an emotional outburst that he came to regret years later.

At the same time, while wisps of smoke were still rising from the ruins of Singasari, the newly crowned King Jayakatwang was back home in Kediri celebrating the city's restored glory and the plunder of his rival's vast treasury. His vow to abstain from earthly pleasures was a distant memory. What's more, he had two valuable hostages, the Singasari princesses. Life was good. Perhaps to avoid further aggravating what was already a tense political situation, he permitted Kertanegara to be revered as a Shiva Buddha at his funeral in honour of his spiritual powers. The king's ashes were scattered at two prominent temples nearby, Sagala and Wairosana.[226]

The city of Singasari was abandoned as people moved to Kediri, the new capital, or disappeared into the villages that dotted the lands. The temple where the stonemasons were working on that fateful day in 1292 was never finished. The site was left undisturbed for sixty years, until Hayam Wuruk, accompanied by Prapanca and the rest of the royal entourage, visited the ruins to honour the memory of King Kertanegara. Centuries later, in August 1815, Raffles and his men would hack their way through the jungle to wake the unfinished temple from its slumber.

Soon a new city would emerge, one even more glorious than Singasari. It would be built close to the holy Wurare cemetery where, in 1292, priests had elevated Kertanegara to the status of an enlightened being, and, two centuries earlier, the sage Bharata had attempted to divide King Airlangga's kingdom in two. Its people called the city Wilwatikta, but it became known for the bitter *(pahit) maja* fruit trees common to the area.

That was the city of Majapahit.

Majapahit rises

Late 1292, the island of Madura.
While the prince felt safe in Madura, he knew he could not stay there for too long. He needed a plan to regain the throne. Then, one morning, his host shared an interesting idea. Wiraraja made it clear to the prince that he was in no position to stage a counter attack. Much better would be to reach out to King Jayakatwang and acknowledge defeat and tell the new king he was willing to work in his service. Once Prince Widjaya had gained the king's

trust, he might be allowed to build a new settlement,[227] with Wiraraja's help of course. After that, anything might be possible.

The prince realised he had little choice. He had no men and no money. A pauper prince without an army was unlikely to rally many to his cause. Wiraraja sent a messenger to inform Jayakatwang that the prince was in Madura, wanted to surrender, and was prepared to serve under him.[228] Jayakatwang was immediately suspicious, as was his scheming *patih*, the man who came up with the brilliant idea of how to capture Singasari. But the more they thought about it, the more the offer started to make sense. After all, the reality was that Prince Widjaya posed no real threat and the new king was indeed very much in Wiraraja's debt. He just had to admire the man's duplicity and the governor of that island backwater deserved better.

And so, it was agreed that the fugitive prince would be allowed to return to Java. A few weeks later, Prince Widjaya and his men rode into the city of Kediri to surrender themselves. The princess, who understandably had some long-standing trust issues, stayed behind in Madura. It was the time of the year when Kediri was abuzz with preparations for the week-long Galangan festival, a time when the gods and spirits of ancestors descended from the heavens and joined in the celebrations.[229]

The highlight of the festival was a large military tournament. King Jayakatwang, whose already large ego was now considerably inflated, wanted to show his people that the famed Prince Widjaya was now his subject. The tables had been turned, and seventy years after the battle of Ganter, when Ken Arok defeated the Kediri forces, it was Singasari that lay in ashes.

The tournament featured hand-to-hand combat and martial arts, from wrestling and sword fighting to archery and jousting. It was a hugely popular event and people poured into town to watch the rare spectacle of military might. As the drink flowed, the guards struggled to keep the unruly crowd under control. This was of course much more than entertainment for the masses; it was pure propaganda. The climax of the festival was a staged battle between the forces from Singasari (*boos from the crowd*), commanded by Prince Widjaya, and the local heroes from Kediri (*huge cheers*). A large stage was erected to ensure that the king and his ministers and priests had the best view in the house.

Unfortunately for the home team, things did not go quite to plan. The first round of hand-to-hand combat was won by the Singasari men, led by Prince Widjaya himself. Jayakatwang stood up, smiled, and told the excitable crowd that a rematch was in order. And in the interests of personal safety, the prince would not compete; it was too dangerous and all that. This meant the Singasari team would start a man short.

Embarrassment soon turned to humiliation when Singasari won the second battle too. The king had lost face and the crowd was turning hostile and all eyes turned to the ashen-faced monarch who sat on the raised stage with the VIPs. But it was Prince Widjaya who stood up and addressed the crowds: 'Clearly the men from Kediri let them, the guests from Singasari, win in battle, as a good host would do. It shows the greatness of King Jayakatwang.' The crowd cheered and the prince noted the broad smile that spread across Jayakatwang's face. It was a masterful piece of diplomacy. The prince had defused a situation which could have easily turned very nasty, and shortly afterwards the king and his vassal adjourned for some serious feasting.

The prince had another reason to be cheerful. During the tournament he had spotted a familiar face in the vast crowd: Gayatri, the youngest Singasari princess who had hidden her identity when the city fell. He had no idea that she was still alive and soon learnt the princess had adopted a new name, Ratna Sutawan, and was working incognito as a servant in the palace. Apparently, the king had taken a liking to her but Gayatri had been able to avoid his advances, at least for the moment.[230] The other two princesses also attended the tournament, so he knew for the first time that all four of King Kertanegara's daughters had survived.[231]

***

Early 1293, Majapahit.
Shortly after the Galangan festival, Prince Widjaya approached Jayakatwang to discuss the sensitive matter of where he and his men were to live on a permanent basis. As Singasari was clearly not an option, the prince suggested a place near a small forest named Trik, halfway between Singasari and Kediri, close to the Wurare cemetery. The strategic location had been originally suggested by the cunning, two-faced Wiraraja. The king, ever suspicious, reluctantly gave his approval on one condition – Widjaya's men could move there but the prince himself had to stay in Kediri, where the palace guards could keep an eye on him.

And so, Prince Widjaya's men rode out to the forest of Trik

where they were joined by some of Wiraraja's men from Madura. They chopped down trees, cleared the area and built houses and an audience hall. One day, some of the men had put down their axes to rest and eat some of the fruit that had fallen from the *maja* trees. But when one took a bite he screwed up his face like a macaque who had swallowed a wasp, and quickly spat out the bitter fruit. Another joked that the whole forest was full of bitter *maja* or '*maja pahit*'. The name stuck and the new town was called Majapahit.[232]

A few weeks later, under the pretext of checking on the progress of the construction work, the prince rode out to Majapahit. It was a place of great beauty, with sublime views and coconut and banana trees growing in abundance in the fertile soil; along both sides of the path stood an expanse of tamarind trees that gave plenty of shade. He noted that the small settlement was in a strategic location at a point where two rivers met, one flowing west and the other north. Small boats ferried supplies up and down the rivers from settlements nearby, and fish were so plentiful they almost jumped into the men's nets. In the evenings, swarms of bats and swallows arrived to devour the mosquitos and flies that infested the riverbanks. Prince Widjaya judged it a perfect place to start again.

The prince was also pleased to see the number of supporters had increased significantly. The word was spreading that he was back. What was once a broken band of fugitives was turning into something far more promising.

His new home was shaping up nicely and it also had a strong spiritual aura as it was very close to the place where

King Kertanegara had been deified at the cemetery at Wurare. In honour of the prince's arrival his men built a makeshift throne, a seat of white stone raised on a dais in a small hall built of wood.[233] To show how pleased he was to see his loyal followers again, the prince gave each of them a special rank.[234] First up was the raw and restless Lawe, who was appointed head of the guards, a 'Rangga', and was now known as 'Rangga Lawe'.[235]

In Kediri, King Jayakatwang was not a happy man. The prince was out of town inspecting his new settlement and there were reports that workers from Madura had arrived in Majapahit to help. He called in his minister Winotan and told him to visit Majapahit, check on the prince, and order him to return: 'Tell him I want him back here for a hunting trip near Kediri.'[236]

When the minister rode into the Majapahit he was taken aback by the scale of the building work at Majapahit. The whole place was a giant construction site. The prince greeted him and had little choice but to show him around. The minister could not fail to notice the large number of workers from Madura. Strange, he thought. What was going on? He then told the prince that the king wanted him to return to Kediri to go hunting.

Winotan joked that he would love to see the Madurese hunt – an obvious sneer at their low status as they were all clearly peasants. That did not go down well with the hot-headed Rangga Lawe who was about to draw his keris and teach the arrogant minister a lesson, when the prince intervened. He apologised and told the minister that he should not take Rangga Lawe too seriously; the man had a good heart but was a bit on the crude side as he had mixed with Madurese peasants during his childhood.[237]

Mollified by these diplomatic remarks, Winotan went on his way and the prince told him he would follow soon.

Prince Widjaya was in a dilemma. He knew that the king was suspicious but if he did not return he would surely be escorted back to Kediri under guard. What then? He asked his three closest friends for advice. The impulsive Rangga Lawe predictably urged an immediate (and unwise) attack on Kediri; Nambi suggested he should return and peel support away from the king by building alliances at court; the thoughtful Sora pointed out the risk in such an approach – some of the noblemen could not be trusted and would almost certainly betray him.

The prince was not convinced by any of these ideas. Better, he said, to consult Wiraraja, who was still the Governor of Madura. The cunning old fox was bound to have a plan. Wiraraja kept it to himself but he was still furious that his mendacity over the fall of Singasari had yet to be rewarded by the powers that be. A messenger was sent and a reply came back in record time. As it happened, Wiraraja had a very good plan. Kublai Khan's armada had been spotted close to the strategic port of Tuban. Perhaps the prince and his men should join forces with the Chinese and rise up against the usurper Jayakatwang?

7

Brawls and Betrayals

(1292 – 1300 CE)

Kublai Khan invades Java and gets played

On a warm, sticky March day in 1293,[238] Chinese admiral Ike Mese gazed out from the deck of his ship across the ocean. He liked what he saw. Hundreds of heavily armed Chinese war junks were under sail for as far as the eye could see; Kublai Khan's mighty armada ready to invade Java. The admiral, a Uyghur from the far northwest, was an experienced captain, navigator and diplomat who had already completed four missions overseas, but he had never attempted anything on this scale. This was his moment.

Three months earlier he had set sail from Quanzhou, a major shipbuilding centre – the same city where, in 1222, Zhao Rugua had collected stories from visiting sailors and written a book about it – which was now the largest port in south-eastern China and an important stop on the maritime Silk Road. The journey was turbulent from the outset – several ships sank during a powerful typhoon and the weather remained foul. Ike Mese wrote in his log: 'The wind was strong and the sea very rough, so that the ships rolled heavily and the soldiers could not eat for many days.'[239]

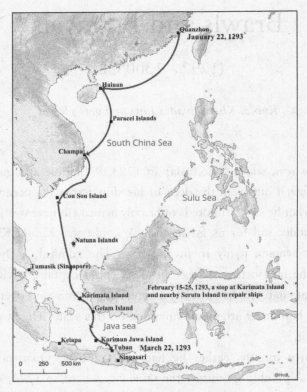

Route from China to Java, 1293.
[Illustration: HvdL; Credit: Hung et. al., 2022]

A few weeks later they reached the coast of the Champa kingdom in what is today southern Vietnam. Reports soon reached King Jaya Simhawarman III that a huge armada had been spotted not far from land. Not again, he thought. In the previous decade Champa had fought off four major Mongol military expeditions but had finally agreed to pay tribute to Dadu (Peking) to avoid further conflict. The king rapidly mobilized his troops[240] only to discover, to his immense relief, that the Chinese came in peace and wanted only to buy food and water. He was further reassured to hear that once the ships had been replenished they would sail on and the wrath of Kublai Khan would fall on the arrogant Javanese further south.

The admiral ordered several ships to sail west to Sumatra[241] to establish a presence in what was an important sea lane. Just a few months earlier the itinerant Venetian, Marco Polo, had sailed the same route to Sumatra on his way home from China in 1292. There, he made the discovery that parts of northern Sumatra were controlled by Muslims.[242]

The rest of the fleet continued the journey south, passing the Riau islands, an archipelago between Sumatra and the southern tip of Malay peninsula, before dropping anchor at a small island (probably Serutu) off the coast of Kalimantan.[243] Here, the thousands of soldiers and sailors rested up while carpenters made repairs and also built smaller vessels that could be sailed up the shallow rivers in Java.

With the ships replenished and repaired, the admiral gave the order to weigh anchor and set course due south for Java. Despite all his years of experience he was apprehensive. This was his moment, his chance to win the everlasting approval of the mighty Khan. Lost in his thoughts, his reverie was broken by a loud cheer. High up in the rigging, a lookout had spotted land. Slowly, light blue mountains covered by cumulus clouds came into view and two hours later coconut palms lining a white sand beach and Tuban's distinctive two large white limestone rocks became clearly visible. After a journey of three months crossing more than 4,000 kilometres of ocean, they had finally reached Java.

The huge fleet moored outside the port of Tuban, the town that for years had served as the maritime gateway to Singasari further inland, now sadly destroyed. The Tuban locals, while accustomed to the coming and going of large numbers of vessels from different countries, had never seen anything like it.

As the draft of the Chinese junks was up to fifteen metres[244] – too deep to enter the shallow harbour – the first task was to commandeer small boats to ferry some of the soldiers to the shore. The admiral was nervous. His troops were vulnerable to a counterattack but he was relieved when he was told that the operation went smoothly and there were no signs of hostile forces.[245] A small boat then ferried over three officials from the splendidly named Office of Pacification who carried a blunt message for the king. He was about to feel the wrath of the Mongol army.

The larger part of the fleet raised anchor and sailed seventy kilometres eastwards to a deeper anchorage at the mouth of the Solo River where they set up camp near a town named Sedayu near Surabaya. Scouts were sent to explore the surrounding area and returned with reports of an impressive 'floating bridge' over the River Mas, a tributary of the Brantas, where local traders gathered to barter goods.[246] As soon as the camp was set up and properly defended, the specially made boats went on the first expedition up the shallow River Solo. A large number of vessels were seized from a local commander, an event worthy of a comment in Admiral Ike Mese's logbook:

The commanders of the imperial army made a camp in the form of a crescent on the bank of the river and left the ferry in charge of a Commander of Ten Thousand; the fleet in the river and the cavalry and infantry on shore then advanced together and Hi-ning-kuan, seeing this, left his boat and fled overnight, whereupon more than a hundred large ships, with devil-heads on the stem, were captured.[247]

So far, so good. But then a message arrived from the Office of Pacification in Tuban. King Kertanegara, the man Kublai Khan wanted to teach a lesson, was dead and his capital city had been destroyed. A new leader – King Jayakatwang – ruled the kingdom from a city called Kediri that was said to be on the other side of the mountains. Clearly, a fresh plan was needed.

The march on Kediri

The Uyghur admiral quickly conferred with his two commanders, Shi-bi, a Mongol, and Gaoxing, who was Chinese. Clearly, the new king must be found and forced to swear allegiance to Kublai Khan. But how? And where was he to be found? They knew very little about this huge mountainous island and that made them nervous. In the meantime, they ordered scouts to map the terrain further inland.

A few days later, a courier arrived at their camp with an

intriguing message. A man calling himself Prince Widjaya, who claimed to be the rightful heir to the throne, had gathered a small force in a place called Majapahit, located further up the River Brantas. The commanders had never heard of him, or Majapahit for that matter. The prince was offering to submit to Kublai Khan if the admirals would help him crush King Jayakatwang in Kediri. In addition, the message read, the princesses in Kediri would accompany the expedition back to China as a token of respect and appreciation. The prince was also offering to supply them with maps to point the invaders in the right direction and, even better, a powerful local landlord named Wiraraja was willing to offer armed support to the prince and the Mongol commanders.

The commanders gathered all the intelligence they could. Senior members of the distinctly nervous local population confirmed that Prince Widjaya was indeed both popular and deemed to be the legitimate heir to King Kertanegara, who had fathered four daughters. Before the king was assassinated and Singasari razed to the ground, the plan was for the prince to marry Kertanegara's eldest daughter, Tribhuwana, who was now held prisoner by the snake Jayakatwang, who no one in that part of Java seemed to trust. One small detail the elders thought fit to omit was that the young prince was present when Ming Qi, the unfortunate Chinese diplomat, had had his nose cut off. Those in the know were well aware that this was the very reason why the huge armada had arrived on their shores.

This was an offer the Chinese admirals could not refuse and so the commanders agreed to work with Prince Widjaya and Wiraraja to crush King Jayakatwang in Kediri. A flurry of messages was exchanged with Majapahit in order to coordinate an attack. First, the Mongols' shallower vessels sailed and poled down the River Mas to Majapahit to rendezvous with Prince Widjaya. First impressions were positive. The prince, a slender man with big lips and an elongated face, came across as intelligent and a born leader, clearly someone the commanders could work with.[248] At the Majapahit court they were also introduced to Wiraraja, the ambitious man who controlled the small island of Madura. He was older, more experienced, and commanded respect. But as they would discover later, far too late as it happened, he was also a double-crossing rogue of the highest order.

From Majapahit, the three forces – one led by the invaders, another by the prince, and a third by the man from the island of Madura – advanced on Kediri, some eighty kilometres inland along the Brantas River. They stayed close to the banks of the river, swollen by regular afternoon downpours in the early months of the rainy season, to avoid getting stuck in dense forests farther inland.

This was a huge army, numbering tens of thousands of soldiers, comprising war elephants, infantry and horsemen armed with pikes, battle axes, bows and rockets, as well as a weapon completely new to the Javanese such as the Chinese *tie pao*, grenades launched by catapults. The army was supported by hundreds of oxcarts that transported food, animal fodder and supplies, and scores of pack elephants which were strong enough to bear the weight of the dismantled parts of the huge siege engines, which later would hurl giant boulders at the Kediri palace walls. At the rear of the column were the doctors and surgeons who watched over the carts carrying their medical equipment and medicines – fearsome saws for amputations, canisters of salves for flesh wounds and thick pastes of turmeric, tamarind and ginger to aid recovery.

Their camp near the city must have made a terrifying sight. There were multiple reports of desperate Kediri nobles trying to bury their riches and hundreds of women and children fleeing to the mountains in panic.[249] But the Kediri army, easily identifiable by its red-and-white banners, was dug in and well prepared, led by the famed general Kebo Mundarung, the man who had nearly killed Prince Widjaya in a muddy field a few months earlier. It was a momentous battle that would shape the destiny of Java for centuries and mark the rise of Majapahit as the centre of power in Java.

The attack came from three flanks.[250] Wiraraja's forces made the first assault, and a second came from the opposite bank of the river, led by Prince Widjaya and his three most loyal lieutenants, Lawe, Nambi and Sora. The main attack, from the north and along the river valley, was made by the Mongol army. The Kediri troops soon faced sustained assaults from a combination of fire arrows, siege engines and *tie pao* grenades, all supported by soldiers on war elephants. The fighting was intense, with large numbers of casualties on both sides. Fortunes ebbed and flowed and neither side would give an inch. After days of slaughter, a ceasefire was negotiated so both sides could regroup, recover their dead, and treat the wounded. But when the battle resumed, the smaller and much weakened Kediri forces soon started to disintegrate. The city was about to fall.

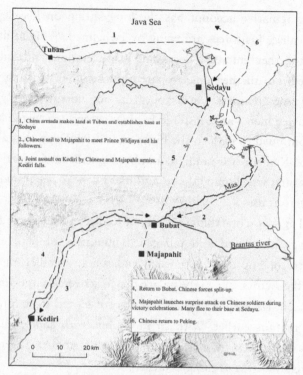

Java Sea

Tuban

Sedayu

1. China armada makes land at Tuban and establishes base at Sedayu

2. Chinese sail to Majapahit to meet Prince Widjaya and his followers.

3. Joint assault on Kediri by Chinese and Majapahit armies. Kediri falls.

Mas

Bubat

Brantas river

Majapahit

4. Return to Bubat. Chinese forces split-up.

5. Majapahit launches surprise attack on Chinese soldiers during victory celebrations. Many flee to their base at Sedayu.

6. Chinese return to Peking.

Kediri

0   10   20 km

@HvdL

Chinese invasion of Java, 1293. [Illustration: HvdL]

Different accounts provide different perspectives on what happened. The Chinese sources were short on detail but described how, when faced with the might of the Mongol army, '*soon Jayakatwang came forward to offer his submission; his wife, his children and officers were taken by the victors, who then went back.*'[251] Other sources were more elaborate and say the king was killed after fighting a heroic rear-guard action as troops entered the city and broke down the doors to the palace. The most imaginative account has the king sitting on his elephant as he realises his forces are being overwhelmed.[252] He folded his hands together, entered a deep state of meditation, and suddenly vanished into the heavens. Apparently his soldiers saw this as a sign of true greatness – a disappearing act worthy of only truly enlightened men – and, inspired by their recently departed leader, they continued to fight to the bitter end.[253] Realising that all was lost, the Kediri royal family committed suicide.[254] General Kebo Mundarung was hunted down and had his head separated from his generous torso.

All agree on one thing: the city of Kediri and the surrounding area was plundered and pillaged. Thousands of people were slaughtered, houses were burned and whole families enslaved. When the victors sacked the palace they discovered large amounts of silver in the Kediri treasury, most of it looted from Singasari a few months earlier. With so much booty to share, all three victorious armies found little to squabble about. There was, however, one area of disagreement.

Prince Widjaya ordered the Singasari princesses, who had been held captive in Kediri, to be escorted back to Majapahit. The Chinese commanders interrupted and reminded him of the deal they had made: the young ladies were for the sole pleasure of the Great Khan. The prince said there had been a misunderstanding. The deal referred to princesses in the Kediri royal family, who unfortunately were no longer available to be sent to Dadu (Peking) on account of their recent deaths. The Singasari ladies – who included the prince's fiancée – were not available. The Chinese felt betrayed and tempers frayed.

At this very tense moment, the cunning old Wiraraja stepped in and used his diplomatic skills to prevent a confrontation. He proposed that these matters should be discussed after Prince Widjaya had been crowned king in Majapahit and declared himself a vassal of Kublai Khan. The Chinese commanders grudgingly agreed and decided that one admiral with two hundred men[255] would keep an eye on the Singasari princesses while the rest of the soldiers ensured that the spoils of war reached their base camp on the coast. The plan was for all parties to reconvene in Majapahit for the coronation of Widjaya and his public submission to the mighty Khan. After that, the armada would sail back home to a hero's welcome.

Widjaya's deception

A few weeks earlier, shortly after the Chinese armada had dropped anchor off the coast of Tuban, messengers were dispatched from Majapahit to Sumatra. Much had changed since King Kertanegara had sent troops from Java to defeat the Melayu kingdom in Sumatra in 1290 in his Pamalayu campaign, making Singasari the most powerful kingdom in the region. The king was dead, Singasari was in ashes, Java was now ruled from Kediri, and a massive enemy fleet was sitting off the coast, seeking revenge for the mutilation of the envoy from Dadu (Peking). The Javanese troops in Sumatra were ordered to return immediately and the Majapahit commanders in Sumatra sailed down the Batang Hari river into the Java Sea and arrived in Tuban about ten days after the fall of Kediri.[256]

They arrived back home to find Majapahit in a state of agitated exuberance tinged with sorrow and loss. Wounded soldiers were pouring back into the city from Kediri, some families were being reunited, others mourned the death of their loved ones, and priests conducted ceremonies in the temples to thank various gods for a famous victory. In the evening, lavish feasts were held to celebrate the living and toast the departed. The whole town was awash in palm wine.

Unsurprisingly, the two hundred Chinese military escorts who were meant to be keeping an eye on the much-in-demand princesses needed no invitation to join in the wild celebrations. They had survived months at sea in foul weather as well as a ferocious battle in an alien land; on top of all that, they would soon return home rich, to be acclaimed as mighty warriors by the great Khan himself. They feasted on roasted goat and chicken, drank toast after toast around blazing campfires, and danced with the tipsy and, by this stage, somewhat lascivious local women.

They remained completely oblivious to the fact that they were about to be ambushed. In all probability it was Wiraraja, the scheming old fox who in his time had double-crossed some of the most powerful people in the land (including Prince Widjaya), who came up with the plan. By now hopelessly inebriated, the Mongols failed to notice that many of Prince Widjaya's crack troops were stone-cold sober. The sign was given and the slaughter began; the two hundred drunken soldiers were no match for the vastly superior force of Majapahit troops.

One of the Chinese commanders in charge of watching the princesses – we don't know which one – managed to escape with a handful of his men and reached the base camp, where the troops were busy loading their booty onto the ships at anchor. But the prince continued to harry the camp, inflicting more casualties. Part of the Chinese forces were cut off from the rest of the army and had to fight through hostile territory while under constant harassment from marauding Majapahit troops.

Once they were all back in camp, the three admirals convened. The situation was perilous – they had lost three thousand soldiers during the battle for Kediri and many more were wounded. And now they had been betrayed by their allies, they were vulnerable to further attacks, and morale among the troops was low. Yet all was not lost as they had looted a staggering 500,000 taels of silver (about 650,000 ounces or 18,400 kilograms) as well as valuable spices, perfumes and fabrics.[257] That would go down well back home. But a counterattack in the dense, hard-to-navigate forests of Java was unthinkable. They all agreed that it was best to cut their losses and leave immediately as the favourable monsoon winds would soon end, leaving them stranded in hostile territory for another six months.

And so, in early November 1293, a year after leaving China for Java, the order was given to weigh anchor and return to Quanzhou.[258] What was meant to be a punitive expedition had been an utter failure. Upon their return to Dadu (Peking), Admirals Shi-bi and Ike Mese were punished but Admiral Gao Xing was awarded fifty taels of gold because he had warned the others of the danger of leaving just two hundred troops in Majapahit territory. Later, the emperor showed mercy on Admirals Shi-bi and Ike-Mese and restored their reputation and property.

But the Khan was now old, obese and sick. Plagued by gout as a result of a great fondness for food and drink, his health started to fail. Soon after the return of the failed Java expedition he died on February 18, 1294, at the age of 79 and was buried at a secret location in Mongolia. In the years that followed, the threat to Southeast Asia faded. The new Khan, Temur, had problems of his own to deal with at home and thought it wise to make peace with neighbouring lands. Given the new spirit of goodwill and harmony, King Widjaya dispatched Javanese envoys to China in 1297 and 1300.[259]

For all their success on the battlefields across the world, it has to be said that the Mongols were pretty underwhelming when it came to long-distance naval campaigns. In addition to the failures in Java and Champa, Kublai Khan made two disastrous attempts to invade Japan in 1274 and 1281 after the Korean kingdom of Goryeo had become a vassal state. He sent two huge fleets but both were smashed to pieces by a combination of violent typhoons and stout defence. The *kamikaze* or 'divine winds' which sank countless ships and the heroic exploits of the samurai warriors still hold semi-mythical status in Japanese culture today.

The Mongol empire was founded by hordes of nomadic warriors who were expert horsemen, not sailors. Kublai Khan built on the success of his grandfather Genghis by building a powerful navy that played a decisive role in defeating the Song Dynasty which ruled China between 960 and 1279. But these battles were fought along China's vast network of rivers, particularly the Yangtze. The ocean-going expeditions to Southeast Asia and Japan were a major disappointment.

Statute of Prince Widjaya (Raden Widjaya),
National Museum, Jakarta. [Photo: HvdL]

Double celebrations

November 1293, the city of Majapahit.
Soon after the Chinese ships had sailed from Java, the hermit
Santamurti left his solitary existence high up on Mount Semeru to
make his way to Majapahit to preside over a double celebration
– the coronation and wedding of Prince Widjaya. The bonds
between the two men were strong and went back a long way.
Santamurti had left the court of King Kertanegara decades earlier
in search of a peaceful life as a hermit and, at great personal risk,
had been quick to offer refuge to the prince and his friends when
they were running for their lives.

Majapahit, now the centre of power in Java, was growing rapidly. The double celebration was a big moment in the city's brief history. The streets were full of builders, carpenters, painters and weavers putting the finishing touches to elaborately decorated pavilions, and excited children tied colourful banners to doorposts and trees. Court officials were busy issuing instructions and no detail was overlooked, not even the precise blend of cow dung, red *andong* blossom and lotus flowers used to decorate walls and buildings.[260]

Upon arrival, the hermit was warmly welcomed by Prince Widjaya and his family. After an exchange of pleasantries, the prince sought his advice about a tricky question. What if a nobleman married one of King Kertanegara's daughters and stirred up trouble by claiming that his wife was the valid heir to the kingdom? This could become problematic, especially if the wife gave birth to a son.

This was a good point, thought Santamurti, especially in light of the bloody history of the dynasty. But he had a simple solution. Prince Widjaya should marry all four daughters in one big wedding. And that was not all. The royals asked what about the two Melayu princesses, Dara Petak and Dara Jingga, who had recently arrived in Java from Sumatra and had been promised as wives to King Kertanegara? Santamurti suggested they could wed important noblemen; after all, the princesses were not of Rajasa blood but rather symbols of the new-found solidarity between Java and Sumatra.[261]

Quite what this assortment of young female royalty thought of this arrangement we shall never know, but the city was now ready for the festivities. The sense of excitement was palpable. Cooks slaved over hot stoves in palace kitchens, livestock was slaughtered in droves, and the smell of incense filled the streets. Foodstalls popped up on every corner, selling dried meat, *krupuk* shrimp crackers, sago cakes, and elephant-shaped biscuits, a particular favourite with the children. Even the royal elephants were given ceremonial baths. Peasants, merchants, hermits, sages and priests from all over Java arrived in town for the celebrations.

The evening before the big day,[262] the female friends and family of the brides arrived at court. Under the guidance of experienced older women who were the custodians of palace traditions, their hair was washed in holy tamarind-infused water as part of a purification ritual. Early the next morning, 21 November 1293,[263] exactly three years after Kertanegara celebrated the unification of Java in the cemetery in Wurare, a host of court musicians made their way to a pavilion at the centre of the palace. As they started to play, some of the princesses started to grumble about the endless preparations and the intense heat. It was going to be a long day.

In the early evening[264] Santamurti greeted the royal family and then proceeded to walk around the town to bless its inhabitants. Meanwhile, noble families gathered early to occupy the best vantage points and commoners jostled for position. Bells were rung to mark the start of the coronation ceremony. The royal family, accompanied by the nervous princesses, entered the city's central courtyard, an open field opposite the palace. Everywhere was bathed in the light of hundreds of torches, and guards kept the huge and happy throng in order.

After an initial prayer, the old hermit proclaimed that:

'With the death of Jayakatwang, the world is clear and without disturbance[265] and under Widjaya the whole of Java most humbly comes forward to pay respect. And all are equally delighted to see the king's consorts.[266]

'From here on, this new king is to be known as Sri Kertarajasa Jayawardhana, a descendant of Ken Arok, King Rajasa, the founder of the royal dynasty in Singasari. Majapahit and Singasari might be different cities, but they are all part of the same mandala kingdom.' And with these words, Prince Widjaya was crowned king[267] and a huge roar went up from the crowd.

Now it was time for the wedding. First, an official read from a scroll that discussed the advantages of a love marriage (tricky in the circumstances) and the merits of marrying an immature girl, in full bloom, as against an older one (no problems on that front). The four princesses then stood up and walked over to choose their husband and the crowds cheered when – surprise, surprise – they all selected King Widjaya. Ceremonial necklaces were draped around his neck and the princesses were carried out of the grounds in palanquins, shaded by umbrellas, to the thunderous beating of drums while spectators stamped their feet in excitement.

The princesses were taken to an inner palace court where they were bathed by nuns[268] to the accompaniment of drums and cymbals. Santamurti read a text to purify the young women, who were then dressed in full bridal attire – heavy on jewels, crowns, and rings on toes and thumbs – and taken to a shrine where the king was waiting. There, Santamurti read another prayer and led the king and the princesses around the shrine seven times. They were then directed to a fire where they offered wood to Agni, the

A temple relief at Candi Penataran near Blitar, East Java,
depicting a queen in a palanquin in a wedding procession.

god of fire, who came down from the heavens to witness the event.
The fire ritual marked the end of the formal marriage ceremony.[269]
All that was left was for the king and his wives to withdraw to the
palace where they were 'like a bee and asana flowers'.

While the bee and the asana flowers were getting to know
each other, the city partied hard. At first light, nobles, brahmins,
priests, peasants and merchants were seen stumbling back to their
homes. In the days that followed, there were puppet and clown
shows, masked dances and sports contests. And, as usual, the
main evening attraction was the huge amount of food and palm
wine available.

A series of ceremonies followed over the next few days.
Tradition required that the new king reward those who had helped
him in the past. King Widjaya awarded Wiraraja the highest
title available to someone outside the royal family – *rakryan* or

honourable gentleman. He also proclaimed that Wiraraja was to rule a large part of the eastern part of Java. So, the ambitious court official who railed at being stuck in the backwater of Madura had finally made it. And it is still not clear if the new king was aware that it was Wiraraja who had suggested that Jayakatwang attack Singasari and depose King Kertanegara. In his defence, he had certainly redeemed himself.

As the incarnation of Shiva and Vishnu, King Widjaya's main task was the spiritual wellbeing of the realm. That involved endless ceremonies, daily prayers and regular visits to shrines and temples across the lands. As such, he declared that the day-to-day running of his kingdom was to be left to his trusted advisors. The thoughtful and diplomatic Nambi became *patih*, the charmingly rude and somewhat bigoted Lawe was appointed governor of the important region of Tuban, and clever Sora became the king's chamberlain.[270] The king also appointed two *dharmadyaksas*, one each for Shiva and Buddhists affairs.[271] The Buddhist *dharmadyaksa* was to be the grandfather of Prapanca, the court poet and historian met earlier who would detail life in Java during the early reign of Hayam Wuruk, who ruled from around 1353[272] to 1389.

The new monarch did not forget the people in the small hamlet of Kudaku. They had, at great risk to their own lives, provided refuge when Widjaya and his men were on the run from Jayakatwang's general, Kebo Mundarung, in the weeks after the fall of Singasari. At the time, he had promised the villagers would be rewarded and he was true to his word. From here on, he stated in a special copper charter, the village was free from taxes and the villagers were owners of all the surrounding lands.[273]

8

Friends Turn Foes

(1300 – 1330 CE)

The rise of the legendary vizier Gajah Mada

Around 1294, Majapahit.

The birth of kings, if the surviving texts are to be believed, were traditionally accompanied by violent earthquakes and thunderous volcanic eruptions. Not so the birth of Gajah Mada, the man whose power would eclipse that of royalty as he emerged from humble origins to become the most powerful man in the empire and the architect of Majapahit's golden age. Even today, he is revered as a national hero and a symbol of both patriotism and Indonesian unity.

Very little is recorded about his early days apart from that he was born sometime after the fall of Singasari and the defeat of the Mongols.[274] His father may have been killed in the fighting[275] and we know nothing about his mother or if he had brothers or sisters. But while his birth might have been unexceptional, his name was a harbinger of things to come. Gajah Mada – or 'rutting elephant' – was not a man to be trifled with.[276]

He was only an infant at the time of the coronation of King

Widjaya in 1293, a ceremony that was meant to unite the kingdom and usher in an era of peace and harmony after the bloodshed and duplicity of King Jayakatwang's reign (some chance!). Gajah Mada was probably raised in a relatively poor household in the area around Majapahit. He would have been about the same age as two powerful members of the royal family – Prince Jayanegara, the son of the new king, and Prince Adityawarman,[277] the son of Dara Jingga, one of the Sumatran princesses who was brought over from Sumatra initially as a gift to King Kertanegara. They both grew up inside the palace walls and enjoyed a far more lavish upbringing than Gajah Mada. But while their background and status differed greatly, over the course of many years their lives would become increasingly entwined.

The trouble started almost as soon as King Widjaya was crowned king. Keen to reward his loyal supporters, he gave Nambi the most coveted job in the kingdom, Patih of Majapahit, and Sora was appointed *demung*, or chamberlain. Lawe, one of his closest friends and advisors, became Governor of Tuban, the important port region. Lawe had been with the king since the bad old days when they were on the run for their lives from the murderous King Jayakatwang after the destruction of Singasari. Lawe and Sora had become close friends and along with Nambi were at the heart of the resistance movement against Jayakatwang. There was something raw in Lawe that the king appreciated on the battlefield. But truth be told, he was a small-minded bigot and completely unsuitable for government. In effect, this promotion pushed Lawe out of Majapahit, the centre of power, something he saw as a huge affront, a humiliation. After the coronation he had expected to be appointed *patih,* the most powerful man in the realm after the royals.[278] To him, a position as regional governor was a slap in the face.

The young king really should have known better. He had seen this story play out before, with horrendous consequences. Back in 1274, King Kertanegara had been casting around for someone to become Governor of Madura. The island was a backwater in the grand scheme of things but someone loyal needed to be in place before the assault on Sumatra. An ambitious young court official was given the job. That man was of course Wiraraja. Like Lawe, he was similarly unimpressed with this 'promotion' and proceeded to drop hints to Jayakatwang that Singasari was vulnerable to attack once the royal fleet had sailed for Sumatra. The rest is a very bloody history. Singasari was destroyed, Kertanegara murdered, Jayakatwang ascended the throne, and Prince Widjaya, as he was then, was forced to flee.

The irony of course is that he was given sanctuary in Madura by Wiraraja, along with his trusted advisors Lawe, Nambi and Sora. Wiraraja then proved himself to be a master of manipulation by patching up a peace between Widjaya and Jayakatwang, arranging a deal between Widjaya and the invading Mongols, and then double crossing them too. Now life had turned full circle. History was repeating itself. Wiraraja was a powerful figure in Majapahit and also in charge of the eastern part of Java, Nambi had been appointed to the exalted position of *patih,* and Sora was now the king's chamberlain. It was Lawe's turn to feel aggrieved, especially as he did not share the king's high regard for Nambi.

This humiliation kept gnawing away at Lawe in Tuban and

one day in 1295[279] he could control himself no longer. He rode to Majapahit, entered the palace[280] and approached an open pavilion where the king was discussing affairs of state with Nambi, Sora and other senior officials. Lawe followed protocol and waited for his turn to speak. He stood up, bowed, put the palms of his hand together as a sign of respect – a *sembah* – and after the mandatory exchange of pleasantries poured out his heart.

'*Your majesty, all of your efforts will be useless because of your nomination of Nambi for the post of Patih Amangkubhumi. If Sora had not been found suitable for this post, certainly I should have been taken into consideration, not Nambi. What was the basis of your nomination? I am convinced that you made a serious mistake in this case, for his appointment will not benefit the state. Without Sora's and Lawe's support sooner or later the state will collapse. You know how Nambi behaved during our struggle. He was stupid, weak, fearful and ugly. He was disappointing in everything he did. Nambi is a man without courage, without prestige, without reputation, without personality. I am sure he is going to destroy the good image of the state and lower your reputation as well. I challenge him for a duel at any time, at any place.*'[281]

A deathly quiet descended on the pavilion. Heads had rolled for lesser crimes than insulting the two most powerful men in the realm. The officials present avoided eye contact with both the king and Patih Nambi, whose face glowed red with anger. One of the religious leaders, *dharmadyaksa* Bhramaraja, broke the silence and reminded Lawe that he would have to bear the consequences of this reckless behaviour. '*They will not inflict damage on you,* but also your family,' he warned. 'I advise you to apologize and to be patient.'

The comments were met by a collective hum of approval. But Lawe was not a man accustomed to heeding advice and instead repeated that he had been treated badly and that Nambi was weak. Then Anabrang 'The Crosser', the man who had led King Kertanegara's naval expeditions to Sumatra years earlier, said he could not listen to any more of this insubordination. 'Lawe, if you are really a man, go home! Gather your manpower and take up your weapons.' Lawe beat his thigh to show that he was ready to accept the challenge and left the audience hall without asking permission.

The king was shocked. Lawe, Nambi and Sora had been with him at his darkest moments. Now two of them were at each other's throats. He held a private consultation with Sora to ask him what he thought about replacing Nambi with Lawe. Although Sora was close to Lawe, he strongly rejected the idea: 'Your majesty, do not do so, otherwise we, Majapahit officials, will be accused of being afraid of facing death. Do not comply with Lawe's desires otherwise its consequences will be that you will lose our respect. It is best to do away with your sympathies for Lawe for he has behaved beyond any order. I am sure Lawe will be defeated, so long as you have Anabrang and my own support.'[282]

Sora then left the pavilion to try to talk some sense into his old friend. He told him that despite the unseemly outburst and his crude manners (he was a ruffian from Madura after all), Lawe was still the king's favourite. The situation could still be salvaged. He should apologize immediately and beg for forgiveness. Known for his hot temper, the governor became even more enraged and shouted: *'There are two alternatives, either to serve the king or to revolt against him.'* And with that, he left the court and rode back to Tuban.

The last option was to send for Wiraraja, that old master of diplomacy, not to mention duplicity.[283] But even he couldn't make Lawe see sense – and his reply was: *'A man has to live for his ideals and strive to reach the highest goals. I want neither fame nor name, but simply a heroic death, which I hope will be followed by a sevenfold rebirth to gradually provide an even more bountiful life.'* War was coming, yet again.

A few weeks later, news arrived that Lawe's heavily armed supporters had left Tuban to move on Majapahit. King Widjaya called in Nambi, Sora and Anabrang 'The Crosser' and ordered them to crush the rebel force. They gathered their forces and left Majapahit, heading due north towards Tuban.

The armies met at the River Tambak Beras, near Gresik, in eastern Java. The first assault was pushed back, so King Widjaya ordered his troops to encircle Lawe's men from three sides. The strategy worked and the rebels were forced back to the river bank.

As the armies clashed, Lawe and Anabrang came face to face on the battlefield. Lawe slashed at Anabrang's horse and the admiral was thrown into the river. Lawe spurred his mount forward and jumped on Anabrang, forcing his head under the water. But Anabrang was not nicknamed Kebo – 'Buffalo' – for nothing. Through sheer brute strength the famed warrior rose from the water and after a ferocious struggle thrust his dagger into Lawe's chest. For good measure, Anabrang proceeded to cut off his head.

At that moment, Sora arrived on the scene. Seeing his old friend lying dead, the usually level-headed Sora was suddenly filled with rage and plunged his spear into Anabrang. The man who had crossed oceans, led armies, invaded Sumatra and had done so much for the empire, was dead, stabbed in the back by Sora, his brother-in-arms.

One man was watching all the action from the river bank, a certain Mahapati, an ambitious young official at court. Unfortunately for Sora, Mahapati proved to be (yet another) deceitful and treacherous man.[284]

A spoilt brat

The 1290s were a tumultuous time. In fewer than five years the royal capital Singasari had been destroyed, the mighty King Kertanegara assassinated, the Mongols seen off, and King Widjaya had been forced to quell an uprising by his close friend Lawe. The people of Majapahit were in desperate need of some peace and quiet.

First, the king had to deal with the ever-ambitious Wiraraja, who, as a reward for his services, had been promoted and put in charge of a large slice of Java. But it still wasn't enough. He always wanted more. The cunning old powerbroker reminded the king of a promise made in very different times, when he was destitute and seeking sanctuary at Wiraraja's palace in Madura. After a particularly heavy night on the palm wine, the king had offered to share his kingdom with his host – should he ever reclaim it, of course – which seemed very unlikely at the time.

King Widjaya was exceedingly reluctant to cut his kingdom in two. A similar exercise had been undertaken back in the time of Airlangga and, much later, King Ken Arok, with disastrous consequences. Such a division of the lands had to be avoided at all costs. Anyway, Wiraraja was already ruling the eastern part of the realm in his name[285] so, arguably, he had already got what he asked for.

Disgruntled, Wiraraja started to shun major ceremonies in Majapahit and was no doubt planning his next move when fate stepped in. In 1301, before he could hatch yet another nefarious plan, the old fox for once did the right thing by dropping dead in Madura, the island for which he had so little time.[286]

For a while, the people of Majapahit enjoyed the peace they yearned for. The city grew rapidly as large numbers of people displaced from Singasari moved to the new capital. Trade prospered, temples and residential compounds were built and luxury of luxuries, terracotta pipes were laid to provide the houses of wealthy merchants and noblemen with fresh water.

As the economy boomed, there was a dire need to replace the huge amount of currency the Mongol invaders had taken back to China with them as booty. King Widjaya sent ships to the wealthy vassal state of Pon-I, now the super-rich oil kingdom of Brunei, to refill the treasury with gold.[287] The state was renowned for camphor, a sought-after incense with medicinal qualities, and its gold mines. Arab and Chinese travellers wrote of 'mountains of camphor' which fetched prices higher than anywhere else in the region. Marco Polo did not visit the place but mentions the abundance of gold and in 1232, itinerant Italian friar Odoric of Pordenone also wrote about palaces with floor tiles made of silver and gold.

This period of peace, stability and growing wealth saw the arts flourish, leaving a powerful cultural legacy. For example, the Panji epic tells of the exploits of Prince Panji, a Javanese hero, who went in search of his beloved Princess Candra Kirana. On his travels he had many adventures, including numerous amorous encounters, before finally being reunited with his lover. This marked the development of a distinct genre of Javanese literature for the first time, and the Panji stories later became popular across the whole of Southeast Asia. They also helped to develop the art of shadow puppetry (*wayang*) for which Java is famed. Panji's adventures were so much in demand that the king ordered engravings depicting the love story to be made on temples across his kingdom.

Meanwhile, inside the royal palace, the usual frictions were surfacing. Queen Gayatri, the playful, shrewd, and favourite wife of the king and daughter of Kertanegara, who had disguised herself as a servant in Kediri for a year to avoid being held as a hostage, was growing increasingly influential. The queen and her sisters were true blue bloods, direct descendants of the Rajasa dynasty, and King Widjaya was all too aware of their importance to his claim to the throne. It was essential that he was seen by all to be the rightful ruler, so he ordered that all royal charters should begin by stressing that King Widjaya was the husband of Kertanegara's daughters and the legitimate ruler of the realm.[288]

Meanwhile, the king's son and heir, Prince Jayanegara, was growing into a spoilt brat. He had an air of entitlement and superiority about him which earned him the nickname '*Raden Kala Gemet*' or 'weak villain'. He was close friends with the well-connected Prince Adityawarman, the son of Dara Jingga, one of the princesses from Sumatra and a Majapahit nobleman.[289] Meanwhile, outside the palace walls, isolated from political intrigues and the lavish life of the royals, Gajah Mada was growing into a smart, perceptive, and exceedingly ambitious young man.

Statue of Gayatri (Prajnaparamita) in National Museum, Jakarta. [Photo: Gunawan Kartapranata]

The fall of Sora

The period of peace and prosperity did not last long. When King Widjaya died in 1309, after ruling for sixteen years, the skies darkened and mountains rumbled.[290] Not a great omen, to say the least, especially as the founder of Majapahit left behind a spoilt, inexperienced heir and a cast of characters who would soon either be scheming together or at each other's throats.

King Jayanegara was still just a teenager at his coronation and soon found himself in the shadow of Queen Gayatri, his father's widow. Her two daughters were appointed queens of (what was left of) Kediri and Singasari,[291] the two parts of the empire over which so much blood had been spilled. Meanwhile, Mahapati, eyewitness to Sora's misdeeds, had risen to a position of influence at court. Far outside the circles of power, Gajah Mada, now seventeen, had joined the Majapahit army's elite force, the Bhayangkara guards.

It was Mahapati who made the first move. Articulate and eloquent, he went out of his way to call regularly on powerful men such as Sora and Nambi at their homes and tell them what they wanted to hear. As he climbed the ranks, he fostered friendly relations with all the major power players at the palace and, whenever possible, was present when the young king made public appearances. Mahapati had one piece of information that he had long kept to himself. He was the only living witness to Sora's murder of the great warrior Anabrang at the climax of Lawe's revolt. He felt it was time to play this card[292] and soon rumours about the strange circumstances of Anabrang's death were everywhere.

One morning, the young king gave a grand audience in the courtyard of the palace. Everyone who was anyone was there. He dressed to impress as he wanted to banish any doubts that he wasn't up to the job – a robe made of parrot feathers, a waistcoat braided with gold, and an exquisite royal *keris*, decorated with precious gems. His crown was adorned with a diamond, and the fragrance of musk oozed from every royal pore.[293]

But something was not quite right. He sensed tensions among the noblemen and his most trusted advisors. Concerned, he sent for Mahapati, the man who always seemed to know what was happening behind the scenes. Mahapati could not believe his luck.

He first told the king that there were concerns that some of the court traditions had not been followed since the coronation. That upset some people. But there was another, bigger problem. Sora may have been one of the king's favourites but everyone was talking about how he had killed Anabrang and many wondered why the king tolerated such wrongdoing.

The king was troubled by these revelations and needed time to think. Meanwhile, Mahapati made his way to the house of Anabrang's son, Taruna, just north of the palace. He found him sitting in the shade of an orange jasmine tree[294] chewing betel nut.[295] Mahapati joined him and after the usual pleasantries casually mentioned that he had heard how much the king regretted the death of his father.

He left the compound and walked over to Sora's compound. He warned him to be careful as there was gossip that Taruna wanted to avenge his father's death. Sora must surely have heard the rumours. Mahapati just wanted to make sure Sora was aware of the danger he was in. Nambi lived close by, so he dropped in to tell the *patih* that the word in palace circles was that the king wanted to replace Sora with Taruna.[296]

Mahapati sat back, admired his handiwork, and waited. First to move was Nambi, who seeing an opportunity to get rid of Sora went to see the king.[297] Jayanegara did not know what to do. Sora had been a loyal friend of his father's but would have to be punished. But this came with risks. Sora was *demung*, a senior minister, and highly popular around town. After some thought, he told Nambi: '*This is my wish, patih: I will follow the laws in this matter and a decision will be made tomorrow – he will either be banned or executed. Make sure Sora is informed.*' Nambi put his palms together in a *sembah* and returned home.[298]

Sora was with his close friend, Gajah Biru – 'Blue Elephant' – when the messenger from the palace delivered the bad news. Mahapati arrived soon afterwards to tell Sora that it was Nambi who had informed the king about the murder of Anabrang.[299] But Sora had never trusted Mahapati and rightly suspected that he was behind all the gossip and court intrigue.

The next morning the king called his senior advisors to the inner courtyard and told them of his decision. As Sora had done so much for the kingdom his life would be spared, but he was to be sent into exile. Guards were sent to inform Sora of his fate but they returned saying he refused to comply and wanted to appear before the king to plead for mercy.[300] The young king was angry and screamed: '*Sora is reckless!*' He then gave the command to muster troops to attack Sora. The palace was in a state of uproar, with emotions further raddled by large amounts of palm wine.[301]

Mahapati rushed off to see Sora who sneered: '*Exceedingly great is the king's grace.*' But he was not going to change his mind. '*I am not like a turtle's neck that can be folded in or out at will. I rather die than change my words.*'[302] He then turned to Mahapati who, as Sora knew very well, was behind it all: '*You only care for yourself and don't mind if you take the kingdom down with you! Don't you think I know what you are doing?*'[303]

A few days later, the king's troops arrived at the cremation grounds outside the city at dawn to confront Sora. It is likely that Gajah Mada, a member of the elite palace guard, was among them. Sora arrived in style, adorned with the jewels he had received as gifts from the king.[304] The two sides clashed and the hand-to-hand combat was brutal. Sora's elephant wrecked Nambi's chariot but then his own elephant was killed and he was thrown to the ground.[305] Taruna, Anabrang's son, moved in for the kill but Sora stabbed Taruna's horse. Sora knocked Taruna to the ground and cut off his head before being struck down by an arrow. His close friend, Gajah Biru, and many good Majapahit men died that fateful day outside the city.[306]

It was a tragic moment. Women wailed in the streets to mourn their husbands, many of the widows committed suicide, became prostitutes, were taken as concubines, or fled the city to become hermits.[307] The king had won the day, but for how long?

***

After all the death and the misery that followed, King Jayanegara knew he had to act to tighten his feeble grip on power and improve his own battered standing with the nobles and religious leaders. Sora was well liked and many mourned his passing. He needed a big, bold idea and what better way was there to enhance his reputation than a major investment in the kingdom's most famous temple? It would bolster his spiritual standing with the religious leaders and provide employment for a small army of stone carvers, wood cutters and labourers. The temple supply chain was both long and lucrative.

Penataran, the state temple of Majapahit, was a pleasant boat ride down the River Brantas and located close to what is today the town of Blitar. It was a spectacular sight, built halfway up a hill with superb views of Mountain Kelud, an active volcano. The temple covered a large area and contained three courtyards, with a main gate guarded by two large statues. The king instructed his architects and builders to draw up ambitious plans to enlarge the whole complex, so it could be inaugurated in his name. The temple played a significant role in Majapahit culture and remains the largest ruined Hindu temple complex in East Java.

But for all his religious philanthropy, the king's court remained riven with factional rivalries. Seven years after the death of King Widjaya, the cunning Mahapati was still up to no good. After bringing Sora down, this time he pitted Patih Nambi and King Jayanegara against each other, spreading rumours doubting the loyalty of the king's right-hand man. Nambi realised immediately what was happening and decided it was best to leave Majapahit for the safety of the island of Madura,[308] where he had taken sanctuary with the king's father all those years ago.

Mahapati advised the king that it would be unwise to let Nambi build up his defences. Royal troops were dispatched – perhaps Gajah Mada, in his early twenties by now, was among them – to attack Nambi's small fortress in Madura.[309] By the time the army arrived, the *patih* had crossed the waters back to eastern Java in an attempt to hide in the mountains.[310] But there was no escape[311] and after a brief clash, Nambi was killed.[312] All of Mahapati's scheming and plotting had finally yielded what he had longed for. Shortly afterwards, King Jayanegara installed him as the *patih* of the whole kingdom.[313]

Young Gajah Mada

The downfall of respected men such as Rawe, Sora and Nambi came with unintended consequences. The king, now in his mid-twenties, was perceived to be increasingly weak, unstable, and prone to making decisions on a whim. Worse still, he was easily manipulated by Mahapati. While Jayanegara poured over architects' drawings of the Penataran project, he was unaware of the discontent building at court and beyond. As the infighting increased, the centre of power was crumbling. Bali, under Majapahit control since the days of King Kertanegara, quietly took back control of its own affairs[314] as did local rulers in other parts of Java.[315]

It was only a matter of time before someone took matters into their own hands. In early 1319, Kuti, a senior court official, persuaded some of the lower-level guards to help him assassinate the king. Under cover of darkness, daggers and spears in hand, they made their way through the inner court to the king's private chambers. This is when Gajah Mada, now in his mid-twenties, officially enters the history books for the first time.[316] Sharp-eyed guards noticed that something was amiss and warned Gajah Mada, the head of the elite Bhayangkara palace guard. He acted quickly, sending some of his men to secure the king and then ordered the other guards to confront the attackers.

But the royal guards were soon overpowered by Kuti's men. Gajah Mada and fifteen men rushed the king to safety, hiding him in Badander, a nearby village. But even here, the king's life was in jeopardy. A supposedly loyal guard made another attempt to kill him only to be intercepted by Gajah Mada's dagger. Clearly, few could be trusted. He ordered that no one was to leave the village and nobody was to know the whereabouts of the king.[317] Now, he needed a plan.

A few days later, Gajah Mada made his way back to Majapahit where he spread the message that the king had been killed while on the run from Kuti. Some men were relieved to hear that their increasingly inept leader was dead, while others were saddened by the news. Gajah Mada paid careful attention to the reactions of the more sympathetic crowd and then probed a little further: '*Do not weep. Kuti is his successor. You like him, don't you?*'

Their less than enthusiastic replies convinced him of the men's loyalty to the king. He could work with them. Gajah Mada then revealed that the king was still alive and, with their support, would soon be back on the throne. Gajah Mada's surprise attack on Kuti, who had installed himself in the royal palace, was a complete success and the usurper and his followers were all killed. King Jayanegara returned to Majapahit and Gajah Mada, the hero of the day, was appointed *patih* of the Singasari region.

Perhaps the most important consequence of the failed revolt was that the young king finally saw through Mahapati's web of lies and deceit. The puppet master had overplayed his hand many times and finally paid with his life. Once he was securely back on the throne, King Jayanegara ordered Mahapati to be executed.[318]

Dawn of the golden age

After barely surviving the latest threat to his crown, the king was even more determined to shore up his hold on power. One avenue he had yet to explore was the immaculate provenance of his nieces, who all carried the Rajasa bloodline. Of particular interest was Princess Tribhuwanatungadewi (one assumes she had a shorter nickname), whose mother was the increasingly influential Queen Gayatri, the youngest daughter of King Kertanegara and the widow of King Widjaya.

The king's logic was simple – if he married even one of these young ladies it would link him directly to the bluest of blue blood. It would also reduce the threat of further challenges to his throne by removing the possibility of claims from over-ambitious suitors. After all, his own father, King Widjaya, had done something very similar to great effect. But when Queen Gayatri heard of the plan, she objected in the strongest terms. The marriage of her daughters was her business, and her business alone. A furious Jayanegara had the princesses locked up in the palace. If he could not marry them, no one could.

As Jayanegara's reign careened from one crisis to the next, Gayatri was emerging as a dowager queen, a powerful figure within the palace. She made it her business to oversee the rise of Gajah Mada, recruiting him into the circles of her daughter, Tribhuwanatungadewi, who was now the queen of Singasari. Gajah Mada was her *patih* and suddenly everybody was talking about this man.

It was probably around this time that Gayatri felt the need to get rid of the king. Her first move was to sound out Gajah Mada. Careful not to give away her feelings about King Jayanegara – she loathed the man – Gayatri asked what exactly had happened during the Kuti rebellion and what he thought about the state of the Majapahit empire. Gajah Mada described in detail the drama at the palace, the flight to safety, his cunning plan to gauge the loyalty of various factions at court, and his subsequent victory. He also lamented the internal strife that had led to the loss of Bali and control of other regions. King Kertanegara had unified the archipelago, so perhaps Majapahit might regain its footing based on her father's ideals.

Gayatri liked what she saw and heard. Here was an intelligent, strong-willed man, who commanded loyalty from his own men and was devoted to the Rajasa dynasty and her father's legacy. She could work with him. Gajah Mada made a similar assessment of Gayatri – a shrewd woman with ambitions for the realm far beyond the petty squabbles of Jayanegara's court. He was also completely new to palace politics so she would offer powerful protection, especially given the erratic behaviour of the king. Trust and mutual respect started to grow between the two (and perhaps a little bit more). For the moment, they were both happy to bide their time.

In 1328, rumours were swirling around the palace that the king was more than fond of the lovely wife of Tanca, a nobleman, legal counsel to the religious leaders, or *dharmaputra,* and a royal doctor.[319] At the same time, the king was suffering from a large, painful boil on his body. All sorts of treatments were tried. First, shredded turmeric and tamarind were brewed with palm sugar and a little salt and given to him to drink. That did nothing to ease the pain and neither did a balm of crushed pandan leaves and ginger, nor did prayers at full moon and the hanging of a holy amulet around the king's neck.

Finally, Tanca decided that the boil should be lanced. The king was moved to his private chambers and was given large amounts of palm wine as an anaesthetic. Once he was heavily intoxicated, Gajah Mada ordered everyone to leave except himself and the doctor.

That is when he saw his chance.

The first attempt to lance the boil was unsuccessful, so Gajah Mada suggested that the doctor should remove the king's under-clothing and protective amulet in order the gain better access to the wound.[320] The king was then rolled over on his side, exposing his whole body. Gajah Mada grabbed one of the razor-sharp surgical knives and stabbed the king in the chest. Even before a very confused Tanca knew what was happening, Gajah Mada grabbed another knife and killed the doctor. Gajah Mada raised the alarm and told the guards that Tanca, humiliated by his wife's infidelity, had murdered the king in a fit of jealousy; he had tried to intervene but only succeeded in stabbing the doctor. No one challenged this version of events, especially after Queen Gayatri agreed that nothing could have been done to prevent what was clearly a terrible tragedy.[321]

Jayanegara was given a grand funeral[322] and buried in Kapopongan.[323] Shortly afterwards, it was announced that Gayatri's daughter, Princess Tribhuwanatungadewi, was to become the new queen.[324] Gajah Mada, the 'rutting elephant', now stood at the heart of the Majapahit court and had a formidable ally in Gayatri, the most powerful person in the kingdom. The two would dominate the empire for decades to come.

It was the dawn of the golden age of Majapahit.

9

Pomp and Splendour

(1330 – 1350 CE)

The Golden Age of Majapahit

1331, Majapahit.

At dawn, birdsong filled the air as a watery sun bathed the red walls of the palace in a pink-orange glow. A troupe of black monkeys crossed an empty street and a lone farmer strolled along a narrow lane on his way to his rice paddy field, where a thin morning mist lingered. Amidst a sea of parrot green paddy fields, the city of Majapahit lay quiet, seemingly – for once – at peace with itself. If only.

Muffled voices came from the religious compound of the *dharmadyaksa* near the southern wall of the palace as servants started to stir. *Dharmadyaksa* Narendra, Prapanca's father, a bald man wearing red ear buds who was dressed in an old, faded orange loincloth, emerged from his room and made his way to the pavilion near the lotus pond. He sat down, started to chew on a betel nut, and was soon deep in his own thoughts. He liked to start the day early.

A *dharmadyaksa's* days were filled with daily prayers, readings, meetings with the *dharmopapati* religious council to discuss arrangements for rituals and ceremonies, listening to people who brought their grievances to the palace, and ruling on matters of law. He spent most of his time at the palace and although very much aware of the different factions scheming against each other – Singasari versus Kediri, Hindus versus Buddhists – he tried as best he could to stay out of court politics.

To his great pleasure, Queen Tribhuwanatunggadewi, who had recently ascended the throne, was a devout Buddhist and had sought his advice when she appointed two new prominent Buddhists to the *dharmopapati* council.[325] She also ordered the restoration of the Buddhist *Candi* Jago, the temple raised in honour of King Wisnuwardhana, the father of mighty King Kertanegara who had fled for his life into the forests nearly a century earlier.

But city politics were never far away. The razor-sharp Gajah Mada – the rutting elephant – was now Patih of Singasari, important, yes, but outranked by the *patih* of the whole of the Majapahit kingdom, Arya Tadah. Narendra liked Arya Tadah. He was shrewd, cultured, had a remarkable command of ancient Sanskrit scriptures, and was widely respected at court. But Arya Tadah was in poor health, frail, and his vision was fading. It was time for him to step down and, as Buddhist teaching advised, wander the lands as a hermit. He was convinced that Gajah Mada was ready to take over this position of great power and influence and that the young queen would agree.

Arya Tadah approached the queen and asked her to release him from his duties. To his disappointment and dismay, she refused. This was a surprise and put him in an awkward situation as Arya Tadah had already discussed his succession plan with Gajah Mada. 'I will take your side, even in what you may do wrong,' Arya Tadah had told him.

But Gajah Mada was a shrewd political operator and was happy to bide his time. Who was he to disagree with the young queen? He was also fully aware that the reins of power at the palace were held by Queen Gayatri, who was not only the queen's mother, the youngest daughter of King Kertanegara and the widow of King Widjaya, but also his patron.

Then, as ever, events intervened. One morning Narendra was sitting in his favourite pavilion contemplating the lotus pond when a messenger arrived with news that a group of rebel nobles in Sadeng, in the far eastern part of Java, were refusing to pay tribute to the young queen. They calculated that the faction-ridden court was too busy dealing with the constant political scheming inside the palace to be concerned about what happened in far-off Sadeng.[326] But they were wrong.

As the news spread about the rebellion, Gajah Mada rushed to the palace and requested an audience with Queen Gayatri. Both agreed that this was a clear act of rebellion and should be dealt with swiftly. Gajah Mada drew up a plan of attack and presented it to the queen, her mother, the two *dharmadyaksas,* and a group of leading noblemen, including a man named Kembar,[327] who was on the outer fringes of the royal family. Kembar, who held the title of prince, envied Gajah Mada's access to Queen Gayatri. In his eyes, Gajah Mada was a mere low-life commoner, while Kembar, a warrior of noble blood, surely deserved a much higher position at court – *patih* of the whole of Majapahit perhaps. It was the chance he had been waiting for. A victorious military campaign against Sadeng was a perfect opportunity to shove Gajah Mada aside.

A few weeks later Gajah Mada and his troops were approaching Sadeng when a message arrived informing him that Kembar's soldiers were already laying siege to the city. Gajah Mada sent a small patrol to ask Kembar to wait for his arrival so they could coordinate the attack. When the patrol arrived, his men were humiliated. Kembar and an ally from Melaka, the port on the Malay peninsula that controlled the sea route between India and China, harangued Gajah Mada's soldiers, lashing at them with a whip.[328] The message was clear – a commoner was in no position to order a nobleman what to do. Gajah Mada fumed. But ever patient, he would exact his revenge later.

With Sadeng surrounded by Majapahit troops, the young queen arrived in person to launch the assault. She too was sending a message – the price for challenging her authority was death. The battle didn't last long; Sadeng's rebel nobles were no match for Majapahit's well-trained and better-equipped troops. The city was soon overwhelmed and the queen celebrated a famous victory by showering her soldiers with gifts. Once they had returned home, the queen called a meeting at the palace and announced that Gajah Mada was to become *patih* of the whole of Majapahit.[329] Kembar seethed.

Empire building

As the new *patih*, Gajah Mada threw himself into the job he had coveted for so long. He met up with district governors, reviewed plans for new temples, inspected the royal warehouses, and sat down with envoys to discuss a diplomatic mission to China, which was set to sail a year later, in 1332.[330] He then revealed the full extent of his ambitions. He wanted a return to the days of the great King Kertanegara, who by the time he died in 1292 had united Java,[331] extended his influence over southern Sumatra, and successfully resisted Mongol attempts to exact tribute from his kingdom. Not surprisingly, Queen Gayatri approved.

A meeting of the most powerful people in the land was called at the imposing 'Amazing Pavilion' in the inner courtyard of the palace. He stood in front of Queen Tribhuwanatunggadewi and spoke of how this was the right time to return Majapahit to the glory days of her grandfather. *'I will not enjoy palapa[332] until all other parts of the archipelago submit to Majapahit.'* It's not clear exactly what he meant, but some scholars believe he was making the ultimate sacrifice – vowing to give up sex until his mission was completed.

He then listed the regions that were to become part of greater Majapahit, from southern Siam (Thailand) and Pahang (the Malay peninsula) to Tumasik (Singapore), the Sunda island chain, Sulawesi, Tanjungpura (Kalimantan) and far-away Seram,[333] part of the Moluccas (Maluku) archipelago, located between the Ceram Sea and the Banda Sea west of New Guinea. At the time, the strategically located Tumasik was growing from a small settlement into a centre of international trade. Hundreds of years later, in 1819, Sir Stamford Raffles would lay claim to what became known as Singapore for the British East India Company; by then, the island's influence had faded and the population had dwindled to a little more than a thousand people.

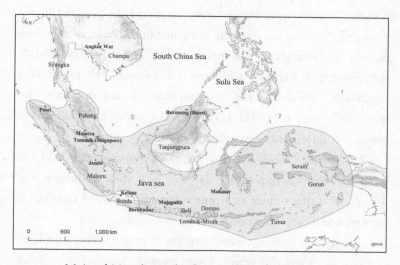

Majapahit's sphere of influence. [Illustration: HvdL]

Gajah Mada finished his speech by presenting his battle plan. First would come the submission of the '*negara agung*', the islands and regions near Majapahit such as east Java, Madura, and Bali. After that, the conquest of the '*mancanegara*', islands such as Lombok and Dompo (now Sumbawa) a little further away. Lastly, they would control the whole archipelago – the *nusantara* – as well as the Malay peninsula; some research points to territories such as

Sulu in the southern Philippines also paying tribute and becoming vassal states. This was not a military conquest, he stated, but an invitation to enjoy the warm embrace of the Javanese motherland with the offer of protection in return. But those that refused would face the wrath of Majapahit's military might.

The queen quickly approved the plan and everybody else nodded in agreement. Afterwards, Gajah Mada lingered in the Amazing Pavilion to enjoy the moment. But instead of receiving plaudits and respect, he was mocked by the old Patih Arya Tadah, the embittered Kembar, and several noblemen. His plans were laughable, ridiculous even. 'Commoners should not have too much ambition,' they said. Gajah Mada remained calm and kept his own counsel. He knew what to do next.

He visited Queen Gayatri the next morning and told her what had happened. Kembar did not share their ambitions and was dividing the nobles at a time when unity was of the utmost importance. Something needed to be done. She agreed.

A few days later, screams were heard coming from Kembar's compound. Soon the whole town knew – Kembar was dead. Murdered. Probably run over by the rutting elephant, the joke went.

The birth of Hayam Wuruk

In 1334, three years after the rebellion in Sadeng, Queen Tribhuwanatunggadewi gave birth to a son, Hayam Wuruk, nicknamed '*Tetep*', 'the cockerel'. Legend has it that at the very moment he was born, the earth shook, Mount Kelud erupted, ash rained down from the skies, and every wretched evildoer died without a gasp. A year later, to the delight of the ladies of the court, the cute, healthy little prince whose birth had caused the earth to tremble took his first step.

Narendra, the religious leader, was a happy man. The kingdom was thriving once again, the queen had produced a male heir, and his own son, Prapanca, had been born around the same time.[334] What propitious timing. As a child, Prapanca spent hours running around the palace courtyards with his friend Prince Hayam Wuruk. They played hide-and-seek near the stables, looked on in fascination as men gambled on fighting cocks and then, as the sun set, sucked sticks of sugar cane under the banyan trees that lined the road along the northern palace walls.

Meanwhile, Gajah Mada was putting his plan into action. He ordered the construction of a large fleet of ships capable of sailing the length of the archipelago.[335] In 1340, a fleet was sent to re-establish control of Sumatra[336] and in 1343, Adityawarman, the son of a Melayu princess taken to Majapahit decades earlier, was appointed viceroy; he became king of Sumatra in 1347.

Bali was next. It had been fifty years since King Kertanegara had taken the island but when the Mongols invaded Java, Bali's leaders had taken the opportunity to free themselves of Majapahit control. In 1343, the same year that Sumatra was retaken, Majapahit troops sailed from Tuban and crushed the resistance of the 'nefarious and vile' inhabitants. Unique in Indonesia, Bali has maintained a Buddhist-Hindu culture ever since.[337] More expeditions followed, and Dompo – now Sumbawa – submitted in 1357. Majapahit had the strongest navy in the region and was admired, respected, or feared across Southeast Asia. Gajah Mada, the most powerful man in the land, was protected by the most powerful woman, the dowager queen Gayatri.

The glorious victories were no doubt re-enacted many times with wooden sticks and rattan shields by the young Hayam Wuruk and Prapanca within the pampered safety of the palace walls. As they grew older, their paths and personalities diverged. Hayam Wuruk was trained as a warrior prince, while Prapanca assisted his father with religious duties. The prince loved hunting, gambling, singing and dancing. Prapanca was more of a loner, taking pleasure in reading old scriptures and long, secluded drinking sessions.

They still met from time to time but these encounters were generally fleeting. They occasionally travelled together on the royal boat sailing south up the River Brantas on the way to Penataran, the state temple of Majapahit[338] before parting ways to attend to their respective duties.

These expeditions were organised by the royal *demung,* or chamberlains, and were planned with the precision of a military campaign. As any experienced *demung* knew, the secret of success was to ensure that the royal bedrooms set up near the temple were so lavishly appointed that the question of who slept where was resolved without much discussion. And the lords of the bedchambers in charge of the royal wardrobe made sure that only the finest tunics, jewels and ceremonial regalia were shipped up from Majapahit. Royals would not be royals if they were not demanding.

Things were different for Prapanca; nobody meticulously planned his wardrobe. But he couldn't complain as two young boys were assigned to fetch him food, water, and copious supplies of palm wine and also massaged his feet when he was tired. They carried his bags stuffed with writing materials and his prized ceremonial garments. The rest of what he needed – bronze bells, incense and oils for religious rituals – was carried on oxcarts. Prapanca was a man of few demands and slept with other Buddhist priests in a small guesthouse, a single room filled with mattresses stuffed with dried grass.

To Prapanca, Penataran was the realm's jewel in the crown. Constructed more than a hundred years earlier, surrounded by dense jungle and set against the backdrop of mighty Mount Kelud, the temple complex was a spectacular sight and it played a significant role in the religious life of the royal family.

The entrance to the temple was guarded by two imposing statues of *darwapala* warriors brandishing clubs – a common architectural element throughout Hindu and Buddhist Java. They seemed to him to grow more convivial on every visit. Inside was a raised platform where entertainers performed under a thatched roof supported by wooden columns.[339] Beyond lay the most sacred part of the temple where only senior religious officials and members of the royal family were allowed to enter; as the son of the *dharmadyaksa*, Prapanca was one of them. As he climbed the narrow central stairs of the inner temple, he stopped at each level to admire the elaborate wall murals depicting ancient legends of good overcoming evil. At the top was a tower,[340] offering stunning views of Mount Kelud, an active volcano, and the surrounding area. Every night, the whole temple was lit up with oil lamps, a sight Prapanca cherished.

This eccentric, oddball of a man would of course go on to play a pivotal role in both recording and researching the history of the empire. He became an important court scribe and poet who would later in life rekindle his close relationship with his old friend the king. In 1365, Prapanca published a volume of manuscripts that gave the modern world a first detailed description of the Majapahit world in the fourteenth century. And in 1359 he would come across an old abbot in a remote Buddhist monastery who shared an extraordinary revelation about the less than savoury origins of the ruling family dating back to 1182. Reading from a long-forgotten text, *The Chronicle of Kings*, the abbot described to Prapanca how King Ken Arok, considered to be the founder of the Rajasa dynasty of the Singasari and Majapahit line of monarchs, was neither, as legend would have it, the son of a Hindu god nor of noble blood. Quite the contrary, he was a brutal robber, rapist and murderer. As the early equivalent of a brand ambassador, Prapanca decided to keep that information to himself.

It was the usual practice for every member of the royal family to join these trips to Penataran. One year, the journey proved too much for Queen Gayatri. The frail old lady was approaching the end of her remarkable life. As a young girl, she fled burning Singasari after her father, King Kertanegara, was murdered, living incognito as a servant in the rebel stronghold of Kediri for a year. She had returned to Majapahit after the Mongol invasion, married King Widjaya, and became the most powerful woman at court. As the dowager queen, she had championed the rise of Gajah Mada and relished the revival of her father's ideal of a unified archipelago, a '*Nusantara*', a proto-Indonesia.[341] In her final years, she shaved her head, became a Buddhist monk, and moved to a monastery just outside Majapahit.[342] She allowed very few visitors but of course one of them was Gajah Mada, the man she created in her own image.

In the year 1350, when Hayam Wuruk was sixteen years old, his grandmother, Gayatri, the most powerful woman the empire had ever seen, died. The body of the last surviving daughter of King Kertanegara was cremated at a solemn ceremony and her ashes scattered in the River Brantas. The head priest, Janawidi,[343] told the large crowd that the soul of Queen Gayatra would roam the mortal world and be released into the realm of immortals twelve years later, in 1362, after a *shradda* ceremony.[344] Hayam Wuruk ordered two temples to be built in his grandmother's name at Kamal Pandak, near Boyolangu.[345] It was a fitting location to honour the woman who had done much to unite the kingdom. This was one of the places where, in 1045, King Airlangga had divided the realm between his two sons, which led to civil war. The kingdom remained divided until the reign of her father, King Kertanegara.

A few years later, Queen Tribhuwanatunggadewi stepped down and, like her mother, in line with Buddhist teachings, became a Buddhist monk in a serene forest retreat on the slope of one of the holy mountains in the region. At the age of nineteen, Hayam Wuruk was crowned king of Majapahit. During the ceremony, the queen announced that her son would officially be called Rajasanagara, the one ruler of a unified Java, 'victorious in all the world, the world conquering king'.[346] To support the young man, a royal council was established[347] but Gajah Madah, now in his early sixties, remained the most feared man in Majapahit.

The new king wanted to make his mark quickly. He ordered a special monument to be built to honour King Kertanegara and the religious leaders who died in the destruction of Singasari in 1292.[348] He also wanted to see business flourish. In 1358, he decreed that ferrymen – increasingly important to traders as local trades networks grew wider – would no longer pay tax apart from annual dues to the king during the Hindu Caitra festival[349] associated with the full moon. He also ordered that if goods fell from a ferry, traders would still have to pay the fee and if a woman fell into the water and the ferryman helped her, he could not be accused of 'touching the woman'.[350] Over the centuries, little has changed; the issues of transport and infrastructure across the vast Indonesian archipelago remain a high priority to this day.

The annual Caitra festival, Majapahit, 1355

King Hayam Wuruk was energetic, handsome, outgoing and gregarious. Even as a child, he loved being the centre of attention, a performer in need of an audience. The annual Caitra festival in March[351] was his time to shine. People came from afar to honour and pay tribute to the new king and enjoy a full month of entertainment and festivities. The young king was in his element.

Caitra was a huge celebration from start to finish and preparations began in the middle of February, when the monsoon rains stopped and when it was easier to navigate the roads and for people from afar to make their way to Majapahit. Canggu, the nearest port, was full of ships from southern China, Siam, Champa and Arabian ports. Many traders were prepared to stay for months and return on the easterly monsoon winds with cargoes of valuable spices.[352] The royal highway between Canggu and Majapahit was crowded with merchants and farmers. As soon as they had sold their goods they joined in the frenzy of drinking and gambling. Across the city, there were cockfights, wrestling competitions, and tug of war contests. Evenings were filled with music, dance and wayang puppet performances (and more drinking). On the diplomatic front, envoys from vassal states gathered to pay tribute to the new king or seek an audience with Gajah Mada.

At sunset on the eve of the first day of Caitra, priests entered the inner pavilion of the royal palace, followed by acolytes chanting sacred Sanskrit texts. King Hayam Wuruk sat on a throne in the Amazing Pavilion, where matted-haired *rshi* hermits and religious leaders sprinkled holy water over him to wash away the evils of the past year.[353] As darkness descended, oil lamps were lit around the palace, a spectacular sight. At the striking of a gong, Gajah Mada led the senior ministers to a large pavilion in front of the palace gates before a growing crowd. It was tradition for an older priest to read out the *Serat Raja Kapakapa*, a text that spoke of the duties of the king to his people – to promote welfare, control crime and to live a life consistent with religious beliefs. But hardly anyone paid attention. The party was just getting started.

The next morning, the first day of the festival, trumpets blared as the king and his family, splendidly attired atop of their equally sartorially impressive elephants, made their way through the palace gates and approached Bubat, the flat, treeless field just outside Majapahit, bordering the Brantas River and adjoining the royal highway to Canggu.[354] It was the city's entertainment centre, perfect for holding boxing matches, tug-of-war contests, dance performances, monkey shows, cock fights and singing competitions. And it was here that the royal party, as dictated by tradition, set up camp for a week in specially constructed pavilions and tents, served by hundreds of palace staff.

In the next few days, the king ate, drank, gambled, and mingled with his people, much to the delight of the ladies who were thrilled to get a glimpse of the handsome young man. He watched puppet and monkey shows, bet on wrestling matches, and judged dancing competitions.[355] Prapanca was there too, gambling, drinking and trying his luck, alas in vain as ever, with the ladies. He drowned his sorrows at the stalls selling palm wine and feasted on grilled chicken skewers, pork neck, hot sambal sauces,[356] fried rice cookies and grilled scorpions.[357]

In Bubat, the king sat in a huge tent protected by mace bearers who kept at bay some of the more enthusiastic members of the public. At particular times of the day, farmers and merchants were permitted to approach the king to offer him *pamuja*, or tribute – bags of rice, bolts of cloth, a cow, some chickens, or a goat. In the late afternoon as the temperature cooled, a ceremony took place to thank the mighty River Brantas for the life it gave to the lands. And on the fourth day officials conducted a land survey to deal with any ownership issues that might have risen in the year.[358] After a week of feasting in Bubat, the sated royals mounted their elephants and made the short journey back to the palace at Majapahit.

In the following week, musicians moved around the city carrying a portable shrine made of carved bamboo stuffed with food. People gathered at the large pavilion opposite the palace gate, where the royal family inspected the shrines. Afterwards, Buddhist and Shivaist priests conducted fire rituals and the next day the whole ritual was repeated so that by the end of the month, the whole pavilion was stuffed with small bamboo shrines.[359] Young children arrived at the crack of dawn to watch the spectacle and inspect the latest shrines.

For Prapanca, the highlight came on the last day of the Caitra festival. In the early hours of the morning, young and old packed into the *alun-alun* square to witness the annual royal parade. It was quite a spectacle. In the morning, men with trumpets, tambourines and drums emerged from the palace gate, followed by boys dressed in white, solemnly singing Sanskrit verses.[360] Next in the procession were the guards, who escorted the royal family in separate palanquins; first, the king's younger sister, then other members of the family, his concubines and, lastly, King Hayam Wuruk himself.

The caravan circled the palace complex, hugging the red-brick walls. Huge crowds formed, boys climbed trees, and men stood on carts to get a better view. Prapanca, ever the observant scribe, noted that several young women ran so fast to catch a glimpse of the king that they lost their balance, suffering what today would be described as a wardrobe malfunction. The crowd roared with laughter.

Later in the day, the royal family, senior ministers, and district heads gathered in the inner courtyard of the palace and sat down in front of the great hall to discuss the economy.[361] King Hayam Wuruk signalled to his uncle, the Prince of Wengker, to begin the proceedings. He spoke about how building and maintaining roads, bridges and waterways was vital for the city and the rest of Java and stressed the importance of opening up new land for cultivation[362] and attracting immigrant farmers and workers.[363]

King Hayam Wuruk then stated that it was everyone's sacred duty to pay their taxes[364] and ordered officials not to take advantage of their positions when visiting peoples' homes. Commoners also had the right to complain about a violent court official, or even royal relatives for that matter.[365] He finished with the words: *'Just like a lion cannot live without the forests, a king cannot live without the country that sustains it.'* All present bowed and then approached him one-by-one, fell to their knees and washed the king's feet.[366]

With the rather dry policy session complete, it was time for (another) lavish communal meal.[367] The feast arrived on golden trays and was laid out around a large conical mountain of rice. After a brief rest, the evening program started. In the *alun-alun* field in front of the palace, there was music, dancing, singing, and even more food. The commoners had to make do with delicacies such as frogs, worms, dogs and rats[368] but no one seemed to care as long as the wine kept flowing.[369] After dark, the crowd was treated to a special performance – 'the mistress of the wind'[370] – a witty yet erotic display of dancing featuring a young girl and a drunken, hopelessly out of step older men plucked from the audience.[371] The spectators loved every minute.

The vast quantities of alcohol ensured that etiquette was temporarily suspended and royals, noblemen and commoners mingled freely with each other. The celebrations reached a crescendo at midnight when, to the delight of the ladies, the still unmarried king performed the '*raket*',[372] a dance based on a court drama telling the story of a lovelorn prince. And with that the month-long party was over. It was time for everyone to go home.[373]

But the next time a party was organized, it turned into a bloodbath.

That was at Hayam Wuruk's wedding.

10

Wedding Disaster

(1357 CE)

*The wedding planner from hell, an exchange of insults
and the Battle of Bubat*

1357, Majapahit.

King Hayam Wuruk, twenty-three years young, was confident
and handsome, he loved to perform on the stage, and was liked by
all. In short, perfect son-in-law material, even before his mighty
kingdom was taken into consideration. However, marrying off
the most powerful king in the region came with all manner of
complications – a limited number of suitable candidates, new
political alliances, and unmatched levels of court politics. In
short, the marriage needed to be planned with the attention to
detail normally associated with a military campaign.

Majapahit exerted its considerable influence over vast swathes
of territory but in the preceding two decades a small power had
emerged, right under its nose, in western Java. The capital of the
Sunda kingdom of Pajajaran[374] was Pakuan, a fortified city in the
cool, leafy foothills of Mount Salak in what is now the Batu Tulis
district of Bogor.

Pakuan, about eight hundred kilometres from Majapahit, tucked away in the ravines and mountains of west Java, was inland, isolated and hard to reach. It was a two-day walk to Sunda Kelapa, a small port on the northern coast of Java at the mouth of the Ciliwung river that meandered through the hills down towards the sea. The name referred to both the Sunda kingdom and 'kelapa' – coconuts – which grew in abundance along the seashore. Today, Sunda Kelapa is a small district in the very north of Jakarta, the giant, sprawling metropolis that is Indonesia's capital.

Pakuan's remote location had served it well and allowed the ruler of Sunda, King Wangi, to retain direct control of his kingdom in the face of growing aggression from his powerful neighbour.[375] Although several minor military incursions had been seen off, the king still paid tribute every year. He was well aware that his realm, small as it was, remained an irritant to Majapahit. He was right.

To no one's surprise, Gajah Mada, the clever, ruthless man who in effect ran Majapahit on a day-to-day basis, had a plan that would resolve the issue of finding his master a bride and also allow him to keep a much closer eye on Sunda. This would also have the added benefit of achieving his ambition of reuniting the whole archipelago, a 'nusantara'.

The solution was simple – arrange a marriage between King Hayam Wuruk and Princess Citra Rashmi, the daughter of King Wangi.[376] The princess was rumoured to be a young woman of great beauty[377] and the union would also satisfy Gajah Mada's imperialist ambitions by putting the Sundanese firmly under the Majapahit thumb. A messenger and an artist were dispatched to

Pakuan to put the proposal to the Sundanese court and obtain a portrait of the princess.

King Wangi immediately warmed to the idea. The marriage would create a powerful political partnership with Majapahit on an equal footing (at least that's what the message implied) and raise his standing in the region. A geomancer was instructed to pick an auspicious date. Back in Majapahit, Hayam Wuruk was in raptures; the portrait confirmed that the rumours were true. The princess, just seventeen, was indeed stunningly beautiful.

Wedding preparations

King Wangi wanted to make a grand entrance. Although he could not match Majapahit's maritime military might, he was determined to make the most of the occasion and impress his hosts. The king was immensely proud of the large fleet of *jong* he had built.[378] What better way to show off his power and prestige than to use these huge junks to transport his beloved daughter to her wedding?

A few weeks later, the royal entourage left the capital at Pakuan and sailed down the Ciliwung river to Sunda Kelapa, where coconut trees lined the seashore. There, a spectacular sight awaited them: two hundred *jong* lay at anchor, flying the king's standard and decked in banners. The boats were filled with a lavish array of wedding gifts, from ivory and silks to caged exotic birds. Still, the king was a cautious man and he also ordered his military commanders to load large amounts of weaponry (Gajah

Mada's reputation had spread far and wide). They raised anchor and sailed eastwards, hugging the northern Java coast, heading to Tuban, the gateway to Majapahit.

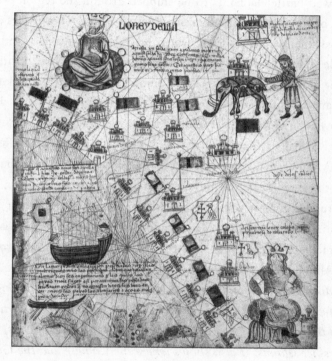

A cropped portion of one of the vallum sheets of a Catalan map by Cresques Abraham featuring a Javanese jong with the caption: 'these ships are called jongs (inchi) and have sixty-cubit hulls with thirty-four cubits of freeboard. They have on top of this between four and ten masts and their sails are of canes and palm.' [Bibliothèque Nationale de France, public domain]

The fleet reflected the extraordinary skill and sophistication of Java's boatbuilders and mariners of the day. These vessels had no peers – they were even larger than the Portuguese ships that arrived in Asia in the 15th century – and could carry up to a thousand men and two thousand tonnes of cargo, which allowed battle elephants to be shipped around the region. They had between two and ten masts, pointed hulls on both sides and massive sails. The Majapahit rulers used them as warships and for trade and could deploy four hundred *jongs* in a single expedition. They were the bedrock of the empire, backed by remarkably advanced technology. Compasses, magnets, maps and deep knowledge of the stars were used for navigation.

Remember that back in 1293, Prince Widjaya had offered the Mongol invaders a detailed map of eastern Java in exchange for their support. And more than two hundred years later, the Portuguese, master explorers and traders, marvelled at the accuracy of maps made by Javanese cartographers. Here is an extract from a letter written by the Portuguese commander Afonso de Albuquerque (1453-1515) to the king of Portugal: *'I am also sending to you an authentic portion of a great map belonging to a Javanese pilot which showed the Cape of Good Hope, Portugal and the territory of Brazil, the Red Sea and the Persian Gulf, and the spice islands. It also shows where the Chinese and the Gores (Ryukyu Islanders and Taiwanese) sail. It strikes me as being the finest piece of work I ever saw.'*

King Wangi's fleet reached Tuban without incident and anchored at the mouth of the River Mas. Smaller, shallow-hulled vessels were used to navigate the wide river inland to Canggu, a short distance from Majapahit. As soon as royal scouts brought news of the imminent arrival of the Sundanese[379] the palace became a frenzy of activity. Huge numbers of pigs, water buffalo, turtles, deer and goats were slaughtered ahead or the immense feast that would be prepared to celebrate the royal wedding.[380] A special dance had been rehearsed by a troop of female performers, pavilions were draped in fine cloth, and royal standards were hung across the whole city.

King Hayam Wuruk could barely contain himself and he was eager to travel to Canggu to greet his bride. But Gajah Mada thought otherwise. 'Let the Sundanese wait for a few days, as is the protocol for such royal visits,' he said, adding, 'they might have ulterior motives, so let's be cautious.'[381] The king grudgingly agreed as his *patih* always knew best.

Meanwhile, the Sundanese had unloaded their ships and made their way to the field at Bubat, just outside Majapahit. A sense of unease started to gnaw away at the Sundanese king. Why had no one presented themselves to offer a formal greeting? If not King Hayam Wuruk, surely at the very least the *patih* and members of the royal family should have been there to welcome them. Something was wrong.

Bad news

The royal entourage quickly set up camp in Bubat. Everything was on a grand scale; hundreds of servants rushed to prepare huge tents, luxurious pavilions and makeshift kitchens. But still they waited. King Wangi, whose impatience had now turned to anger, summoned his *patih*, Anepaken, who also thought the lack of any official reception was both strange and suspicious. After a brief discussion it was agreed that the *patih*, *demung* (chamberlain) and *tumenggung* (army chief) should pay Gajah Mada an official visit under the protection of three hundred guards.[382] Perhaps a civilised conversation between equals could help to avoid any misunderstandings.

After the short ride to Majapahit, they made themselves known to the palace guards and were told to wait inside a pavilion in the grand residence where they were offered food, betel nuts and cold water. But when Gajah Mada finally appeared, the diplomatic exchange went downhill rapidly, at least according to the Sundanese record of what happened.[383]

Gajah Mada looked disdainfully at the three men. 'There is Patih Anepaken. Be welcome. I don't know your ranks. But why are you all so rude to just arrive here and storm into my house uninvited?'

Anepaken bristled. 'We are sent by our king to see why we were not given a proper reception by the king of Majapahit. And you call me impolite? We are here to see when we can get our ships in from the coast – filled with presents for the king – and we want to know the arrangements for when the king will ask our princes to marry him.'

Gajah Mada spat back: 'Well, you seem to be able to talk. But you don't behave like a proper *mantri* (minister), coming here and demanding all sorts of things, like a whore. Let me teach you how subjects typically behave here. They ask for an audience, humbly, and offer presents. I understand you have a princess as a gift. If you come with me, I can make sure she is presented to the king.'[384]

At that moment, Gajah Mada's real intentions became clear to the Sundanese. This was not to be a marriage of equals. Majapahit wanted to take the princess as a concubine and Sunda would be absorbed into the Majapahit empire. That was not what had been agreed a few weeks earlier. All pretence of diplomacy immediately vanished. Anepaken was furious: 'What does this mean? You want us, the Sundanese, who never lost a battle, to become subjects to your king? In the past you tried to capture our lands but we drove your people back and they died begging for their lives. And now you spew words that sound like the fart of a cricket and smell like dogshit.'

Gajah Mada, normally reserved and calculating, shouted back: 'You clearly don't know how to behave, but let me talk with the king and send you a messenger if we allow your ships to come inland. Meanwhile, you wait in Bubat. And if you move only an inch from that spot, I will send orders to kill you all.'

The Sundanese leaders had heard enough. They rushed back to Bubat to tell King Wangi that the marriage was simply a ploy by Gajah Mada to force Sunda to submit to Majapahit. Anepaken suggested that Princess Citra Rashmi be sent straight back home for her own safety. But the young princess refused to leave her father, no matter the consequences. The people of Sunda did not back down.

Back at the palace, Gajah Mada arranged an urgent audience with the king. As predicted, he said, the treacherous Sundanese came with bad intentions. To make matters worse, they were rude and when he put them in their place, they stormed off. The marriage was off and they should expect trouble. These arrogant Sundanese, he said, were up for a fight.

King Hayam Wuruk was distraught and angry. He had been looking forward to his wedding night with the beautiful princess with great anticipation and now he found himself preparing for bloodshed. He sent a message asking Wengker, his uncle based in Kediri, to send reinforcements as soon as possible. Gajah Mada ordered his guards to beat the *basantaka,* the city's giant war drum. Instead of celebrating a royal wedding, the city prepared for battle on its own doorstep.[385]

The battle of Bubat

The next day found Gajah Mada in his element. Mounted on his favourite horse, he paraded himself in front of thousands of troops, holding aloft his banner of a gold brocade elephant with its trunk pointed skyward. Behind him was King Hayam Wuruk, dressed in white sitting in a howdah mounted on an elephant. The signal was given and the army moved towards Bubat.

Gajah Mada ordered scouts to ride to the Sundanese camp with an offer of peace on the condition that they submitted immediately. The scouts found their soldiers drinking palm wine to find the courage for the coming battle. They knew that they were heavily outnumbered. King Wangi dismissed the offer with a contemptuous wave of his hand. The Sundanese were in no mood to surrender.

It was now late in the day and the plan was to attack the next morning from three sides and push the Sundanese back to the Brantas river. When the sun rose, King Wangi's men were prepared. They had brought their ships further up the river, bringing the enemy into range of their *cetbang* cannons.[386] These primitive pieces of artillery, introduced to Java by the defeated Mongol invasion force, were made of bronze and could fire arrow-like projectiles, bullets and stones. The opening salvo marked the start of the Battle of Bubat and when part of the Majapahit forces were trapped near the river and came under heavy bombardment, the Sunda army held the upper hand.[387]

The situation deteriorated further when the Sundanese breached the Majapahit lines and were able to attack Gajah Mada, who fell from his horse. Legend has it that he hacked his way through the enemy soldiers – quite a feat for a man well into his sixties – which allowed his men to come to his aid and chop off the head of a Sundanese army commander.

The tide turned when Wengker's reinforcements arrived from Kediri. The Sundanese were now seriously outmanned and their resistance crumbled like dust. When King Wangi realized that his cause was hopeless, he rode his elephant into the heart of the battle. After a lance pierced his body and hurled him onto the elephant's back,[388] Majapahit men hacked him to pieces. In a matter of hours, the Sundanese forces were completely wiped out. Chroniclers later spoke of a sea of blood and mountains of corpses.[389]

Princess Citra Rashmi watched in horror from a small hill near the edge of the battlefield, crying out in anguish as her father and his troops were cut down. Her guards urged her to flee – they could surely still find a way back to Sunda – but the princess would not hear of it. Seeing that all was lost, she grabbed a *keris* from her guard and stabbed herself to death. Her tragically premature departure into the afterlife marked the end of the Battle of Bubat.[390] The schism with Majapahit never healed and even today Sunda has its own language and resentments, as well as a separate identity from the rest of Java.

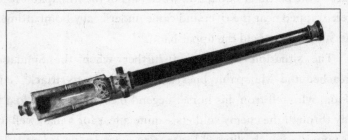

Majapahit 'cetbang' cannon. Cannons were introduced to Majapahit when Kublai Khan invaded Java in 1293. [Metropolitan Museum, New York; public domain]

Wengker wins

There were no feasts or victory celebrations at the palace and the performers who had rehearsed a new dance for the wedding were sent home. King Hayam Wuruk was seething with anger. He realised that without the timely intervention of his uncle Wengker the outcome of the Battle of Bubat might have been very different. The moment had finally arrived for the king and his uncle to acknowledge that they had ceded far too much power to Gajah

Mada, whose imperial ambitions had caused this whole bloody mess. He had played the royals like a *wayang* puppet show.

After the battle, King Hayam Wuruk met his uncle at the king's residence inside the palace complex. Wengker had long resented Gajah Mada. The *patih* wielded too much influence at court and behaved as if the kingdom was his. While the young king spent his time overseeing ceremonies and rituals, attending dance performances, or enjoying himself at the annual Caitra festival, Gajah Mada ruled the lands with an iron first.

Over the years, he had become more and more controlling and oppressive, especially after the death of Queen Gayatri. The *patih* had a wide network of informants providing him with vital intelligence from across the empire. People turned to him, not the king, for advice or to settle disputes. His judgement was final.

What complicated matters further was that the *patih* was an army man, a former commander of the elite Bhayangkara guards, who commanded the respect of the troops. A number of commanders had him to thank for their move up the greasy military pole as the *patih* always took great care to oversee who was promoted, and who was not. Many of these officers were loyal to the *patih*. Gajah Mada was not a man who could easily be dismissed, even by the royal family.

The king and Wengker both agreed that it was completely unacceptable that what should have been a glorious wedding had turned into a massacre. Gajah Mada had also lied about what exactly had happened during the meeting with the three senior delegates from Sunda. Enough was enough. Uncle Wengker urged the king to fire the *patih* and arrest him.

Hayam Wuruk agreed. The order went out and troops rushed to Gajah Mada's compound and battered down the door. Despite a thorough search, the *patih* was nowhere to be found. The next morning the king ordered his soldiers to look 'in forests and mountains, in remote hermitages, in the dwelling places of the abbots and in villages, in inaccessible regions, in ravines and caves, on impassable roads, in gorges, by gullies and in stone fields.'[391] Gajah Mada was nowhere to be seen and had disappeared like a puff of smoke.

Gajah Mada knew very well that, for once, he had seriously overplayed his hand. After the battle he dressed like a commoner and immediately fled the city and went into hiding. Even his wife, who scoured the countryside for weeks, could find no sign of him. Everybody had a different explanation for his sudden disappearance. His enemies revelled in the thought that this overambitious man was cursed or, even better, had been murdered. The palace monks were convinced the gods had punished the man and banished him to the afterlife. Local magicians blamed sorcery and there were stories that the missing *patih* had been seen meditating on a remote mountain top. Meanwhile, merchants arriving in the city were certain they had seen him walking the countryside dressed as a flea-bitten hermit. But subsequent investigations into the leads all led to northing. Yet again, Gajah Mada had outsmarted his adversaries.[392]

Not that he had to stay out of sight for long. The king appointed Wengker to manage the kingdom[393] and it was agreed that his uncle would spend more time at the palace in Majapahit and less in his hometown of Kediri on the other side of the mountains. But at the palace it soon became painfully obvious that Wengker, the king, and his council had no idea how to run the kingdom.

They knew very little about the legal system, governance and taxes or how to manage royal warehouses and food stocks. When the heads of villages arrived at court seeking to settle disputes, they were clueless. All these matters had been handled by Gajah Mada. They needed him back. The message went out that the king's fury had cooled and a few days later Gajah Mada returned to the palace. He was formally reappointed at a short, frosty ceremony and, to keep him on a tight leash, there would be no further diplomatic initiatives without the consent of the royal council.[394]

One problem remained – Hayam Wuruk still needed a wife. The royal council was convened to discuss the matter as it was of the utmost importance to have an heir to the kingdom. Rather than scour the land to find a daughter of a loyal nobleman – that would be below the king's station – all agreed that it was better to keep it in the family. Hayam Wuruk would marry his niece, Paduka Sori, the daughter of uncle Wengker.[395]

Geomancers selected a propitious day, a lavish wedding was organised, and Paduka Sori soon gave birth to a daughter, a shy girl, Princess Kusumawardhani,[396] and later Hayam Wuruk would also have a son, Wirabumi, by a concubine.

While the Battle of Bubat was a diplomatic disaster, Majapahit's power and influence remained unchallenged. A few years earlier, around 1350, four hundred Majapahit *jong* painted in black and red had sailed north. They made a stop in Tumasik, what is now Singapore, and sailed on to Pasai on the very northern tip of Sumatra, opposite the island of Penang off the Malay peninsula. More than two thousand miles from Tuban,[397] Pasai was home to many of the region's first Muslim traders and in the perfect location to monitor the sea lanes entering the strategically significant Malacca Strait. The whole *nusantara* archipelago was united under one banner.

It is hard to overstate the maritime power of the empire. There are unconfirmed reports that Majapahit ships later reached some of the remotest parts of the planet. Ludovico di Varthema (c.1470-1517) was an Italian traveller and diarist and the first European to write an account of the pilgrimage to Mecca. He also visited Bengal, Malacca, Sumatra, the Spice Islands and Java. In his book *Itinerario de Ludouico de Varthema Bolognese*, he wrote that the southern Javanese people sailed to 'far Southern lands' up to the point they arrived at an island where a day only lasted four hours long and was 'colder than in any part of the world.'[398] It's improbable that they sailed all that way – the Italian's imagination may have got the better of him – as modern studies have determined that such an island would have been located at least 900 nautical miles (1,666 kilometres) south of the southernmost point of Tasmania. But it does suggest that Javanese seamen knew of Australia.[399]

But even at the peak of his power, the ever-popular King Hayam Wuruk was eager to raise his personal standing with his people throughout eastern Java, the core of his kingdom, the heartland of the Majapahit empire. And to achieve that goal, he planned a series of royal tours.

11

The Royal Progress

(1359 CE)

Epic journeys and the seeds of decay

Ever the showman, King Hayam Wuruk was keen to inspect his lands and bask in the adulation of his loyal subjects.[400] After his coronation, he made regular tours around large parts of Java, visiting villages, towns, shrines, temples, monasteries and, of course, the people. These journeys lasted up to three months and took place during the dry season as many roads were impassable and flooding became a problem (as it still is today) when the rains came. It's no coincidence that ferries, road maintenance and bridge building were always high on the king's policy agenda.

The royal inspections required months of preparations. The route was meticulously planned, and scouts were sent out to assess road conditions and alert local dignitaries that they would be expected to host and entertain the king. There was of course only one man for the job. Gajah Mada oversaw the whole operation with his usual efficiency, down to the very last detail. He was a meticulous planner, and nothing was left to chance.

And, from 1359 onwards, Prapanca, the loyal if rather

bibulous scribe, was there to manage all the religious ceremonies and record every detail of the journey, or at least those that glorified the king's reign. Prapanca's father had accompanied the royal family on earlier tours but as he entered his eighties the journeys had become too arduous for the old *dharmadyaksa*. That is why the king had summoned Prapanca to court to order him to take his father's place.

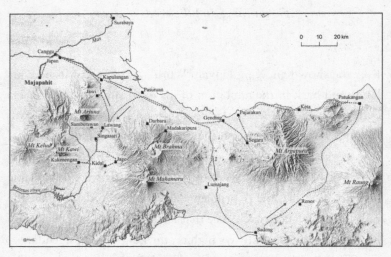

Hayam Wuruk's journey of 1359.
[Illustration: HvdL; Credit: Bullough, 2007]

In total, seven such tours were made between 1353 and 1363[401] and only when the king had pressing business were they shelved. One year he devoted his time to constructing a shrine to honour his late mother. Candi Rimbi was richly and rather strangely decorated with multitude images of floppy-eared animals as well as a relief of two people being boiled alive in a cauldron.[402] In 1362, he presided over a *shraddu* for his grandmother, Queen Gayatri, whose soul, twelve years after her death, was finally ready to enter the abode of the immortals.

Departure

September 1359, Kapulungan.

Kapulungan, just south of Surabaya and a day's walk from the capital, Majapahit, was a tranquil place where little had changed over the years; each day was pretty much the same as the one before. Farmers worked the fields, village elders chewed betel nut under shady *kapok* trees, and village women sold food to the few merchants passing through. But Kapulungan did have one claim to fame. Its proximity to Majapahit and a well-kept and wide road made it the perfect starting point for what became known as the Royal Progress.

And so it was that in the early days of September 1359 that this quiet village, for a short time at least, became a bustling town. Hundreds of people – soldiers, officials, family members and their servants – poured in from the capital. A sea of carriages and bullock carts filled a large open field, temporary stables were built for the horses, while the royal elephants sought shade under the trees. The amount of baggage was simply staggering: tents, carpets, provisions, cooking utensils, animal feed, ceremonial bells and gongs, bamboo containers full of palm wine, fighting cocks in cages and, of course, the voluminous wardrobes worthy of a royal entourage.

The young ladies of Kapulungan could hardly contain themselves, as they had never seen anything quite like it. First, they sneaked past the guards to admire the highly decorated royal carriages. For the king's sisters there were emblems of a bright sun for the Princess of Pajang and a white bull for the Princess of Lasem, and flowers for the Princess of Kediri, his aunt; the king's carriage carried the emblem of the bitter tasting Majapahit fruit.[403] Then they adorned themselves with a special type of betel nut leaf, a flower without a stem, known as 'weeping leaves'. It was said that if you wore them in your hair a handsome young man would instantly fall madly in love with you and weep tears of joy. Suitably accessorised, they gorged themselves on sweet sugar palm juice and ogled the hordes of handsome city boys arriving from the capital.

On the evening prior to departure the whole area was lit up by a sea of small campfires and oil lamps. Before dawn, the royal family gathered to conduct a brief religious ceremony under the stars. At precisely six o'clock in the morning as the sun appeared on the horizon, the astrologers gave the sign. Drums were beaten, conches blown, and the long, snaking caravan moved off.[404] The three-month journey through eastern Java had begun.

Gajah Mada led the way, turning his horse east onto the royal highway,[405] followed by guards and mounted noblemen. The king and the royal family rode in carriages in the middle of the caravan, attended by trusted attendants, who served food and water, and carried parasols[406] to provide shelter from the sun. At all times, the king's female bodyguards, the *bhayangkari*, were near. On most days, the caravan would rest up until the afternoon to avoid the midday heat and then travel into the cooler evening,[407] when servants would pitch camp and collect food and water.[408]

The royal procession was an incredible sight and sent ripples of excitement though the countryside as scouts arrived in towns and villages to announce that the king was approaching. Village elders, the *buyut*, dressed in their finest and stood in line to greet him. Young boys studying at religious schools put aside their books, and wrinkled farmers rushed from the paddy fields to the roadside, hoping to get a glimpse. Priests from remote Buddhist and Hindu temples and monasteries deep in the forests and mountains came down to the valley and waited for days to pay homage.[409]

A three-day stop was scheduled in the town of Bhayalango to secure provisions and rest the horses and oxen. The next stop was Mdakaripura, a place of great spiritual significance for Gajah Mada. It was here that he had come to meditate (and hide[410]) when he lost his job as *patih* after singlehandedly sabotaging the king's marriage to a beautiful princess, poisoning diplomatic relations with the neighbouring Sunda kingdom in the process.

Mdakaripura was simply spectacular, the site of a mystical, giant waterfall a thousand metres above sea level set against the backdrop of Mount Bromo, an active volcano. Here, after taking a ritual bath in the waterfall, the king made a grand gesture to show that all was forgiven. He rewarded Gajah Mada for his loyal service by granting him a large area of land.[411]

The caravan continued along the northern shore of Java and

then bent south, inland, along small roads through valleys and dense forests. Deep ravines and steep hills made travel difficult and at times the horses were replaced with oxen to pull the royal carriages over the mountains. Prapanca was not at ease in this treacherous terrain and was delighted when they eventually stopped at a beautiful lake covered with red and white lotuses. He saw local people catching shrimp[412] and young men with blowpipes hunting waterfowl. There was duck for dinner that night. They had entered Sadeng, a region now firmly back under the full control of Majapahit after a failed uprising back in 1331. The king remained there for a few days to rule on minor local disputes, receive and hand out gifts, and, most important of all, to make sure that the people had not forgotten who was in charge.

Salt

Three weeks into the royal tour, the caravan reached the vast, windswept beaches on the northern shore of Java. Prapanca, like most people from the capital, was more accustomed to foodstalls, paddy fields and forests. He found the constant movement of the ocean rather unsettling and looked on in puzzlement as some of his braver travelling companions rushed into the water to frolic in the waves. Prapanca preferred the company of a good book, the shade of a sturdy tree, and a cup or two of palm wine.

But it was here that he caught his first glimpse of one of the kingdom's biggest growth industries – salt. Majapahit was prosperous and its people liked the finer things in life: cloth from

India, porcelain from China, and, closer to home, that culinary wonder that was salt. But making the stuff was hard work. Under blazing sun, bondsmen had to scrape the dried crust of the salt ponds, rinse the soil, and shovel it into woven bags.

As Prapanca witnessed first-hand, the towns of Biluluk and Tanggulanan, north of Majapahit, were blessed with the presence of a saline spring. Salt water simply bubbled up from the depths of the earth and spilled into the neighbouring fields.[413] This was obviously a gift from the gods for the blessed people of Majapahit, as well as a commercial opportunity not to be missed. Royal oversight was clearly required and Prince Wengker, the king's uncle, and two powerful local noble families – the Biluluks and Tanggulanans – acquired a vast number of salt ponds. It was a highly profitable business. Soon, they became Majapahit's salt oligarchs as money literally spewed out of the ground and Prapanca noted that they were men of great wealth and influence at court.

To ensure that the salt trade flourished across the realm, the king announced that small peddlers – those who carried less than sixty kilograms on their shoulder-poles – did not have to pay taxes. But big businesses were expected to pay up and the salt oligarchs knew very well that the royals expected to get their share. Each year, they went to Majapahit to join in the Caitra festivities to make lavish *pamuja* contributions to the king. They also made sure that they made regular purchases from the royal family – rice, cloth and so forth – at inflated prices in order to keep the peace (and their heads and salt ponds).

But once a year, for five days during a religious festival, the salt rights in the two towns were suspended. Anyone and everyone could scoop the salt water from the bubbling saline spring for free. Chaos ensued amid the scramble to make an honest buck. While the salt oligarchs became wealthy, the commoners also made a good living selling food to merchants who travelled from afar to buy this precious commodity, which was exported far and wide. Some of the more entrepreneurial citizens salted, cured, dried and spiced sheep, goat, buffalo and fowl and sold them as *dendeng*, a Majapahit delicacy. Prapanca enjoyed this dish immensely and was regularly seen chewing on the hard, dried salted meat, washed down with liberal quantities of wine.

Celestial nymphs

The Royal Progress made camp close to the sea. This presented an opportunity for local officials and envoys from Bali and other islands to arrive by boat and pay homage to the king and shower him with gifts. In the nearby town of Patukangan, the local governor was determined to make a particularly good impression. He escorted the king to a specially constructed bath house built on poles in the sea, accessible by a boardwalk. He said a sacred ceremony had been arranged, a ritual that would be performed by 'celestial nymphs'.[414] And with that, he left the king at their service.

A few days later, the caravan was back on the road heading towards Keta,[415] a rebellious town in the Kalayu region on the northern coast that Gajah Mada had taken in 1331, some twenty-eight years earlier. Perhaps the word from Patukangan had gotten out. Here, erotic dances were staged late at night for the king's pleasure, and in nearby villages he was presented with several 'wives', some of them the daughters of local officials who were keen to please.

From there, they moved inland towards Segara, home to Hindu priests and hermits high in the forests up in the hills. The handsome king caused considerable excitement among the nuns who lived there. Clearly, the divine spirit was not altogether hostile to worldly matters. Indeed, the stop at Segara was arranged so the king could resolve a longstanding quarrel about the amount of tribute the priests should pay at the annual Caitra festival in Majapahit.[416]

Despite this petty squabble over money, Prapanca liked the place. At this hermitage, his Hindu counterparts were busy with meetings and ceremonies. But for a Buddhist, there was little to do in terms of official business in this Hindu enclave and he had time to walk in the woods and valleys and enjoy the stunning scenery. There were flame trees, in full bloom this time of year, fragrant jasmine and frangipani, willow, teak, cashew and large, shady tamarind trees. Segara was also blessed with an abundance of fruit – rambutan, mangoes, jackfruit and mangosteen. Best of all, there was a pond completely covered with lotus flowers. Segara was quiet and tranquil, just how he liked it.[417] It was also surprisingly sophisticated in some ways. Most of the houses had roofs made of palm fibre, which was strong and waterproof; in Majapahit this was only reserved for temples. Ever inquisitive and observant, he noted that down.

The caravan then made its way down through the hills, through dense forests towards the plains near the northern shore. The next stop was Pasaruan, a town that was close to the heart of the ruling Rajasa dynasty. It was located near Candi Jawi, the temple built on the north eastern slope of Mount Welirang dating back to the Singasari kingdom. The king held ceremonies there to honour his famed great-grandfather, King Kertanegara, in whose memory the temple had been built. The royal family then visited the ruins of Singasari, the old capital where his forefather had ruled a century earlier.

It was in Pasaruan where Prapanca broke off from the royal entourage to visit his father's old friend, Abbot Ratnangsa, at the remote Buddhist monastery in Darbaru. That was where he learned about King Hayam Wuruk's royal lineage, which could be traced all the way back to King Ken Arok, who died in 1227 and was the founder of the Rajasa dynasty of the Singasari and Majapahit line of monarchs.

After a short diversion to Kagenengan to honour Ken Arok, the caravan snaked back towards Majapahit. It was mid-November, some ten weeks after they had departed, and the king received a rapturous reception on his return. In the years to come, he would make more royal tours of eastern Java,[418] but three years later he had other business to attend to. His revered grandmother, Queen Gayatri, had passed away twelve years earlier in 1350 and it was time for him to arrange a different kind of journey, one that would take her to the world of the immortals.

Queen Gayatri joins the immortals

1362, Majapahit.

Preparations for the *shraddu* began in earnest two months before the week-long ceremony. A Buddhist priest placed an effigy of Queen Gayatri made of flowers at the centre of a large circle of uncooked, coloured rice piled high in the great *witana* meeting hall in the palace. The beating of drums and gongs accompanied dancers who worked themselves into a trance-like state, chanting in rhythm to invite the soul of the queen to enter the effigy.[419]

On the first evening, Gajah Mada, the commoner who was closest to her in so many ways, stood up and made a speech in the *witana*, which had been decorated with red cloth and hundreds of oil lamps. Every member of the royal family was there, as were nobles and ministers. Now seventy years old, Gajah Mada spoke of his great admiration for the woman who had guided his career and acted as a power behind the throne. What an extraordinary life the queen had led. She had seen the fall of Singasari after the assassination of her grandfather, King Kertanegara, and been taken by force to Kediri, where she had lived incognito as a servant. She had married King Widjaya, the man who had founded the city of Majapahit and reunited the kingdom. Towards the end, she had offered guidance to her grandson, the young Hayam Wuruk.

When he sat down, he called for a moment of silence. This was an emotional moment for him. The effigy of the queen was then placed on a 'lion throne', a brightly painted chair made of bamboo. Accompanied by chanting priests, it was carried to the large pavilion on the *alun-alun* square opposite the entrance to the palace. Huge bamboo stands had been built to accommodate the throngs of grieving commoners; thatched roofs offered shade from the burning heat.[420]

For seven days, the whole city – from humble farmers and hunters to members of the royal guard, nobles and religious leaders – came to pay homage to the queen. They said prayers and laid food in front of the effigy. The long line of mourners filled the field and musicians playing flutes to the beat of a single drum kept the procession moving. One evening, ladies at the court came out to dance, a performance witnessed only by women, including the king's wife and his sisters.[421]

After seven days, the effigy was carried to the river, where it began the next stage of the queen's journey. The people then made small offerings around the city – in gateways, trees, at crossroads and entrances to homes and temples – to ensure the other deities and spirits did not feel neglected as Queen Gayatri joined the immortals.

The death of Gajah Mada

1364, Simping, near Blitar.

Despite his advancing years – he was now in his early seventies – Gajah Mada was still full of energy and very much involved with running the day-to-day affairs of the kingdom, while at the same time writing a book about Majapahit's laws and rituals, the *Adigama*.[422] A year after the *shraddu*, King Hayam Wuruk, now twenty-nine years old, journeyed to Simping[423] on the southern coast of Java to inspect the restoration of a temple, a shrine for King Widjaya, the founder of Majapahit. An earthquake had caused the temple to collapse and the king wanted to move it to a more auspicious location, a little to the west.[424]

His inspection tour was cut short when he received word that Gajah Mada had fallen ill. The king immediately returned to Majapahit. Royal doctors gave the now frail old man daily potions of cloves, pearl grass and soursop, a plant which reduced inflammation and pain. Sorcerers rubbed his body with ashes and chanted incantations. Every day, people gathered outside Gajah Mada's compound to pray, and women and children would light oil lamps at home to honour the great man. Despite all these efforts, the respected *patih* passed away a few weeks later.[425]

Gajah Mada may have come from humble origins but he had risen to the pinnacle of power and, despite the Battle of Bubat fiasco, the king wanted to honour this extraordinary man with a state funeral; a few days later, his body was cremated and the ashes scattered in the River Brantas.

But a new question soon arose – who could possibly replace Gajah Mada?[426] As the court had already discovered to its cost, the man was irreplaceable. He was a brilliant administrator, a shrewd powerbroker, a fine military commander and an unscrupulous autocrat who left little room for disagreement at the Majapahit court.[427] Gajah Mada was more feared than loved[428] and, with the old schemer out of the way, long suppressed tensions between rival factions – Hindus against Buddhists, Kediri versus Singasari – were sure to bubble back to the surface.

The members of the seven-strong royal council knew they

needed to act quickly. Well aware that appointing another strongman was not in their best interests, they decided to appoint two men as 'the hands and feet' of the king and keep them both on a tight leash. Only when Hayam Wuruk reached the age of thirty and had become more confident and assertive[429] would a single *patih* be appointed.

For the next twenty-five years King Hayam Wuruk ruled alone. He had leaned heavily on and learned much from Gajah Mada, his mother, his famed grandmother and uncle Wengker, and he was now a wiser man. It was a time of peace. There were no rebellions or uprisings and nobles from afar arrived in Majapahit each year for the Caitra festival to pay tribute and homage. The king was content and devoted much time to his favourite sanctuary, the Penataran state temple complex near Blitar, where he oversaw the construction of what is today called the Dated Temple. It was richly decorated with *naga* dragons, mythical semi-divine beings that are half human and half cobra.

First signs of strain – a diplomatic incident with Sumatra and China

After years of peace and prosperity, signs of trouble started to emerge in Sumatra. The huge island neighbouring Java had long been under the control of Majapahit and was ruled by a man called Adityawarman, whom King Hayam Wuruk had every reason to believe was a loyal subject. After all, he was the son of one the Melayu princesses from Sumatra who had been sent to the court of King Kertanegara as a gift back in 1293. He had grown up in the palace at Majapahit, knew his way around court politics, and even shared Kertanegara's interest in Buddhist tantric sex rituals.

Well regarded, Gajah Mada had sent him to Sumatra in 1343 to take control of the Melayu kingdom at the time when the empire was expanding. At some point, Adityawarman's ambitions grew well beyond his relatively modest station. He was first appointed viceroy of Melayu but two years later declared himself king of the region. In 1375, he made the bold decision to dispatch diplomatic envoys to China[430] without consulting Hayam Wuruk in Java. To make his point, he also ordered a stone inscription to be made that showed a list of kings, with his own name mentioned before the rulers of Majapahit.[431]

In Peking, the Emperor Hongwu responded by sending an envoy to Sumatra carrying gifts for Adityawarman. When word reached King Hayam Wuruk that Melayu had reached out to China, his reaction was predictably volcanic. Melayu was part of his empire and Adityawarman had no authority to contact the emperor of China. Clearly, the whole business made the king look weak, so a strong message needed to be sent to Peking. He ordered the Chinese envoy in Sumatra to travel to Majapahit and on arrival had him come to the Amazing Pavilion. There, he told the diplomat he would not tolerate China having anything to do with Melayu and that Peking should know better than to intervene in his business. To send a stern message, the envoy was promptly put to death and sent back home in a bag.

The news soon reached China. While the emperor was angered by the death of his envoy, he had never meant to challenge the authority of Majapahit in the king's own backyard. It was all a mistake. And with Kublai Khan's disastrous campaign in Java nearly a century earlier still fresh in the mind, he had no desire to start another war. Relations between China and Java soon returned to normal. As a sign of goodwill, in November 1381 Hayam Wuruk dispatched a letter and three hundred slaves to China; in return the Chinese emperor sent rich fabrics and paper money to Majapahit.[432]

The king now turned his attention to his man Adityawarman in Sumatra. He was in no mood to tolerate his disobedience and sent three hundred warships and two hundred thousand soldiers to Melayu, and the upstart Adityawarman was never heard of again. It's safe to assume that he was either executed, committed suicide or died of a combination of stress and old age (he was well into his eighties).

On the way, the king's troops intervened in a local power struggle by laying siege to Tumasik, which was by now the walled city of Singapura.[433] After a month of resistance, the Majapahit soldiers broke through and massacred the inhabitants. The local king, Parameswara, fled north to the mouth of Malacca River. There, he converted to Islam, changed his name to Sultan Iskandar Shah, and founded the kingdom of Malacca on the coast of the Malay peninsula, which was traditionally Majapahit country.

As the sultan's power grew, so did his influence over the narrow Malacca Strait, the most direct route between the Indian Ocean and the South China Sea, and the main sea lane that carried trade between India, Southeast Asia and China. Muslims had always had a presence in Majapahit. For centuries, they had come to Java to trade and many lived in the city but their numbers were small and they were not involved in court politics. But the rise of Malacca was significant – it was the first time a powerful Muslim presence had been established on Majapahit's doorstep.

12

Death and Distrust

(1400 – 1430 CE)

Changes at the top lead to civil war and decline

1389, Majapahit.
On a steamy, sweltering afternoon, at that time of the year when the flame tree was in full bloom, the jackfruit was ripe, and rambutans were in abundance, a storm was about to break over Majapahit. A drumbeat was heard from the palace and brass gongs sounded across the city. The king was dead and the heavens wept.

The terrible news spread like wildfire. At the age of fifty-five, King Hayam Wuruk had joined the immortals.[434] The massive downpour had cleared the heavy air and a large crowd soon gathered to lay flowers and strings of jasmine garlands at the palace gate. Some prayed, while others stood in silence, heads bowed. The city was soon in a tumult of grief. As the skies turned from red to purple and night set in, huge numbers of mourners descended on the city's temples to honour their beloved king. The slow, rhythmic beating of the drums continued until morning.

Inside the palace, preparations for the funeral were soon

underway.[435] Everyone wanted their say, from the *patih* to the religious leaders, the *dharmadyaksas*, and, of course, the many different members of the royal family. Plans were drawn and redrawn. Eventually, it was agreed that the master of ceremonies, the *kanuhuran*, would be in charge of funeral arrangements and the Hindu priests would be responsible for embalming the king's body with honey and fragrant oils. A large sarcophagus in the form of a blue-black ox, with enormous curved horns was constructed; messengers rode to villages, towns, cities, and monasteries to announce the tragic news. Diplomatic letters were sent to kings and nobles in vassal states like Siam, Sumatra, and smaller kingdoms to inform them of the king's passing and remind them, politely of course, that Majapahit was still firmly in charge.

In the weeks that followed, Majapahit experienced a huge influx of people. There were those who wanted to pay their respects, those keen to attend what was bound to be a once-in-a-lifetime spectacle, and those who simply wanted to make a buck or two. Funerals, after all, were big business, especially one on such a grand scale as this. Ever observant, Prapanca watched stalls selling rambutan, jackfruit, bananas, coconuts and mangoes spring up all over the city. Others peddled small amulets, cooked rice with chicken, vegetables wrapped in banana leaves, or *jamu* herbal cocktails. Priests arrived from afar to recite prayers (and collect payments for doing so).

There was no shortage of fortune tellers either. While Prapanca was happy to seek guidance from a well-known wandering astrologer, he had no time for the roadside palm readers whom he regarded with contempt. In the evening he enjoyed *wayang* puppet shows, watched in amazement as a juggler balanced a knife on his nose while standing on one foot, and stood in the crowd to watch a performance of the king's favourite dances. The city had an almost celebratory air. King Hayam Wuruk, no stranger to a good party, would no doubt have approved.

A year earlier

The previous year, Hayam Wuruk's wife, Panduka Sori, had passed away, raising the issue of Hayam Wuruk's own succession plans. As things stood, his daughter, Princess Kusumawardhana,[436] a quiet, shy and introverted young woman, was heir to the throne.[437] The princess took after her father in one way though – she was far more interested in the arts, dance and music than land disputes and diplomacy, which she found both boring, tedious and confusing.[438]

Her husband and nephew, Prince Wikramawardhana, was soft spoken, easily offended, and prone to wild emotional swings. Some considered him arrogant, others thought that he was just distant. The two stood in sharp contrast to Prince Wirabumi, the son of Hayam Wuruk by a concubine, who was liked for his playful, good-humoured demeanour and lack of royal grandeur. He was much more popular with the people of Majapahit than his half-sister.

But the king had made up his mind. He called his family and ministers to a meeting at the palace's famed Amazing Pavilion. After his death, he proclaimed, the kingdom was to be ruled by his daughter and her husband. Prince Wirabumi was given the task of governing the eastern parts of Java, all the way from

Lamongan, north of Majapahit, to Blambangan on the east coast. His daughter would have the final say in case of disagreements.

It was a short meeting with long-term consequences. Prince Wikramawardhana disliked Prince Wirabumi intensely and thought the existence of what he considered to be a parallel centre of power would inevitably lead to problems.

Patih Enggon may have held nothing like as much influence as the mighty Gajah Mada but he was nonetheless an astute observer of palace politics. After the meeting, he fell into conversation with another senior official, the *demung*, the royal chamberlain, who complained that Majapahit was a land where amnesia ruled; its rulers had forgotten the lessons of the past. Had the Rajasa dynasty learned nothing from the previous mistakes made by rulers going all the way back to King Airlangga, who had divided the kingdom in 1042 with disastrous consequences? The *patih* nodded. He had conveyed the same thoughts to the king. 'Things,' said Enggon, 'will get messy very soon.'

He was right. Prince Wirabumi left the palace soon afterwards and moved east to rule what he considered to be his own kingdom. The omens were not good, especially after Prince Wirabumi dispatched his own diplomatic mission to China. The Chinese emperor was confused – were there now two kings in Java?

But King Wikramawardhana's attention soon shifted to happier family matters closer to home. Princess Kusumawardhana gave birth to a boy[439] and, a year later, a daughter, the lovely Suhita. Hayam Wuruk's last days were spent spoiling his two grandchildren. He took them to see the palace elephants and watch cock fights and they shared the best durian in the land on trips to the temples of their forefathers. That is, until that sultry afternoon when it started to rain and Hayam Wuruk entered the afterlife.

Hayam Wuruk's funeral

Each day at dawn, white lilies were placed on a statue of the king on the pavilion outside the north palace gate as hundreds of women sang songs of mourning. Then, exactly five weeks after Hayam Wuruk's death, a huge throng gathered for the funeral. The early arrivals squatted under the expanse of banyan trees looking for shade. But soon the crowd spilled over into the large open *alun-alun* field and thousands lined the road to the cremation grounds outside the city.

As was tradition, the king was provided with a new name for the afterlife – Hyang Wekasing Suka. Inside the palace, the king's embalmed body was placed in the specially made sarcophagus. The elite Bhayangkara guards then carried it to the inner courtyard, where priests and the royal family stood waiting. The clash of cymbals and the beating of gongs signalled that the funeral procession was about to start.

In front walked the concubines who were to die with the king after enjoying a last ritual bath earlier that morning. Barefoot and dressed in white silk garments, with their hair let down to the waist, they stepped solemnly forward. Next through the palace gate stepped a thousand wailing young virgins, followed by court officials carrying royal regalia: the king's *sirih* box, a crown and his jewels. For a moment, it seemed as if the procession had come to a halt but then the Bhayangkara guards emerged, carrying the sarcophagus with the pointed ox horns.

Behind the sarcophagus walked the royal family, including the king's nine-year-old granddaughter Suhita, dressed in white and red. They were followed by nobles, the *patih* and his ministers, Prapanca – who wore a saffron loin cloth and a garland of yellow flowers around his neck – and district governors and the royal guards.

Thousands of spectators desperate for a last glimpse of the king on his final journey at times surged forward to touch the coffin, only to be pushed back by guards. An endless line of people snaked through the city on the road to the ceremonial burial grounds on an elevated field populated with fragrant plumeria trees, near the River Brantas just outside the city.

There, a large pyre made of perfumed sandalwood laced with cloves, garlic, cinnamon and cumin seeds had been prepared. The hushed crowd spread out to form a crescent around the riverbank as the coffin arrived. Hindu priests threw burning torches on to the pyre and flames shot up towards the sky.

What followed left young Suhita distraught. As the sarcophagus burned, the concubines who she knew so well, the women that had played with her and pampered her since she was a baby, said farewell to each other and walked into the fire without flinching. There were no screams as they burned in silence. Suhita could hardly breathe. The smell of their burning flesh would stay with her for the rest of her life.

When it was all over, the king's ashes were collected in a

golden bowl. Matted-haired *rshi* hermits then scattered them in the waters of the River Brantas. By now, it was late in the afternoon and the crowd started to disperse.

Suhita walked home in silence. The funeral had changed her, forever. It was as if the universe was sending her a message urging her to breathe, see, smell, hear, taste, talk and learn. A great calm came over her, like a soft cloak. Unlike the poor concubines, she vowed she would lead a long and fulfilling life.

For Prapanca, the funeral marked a turning point. He had shared so much with his friend, lord and master. Cockfights as children and, later, epic journeys around the kingdom that he faithfully documented. It was twenty-five years since he finished his immense narrative poem, the *Desawarnana*. A shroud of emptiness fell over him. It was time for him to relinquish his court duties.

Prapanca and a handful of priests carried some of the king's ashes in a small bronze container to a special shrine in Candi Ngetos, near Kediri, right in the heart of the kingdom.[440] It was Prapanca's last official task. In his twilight years he enjoyed the simple life in a quiet mountain hermitage. There were no kings, no *patih,* no grand tours or ceremonies to worry about. He ate when he was hungry and slept when he was tired; when he did neither, he prayed, walked, or talked with fellow monks in a pavilion. In the evenings he enjoyed a cup or two of palm wine. Prapanca was at peace.

Twelve years later, in 1401, Prapanca returned to Candi Ngetos for Hayam Wuruk's *shraddu.*[441] He was an old man holding a staff, his mind slow and his duties long passed on to others. Not long after that, Prapanca closed his eyes and joined his king in the world of immortals. The Buddhist monks at the hermitage scattered his ashes in the surrounding fields.[442]

Start of the Paregreg civil war

King Wikramawardhana was eager to make his mark. He did not want to be seen as a second-rate leader who spent his time dealing with third-rate issues such as routine temple inspections. He wanted to be remembered as one of the all-time greats.

The day after the cremation, he summoned Patih Enggon to discuss the state of the nation. The mood was upbeat. The warehouses were well stocked with rice, taxes were being regularly collected from markets and traders, and while some work was needed to repair irrigation projects this was largely in hand. New temples were under construction and the priests said (as they would) that the gods very much favoured the new queen and her king. 'In short,' the *patih* concluded, 'all is well and there is little you have to do.' He waited for a moment and continued: 'But what needs your urgent attention is Sumatra.'

After the death of Hayan Wuruk, several minor kings in Sumatra had started to behave as if the lands they controlled were no longer vassal states. The *patih* suggested sending soldiers to the island to secure the region. A show of force would make clear that Majapahit's hegemony across the archipelago was absolute.

But it was not that simple and it would be eight years before these vassals again sent tribute to the king.[443] During this period the cost of the ships, weapons and soldiers blew a huge hole in the king's treasury. And reports came in that fewer trading vessels were arriving at Majapahit's ports. It was said that many merchants were flocking to the strategically important city of Malacca on the Malay peninsula.

This news was confirmed by Siamese diplomats who had arrived in Majapahit for an audience with the king. But it was not trade they wanted to discuss, they said, but to pass on a message from Chinese emperor Hongwu. Majapahit had not sent a diplomatic mission to Peking for several years. Perhaps Siam could help to get the message across:

'How is it possible that Java and other countries can refuse the favour of heaven [meaning the emperor] and discard the master-servant relationship? Only Java obstructs our culture. Java, an insignificant country, supports criminals. You, king of Siam, still fulfil your obligations as a subject. Thus, the Emperor would be grateful if you would convey this instruction to Java, so that they can learn the True Great Principles of Behaviour.'[444]

The *patih* appreciated this warning and said that a mission to Peking would be dispatched soon. The problem was, he told the diplomats from Siam, that the king was rather distracted. He explained that a few days before their arrival, the king's youngest son, not even twenty years old, had fallen sick. Priests prayed at the prince's bedside, doctors prepared herbal concoctions and crawled on all fours around the patient and swung a magic coin-like amulet above him while whispering incantations.[445] It was all to no avail. A few months after the Siamese sailed off, in 1399, the young son died.

The boy's death left King Wikramawardhana and Queen Kusumawardhana distraught. After the funeral[446] the queen took to her bed and suffered a complete mental and physical collapse. She was convinced she was under a spell and not even the most powerful herbal baths, candle rituals and spells could break the curse. The king was coping little better. He was withdrawn and spoke to hardly anyone. Eventually, he temporarily retreated to a forest hermitage and instructed the newly appointed Patih, Manguri – Gajah Enggon had died in 1398 – to deal with the day-to-day matters of state.

Princess Suhita was by now a confident young woman. In her opinion, like the poor concubines, her parents were giving up on life too soon. In her father's absence, she was anointed queen although he retained the title of king. Suhita soon became an influential member of the royal council.[447] At one of the first meeting she attended, it was ruled that the people who took care of a temple at the holy Mount Bromo would no longer have to make annual payments of rice to the royal family.[448]

Meanwhile, several hundred kilometres to the east, Prince Wirabumi was furious when he heard the news that Suhita had been appointed queen. As the only son of King Hayam Wuruk, he was the rightful heir, not that innocent young girl. His family were clearly not treating him with the respect he deserved and he complained to his advisors that his half-sister's breakdown was to be expected from one so fragile. After all, he had continued to run his realm when his first son had died during a hunting accident.

Out of respect for his father, Prince Wirabumi remained quiet until after Hayam Wuruk's *shraddu* in 1401, twelve years

MAJAPAHIT

after his death. Prapanca had attended the ceremony and was saddened to discover that the king's children were at each other's throats. Things soon span even further out of control. When King Wikramawardhana heard that Prince Wirabumi had sent diplomats to China, he flew into a rage. His days of grieving were over. He was the one and only king of Majapahit.[449]

It started with a few skirmishes, insignificant needle pricks. King Wikramawardhana ordered his troops to make a bit of a show – burn a few houses and then retreat. In return, Wirabumi pursued a similar strategy. These tit-for-tat tactics inevitably led to more serious confrontations over the next few years. Once again, war was coming to Java. Farmers became soldiers, trenches were dug, and forests were chopped down to construct fortifications. By 1404, Java was engulfed in an all-out civil war, the *Paregreg*.[450]

Neither side was able to advance and by early 1406 the battle lines were much as they were in 1404. On the dividing line lay the old capital of Singasari which, after years of slumber and neglect, suddenly regained strategic importance. Both sides wanted access to the city and its roads and lobbied hard for the support of the local regent. Gifts were offered, priests arrived to utter benevolent incantations, and all manner of promises were made. After keeping his cards close to his chest in order to extract as much as he could from both rulers, the regent sided with Majapahit. Then things got even more complicated.

Far away in China, the new Ming emperor, Yongle, was completely unaware of what was happening in Java. In 1405, seeking to shore up his influence, he dispatched a fleet under the command of Admiral Zheng. By 1406, right in the middle of

Paregreg civil war, the emperor's ships sailed into the Java Sea[451] and Chinese diplomatic envoys had landed to have discussions with Prince Wirabumi.

In Majapahit, King Wikramawardhana mistakenly thought that his rival was receiving military support from the Chinese, who were totally unaware of the dangers they faced. It was as if the emperor had disturbed a bee colony. One day in 1406, as the Chinese relaxed in a market place while the diplomats held an audience with Wirabumi in his palace, gunshots were fired. Chaos and panic ensued as people ran for cover. Soldiers carrying King Wikramawardhana's banners moved into the market place and cut people down without making any distinction between Javanese and Admiral's Zheng's men. A few moments later, the attackers retreated and a hundred and seventy Chinese lay dead on the ground.

The Chinese survivors hurried back to their ships and sailed off – a case of history repeating itself yet again – while the Javanese continued to fight among themselves. A few days later, the king's men broke down the gate to Wirabumi's palace. Wirabumi fled to the coast where a ship lay waiting for him, but a Majapahit nobleman named 'Prince Elephant' – possibly a reference to his heavy build – was able to intercept the vessel. He killed Wirabumi and cut off his head.

Prince Elephant carried his trophy back to Majapahit and presented it to the rejuvenated king, his aloof queen, and their daughter Suhita,[452] who looked on in disgust. It was late 1406 and the Paregreg was over. Java was at peace again.

The king proclaimed that, after years of war, the days of

Majapahit's greatness had returned. To celebrate, ritual baths were to be constructed at Penataran, the large state temple near Blitar.[453] The crowd cheered and then feasted on the lavish amounts of food and palm wine provided by the king.

Cracks appear

The court officials were no fools. Despite the wild celebrations, they knew that the civil war had damaged Majapahit's prestige and influence in the region. Reports soon arrived that local leaders across the archipelago were trying to peel away from Majapahit. First to move was the king of Brunei,[454] who had always been a reluctant supplier of camphor and gold to Java.[455] As soon as he heard about the civil war, he dispatched a mission to China. He told the emperor that Java demanded forty kati[456] of camphor from Brunei each year. He would be happy to send this to China instead should the emperor be willing to officially inform Majapahit about this change in arrangements.[457]

The emperor got the message. Majapahit was now weak and he had a score to settle. If Brunei wanted their protection, perhaps others did too. He sent letters to the rulers of the city of Palembang in Sumatra and, to his delight, in 1403 that city sent tribute to China. Soon afterwards, news arrived that Pasai in north Sumatra also wanted to become a vassal state.[458] Clearly, Majapahit's sway in the region was waning.

By that time, the Chinese mission which had been caught in the crossfire of the civil war had returned. The emperor now knew that a hundred and seventy of his men had been murdered. He was furious. These men had come in peace and the attack was an affront to his status. A letter was dispatched to Majapahit demanding sixty thousand taels of gold in compensation.[459]

King Wikramawardhana was in a dilemma. As a result of the war, he did not have anything like that kind of money. But at the same time he could not ignore the demands of an angry Chinese emperor. In 1408 a Javanese ship arrived in China with ten thousand taels of gold on board. An accompanying letter explained that it was all Majapahit could afford. The emperor, happy to have made his point, sent a message back to Majapahit that settled the issue:

'What I want from those people who live far away, is that they acknowledge their guilt, but do not want to enrich myself with their gold.'[460]

To keep the peace, Majapahit regularly dispatched slaves, spices, gold ornaments and exotic birds to China.

But there was another problem closer to home – the upstart port of Malacca. In 1415, its leaders spread false news that they had control over Palembang in Sumatra, and in turn the strategic Strait of Malacca, with the backing of the Chinese.

The emperor quickly sent a letter to Majapahit to say that Malacca was spreading lies, a sign that China was keen to maintain the status quo in the region.[461] While Malacca's bluff had been called, the affair sent a message to the fast growing Islamic centres on the north coast of Java: Malacca was now a city to be reckoned with,[462]

Back in Java, the situation was going from bad to worse.

A series of earthquakes shook Majapahit and the surrounding area; roofs collapsed, shrines were destroyed, and there were widespread reports that landslides[463] had damaged roads, paddy fields, canals and dams.[464] Irrigation officials told ministers that the River Brantas was silting up and becoming narrower and difficult to navigate in some places. It seemed likely that Majapahit would eventually lose direct access to the sea.[465] This was of grave concern to the ferrymen and local traders who depended on the river and prominent soothsayers around town were convinced the earthquakes, landslides and changes in the course of the river were stern warnings from the gods and harbingers of impending doom.

The irrigation officers had requested money from the palace but after the payment to China there was not a lot left. While a few new canals were dug and parts of the Brantas widened,[466] the harvest suffered as farmers left fields close to the river abandoned. Trade was hit hard too, and ferrymen reported fewer and fewer merchants crossing the river. Each year, the number of bags of rice offered to the king at the annual Caitra festival was much lower than in the previous year.

In 1426, Java, an incredibly fertile island lush with vegetation, was struck by famine. Warehouses were empty, nobles became beggars, and children starved. But then things got even worse – just as the astrologers had foreseen, King Wikramawardhana died in 1429.

It was now up to his daughter, Suhita, to deal with the mess he had left behind.

13

A Stroll Around Town

(1415 CE)

An eyewitness account of life in Majapahit

The port of Liujiagang on the Yangze River, near present-day Suzhou, must have made an awe-inspiring sight on that auspicious day in 1413. Armed ships dotted the horizon for as far as the eye could see. On board were admirals and sailors, generals and soldiers, along with diplomats, translators, doctors, blacksmiths, carpenters and a sprinkling of geomancers and astrologers. Admiral Zheng He's armada was ready to set sail.

The Ming dynasty sponsored seven 'treasure fleets' between 1405 and 1433, all leaving from Liujiagang, known at the time as the 'No 1 Port Under Heaven'. These naval expeditions – part military, part trade missions, part diplomacy – projected Chinese power and wealth to the known world and returned with foreign ambassadors from states and kingdoms willing to pay tribute to China. The 'treasure' refers to the array of goods and commodities on board that were new to many of the places visited on these epic voyages. While this impressed the locals, trade flowed both ways. For example, black pepper became common in China for the first time and cobalt oxide from Persia was the main source for the blue and white porcelain that became synonymous with the Ming dynasty.

The fleets visited Brunei, Java, Thailand and other parts of Southeast Asia, India, the Horn of Africa, and Arabia. After the failure of Kublai Khan's overseas adventures, the Ming dynasty succeeded in establishing control over an expansive maritime network of cities across the region, connecting many countries at both the economic and political level.

Zheng He, a mariner, explorer, diplomat, admiral and court eunuch, is often regarded as the greatest sailor in China's history. He was known for his military acumen, strong personality and broad religious views – he was born to a Muslim family in Yunnan and was a practising Buddhist. Most importantly, he had the complete trust of the emperor, Zhu Di. This was his fourth voyage of exploration[467] and he had more than three hundred ships and twenty-eight thousand men under his command.

On board was an adventurous, inquisitive and open-minded man named Ma Huan, who accompanied Zheng He on three of his seven expeditions. A Muslim from Zhejiang province, fluent in Arabic and Persian, he had a sharp eye for detail and today would be called an anthropologist. Everywhere he went, Ma Huan took notes on the weather, diet, vegetation, animal life, local customs, geography, politics, economy and methods of punishing criminals. He was factual, fair and without prejudice. Thanks to him, we have the only eyewitness account by a foreigner of what life was like in Majapahit in 1413.

Arrival in Java

Ma Huan, more linguist than sailor, was delighted to set foot on dry land after such a long voyage on a cramped war junk. The port of Tuban was busy, appeared mildly prosperous to his eye, and smelled of fish, fruit, cabbage and burned wood. The local market was crowded and multi-tongued, with Chinese, Indian, Arab and Javanese traders busy selling their wares to each other and to local residents. Once he had made his way through the crowd, he found a place in the shade and scribbled down his first (if not exactly startling) impression: 'The climate is hot, like summer.'[468]

He sat down for a while and watched this small world go by. The harbour, while busy, was not a patch on mighty Liujiagang. He found it difficult to comprehend that more than a hundred years ago Kublai Khan's mighty armada had been forced to beat such a hasty and humiliating retreat from this land. It would never have happened under Zheng He, he chuckled to himself.

Ma Huan didn't want to linger as he was keen to reach Majapahit, the city about which he had heard so much. He took a broad dirt road cluttered with traders and local people going about their business, some on foot, others on horseback, and then turned east along the coast towards the town of Gresik, a two-day walk, and onward to Surabaya, then just a humble seaside village. There he saw women feeding long-tailed monkeys. Legend had it that if the monkeys mated after being fed, the women would become pregnant. All 'very remarkable', Ma Huan wrote in his notebook.[469]

In Surabaya he boarded a small boat and sailed along the

River Mas towards Majapahit. He saw majestic volcanos on the horizon as he passed open fields where farmers and bondsmen were hard at work. He noted that rice was harvested twice a year – presumably why people had money to spend – but there was no wheat or barley in these lands. On the road that snaked along the banks of the river he saw a small caravan of traders, a couple of Indian astronomers – very much honoured at the court of the Majapahit[470] – and a pack of scrawny dogs. Then, open-jawed, he caught sight of his first rhinoceros, which was wallowing happily in the mud.[471]

He thought the local men looked scruffy, bare footed with messy hair and a simple piece of cloth strung around their waist. He was more impressed by the ornate daggers – the *keris* – which they all carried:

'From little boys of three years to old men of a hundred years, they all have these knives, which are all made of steel, with most intricate patterns drawn in very delicate lines. For the handles they use gold or rhinoceros horn or elephants' teeth, engraved with representations of human forms or devils' faces, the craftsmanship being very fine and skilful.'[472]

The women pinned their hair in a knot on the back of their heads. Some were bare-breasted but most wore a garment covering the upper part of the body and a kerchief around the waist. He learned that patting someone on the head was to be avoided:

'The people of the country, both men and women, are all particular about their heads. If a man touches their head with his hand, they at once pull out these knives and stab each other.'[473]

Onwards to Majapahit

The boat sailed on to Canggu,[474] another busy market town that long ago had been singled out as an important trading hub and fortified by King Wisnuwardhana back in the 1250s. The docks were crammed with ships and men were busy carrying baskets to the market located on an open field on the bank of the river. Again, he was impressed how cosmopolitan the place was, spotting Indians, Arabs, Moluccans and Chinese living in wooden houses close by. The market was hot, crowded and colourful, with stalls piled high with coconuts, bags of spices and rice, linen, dried fish, ceramics, parrots and other types of exotic birds in cages.[475]

Ma Huan was close to Majapahit now. He walked along the wide, unpaved *rajamarga*, or royal highway, to Bubat, a flat, bare, treeless area outside the city.[476] It was a place of entertainment, with stands full of noisy spectators watching and gambling on wrestling matches and cockfights. And, just as in China, where there was sport there was food. He wandered through the clutter of stalls and marvelled at the range of treats on sale. There was everything from cuts of pork neck, grilled meat on skewers, and cooked vegetables with hot *sambal* sauces,[477] to mushrooms, fried rice cookies, black scorpions, birds, squid and crab.[478] Other, more exotic offerings, he could not put a name to.

He walked on and, to his surprise, found that there were no city walls.[479] A sign of strong, confident rulers, he wondered? Small bamboo huts soon gave way to brick houses with courtyards, and at regular intervals he came across ornate temples, some as much as twenty metres high. He then saw a workshop where Majapahit's famed terracotta manufacturers were hard at work. Boys carried in sun-dried clay, others attended a small oven near where craftsmen, sitting cross-legged on the ground, were working. Out front, the fruits of their labour were on sale – pots, bowls, piggy banks so beloved by children (as they are in Java to this day),[480] and cremation urns, all with the sunburst motif of Majapahit. For a little extra money, more elaborate items were available, such as small replicas of temples and ornaments decorated with fierce looking sea creatures.[481]

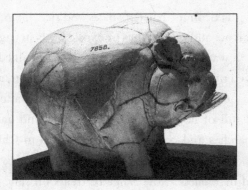

14th/15th-century terracotta piggy bank in National Museum, Jakarta, discovered in Trowulan, East Java. The world's earliest-known pig-shaped money containers date to 12th-c. Java. The term *celengan* – from the Javanese *celeng* or wild boar – is still used today for 'piggy bank' and 'savings' in Bahasa Indonesia. [Photo: HvdL]

It was getting late, and Ma Huan needed somewhere to stay. One of the traders he had met on the royal highway had told him of a lodge that took in foreign visitors. It was in the middle of a lively, bustling neighbourhood connected by small alleyways.

Almost all the dwellings were bamboo huts but there were a few larger houses that had their own family shrine in a front courtyard and were surrounded by a small wall. At the entrance to the lodge, he came across a young boy, barely a year old, wearing a Chinese jacket but no pants. He looked at him in a childish fascination. The owner was Chinese and told him that there were as many as two or three hundred foreign families living in the city.[482]

The friendly trader, who spoke a little Chinese, also invited Ma Huan to join him for a meal at his home, which was nearby. It was a simple abode, little more than a tiled roof supported by a few pillars, with a raised wooden floor where people sat cross-legged on rattan and patterned grass mats. When the food was ready to be served, the men spat out the betel nuts they were chewing, rinsed their mouths with water, washed their hands and sat down in a circle. Banana leaves were passed around and, with their right hand, they scooped up the food in front of them – steamed rice, boiled papaya leaves, salted eggs, fire-roasted snakes, minced tripe, sizzling turtle dripping, a beef soup called *rawon*, and sweet banana hearts.[483] This was way better than the slop served on the Chinese junks.

He had no idea what the others were talking about but liked the sound of their strange but melodic language and the palm wine was slipping down well. It transpired that one of the neighbours, a man called Pakararas, was training to be a palace guard, a good job which also came with useful connections in high places. In a corner, he saw several decapitated terracotta figures. He was told they were part of a ritual to transfer the risk of childbirth to the pregnant woman's ceramic counterpart.[484] He then pointed at a brick-covered hole in the soil, about one metre deep. This is where the family's few valuables were kept.[485] For dessert they ate coconuts, bananas, sugar cane and mangosteen.[486] These people had no knowledge of tea and instead served a mix of lime, nuts and water. Not bad at all. After dinner there was time for more betel nut while the servants ate the leftovers.

Ma Huan bade his host good evening and returned to the lodge. Before going to bed, he sat outside and watched the world go by. A few hawkers selling snacks from handcarts took evasive action when a well-dressed man on horseback shooed them out of the way. Then he heard what at first sounded like trouble at the end of the street. Instead, it was a cheerful, tipsy wedding party complete with brass drums, gongs and firecrackers. The married couple walked in the middle surrounded by friends and family with *keris* and shields. The celebrations continued well into the night.

The next day at dawn Ma Huan bought breakfast – rice with coconut milk and vegetables, wrapped in banana leaves – from a friendly woman who ran a makeshift kitchen opposite the lodge. She also offered him a brownish brew bubbling away on a small fire. The mix of sour tamarind, ginger and palm sugar was delicious and good for indigestion, apparently.

A stroll around town

In the days that followed, Ma Huan made a habit of going for long walks around Majapahit. He was getting a feel for the place and wanted to see more. He soon learned to distinguish between the area around the central palace compound, the *pura*, and the rest of the city, the *nagara*.[487] Although Majapahit was not large by Chinese standards, it still took nearly two hours to walk from one side of the city to the other.[488] He liked the sense of bustle and enterprise, from the street stalls selling fried dough or meatballs on skewers to the hustling wood carvers, basket weavers, perfume sellers and goldsmiths. There was a sense of space, too, with banana groves and trees offering regular shelter from the busy streets and ferocious sun.

Ma Huan soon felt very much part of this warm, welcoming and diverse community. He was struck by the variety of people walking the streets, from proud Brahmins with their partly shaven heads and recluses with matted hair, to widowed women dressed all in white, and Chinese and Arab traders. He saw how babies had their heads shaved and looked on as an elderly lady coached young female dancers ahead of the next religious festival.[489]

He strolled on and entered a noticeably cooler stretch of road that was heavily shaded by *waringin* fig trees. There were wooden benches where an elderly woman made a living selling herbal drinks – *jamu* – and giving massages. He couldn't resist. The old lady may have been frail and had lost all her teeth but her fingers and hands were like steel. Refreshed and relaxed, he continued to explore. Moments later, he was stopped in his tracks by the racket being made by a flock of birds gorging on a cluster of *jamblang* plum trees. He laughed as black monkeys with bulging cheeks made sure that they got their share; there was never a dull moment in Majapahit.

The road opened up onto a large open square in a field, the

alun-alun.[490] On his left, an imposing red-brick gate became visible through the trees. This is where the powerful *patih* – the senior court advisors – lived. Further on, there was a cluster of small temples where priests, one a hunchback, with white and yellow robes, lit incense and chanted prayers.[491] By now he was hungry, and the smell of barbecued meat was wafting in from the main market. Curious as ever, he asked about the prices of some of the vast array of goods on sale. Mistaken for a Chinese merchant, he was immediately assailed by a swarm of pushy traders seeking to buy blue porcelain and gold-flecked silk.[492] Disappointed, they soon walked back to their stalls. It did not take him long to work out that chickens, ducks, goats, fish and vegetables were relatively cheap in Majapahit.[493] He ate his fill without straining his limited budget.

When he returned to the main road at the end of the *alun-alun,* he found himself at the famed *catuspatha*, the crossroads at the heart of the city. It was a holy place, marked by an imposing statue of Ganesha, the elephant-headed son of Shiva, a popular deity who clears obstacles and paves the way for a better life.[494] It was busy too, crowded with bullock carts, commoners on their way to the market, mounted noblemen heading to the palace, minor officials making their way there on foot, and hunters returning from a long, hot day in the forest.

Looking to his right, to the west, he caught his first glimpse of one of the red outer walls of the royal palace at the end of a broad road lined with fig trees. It was an impressive sight, ten metres high and over two hundred metres long. A troop of uniformed guards and two elephants were stationed at the palace gate. Straight ahead, due south, lay the residences of the *dharmadyaksas*, Majapahit's influential (and often feared) bishops and religious judges.

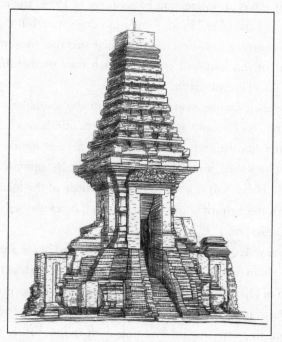

Bajang Ratu in Trowulan, East Java. [Illustration: Ilyazsa]

Ma Huan then turned east, away from the palace. He had been told of a temple complex on the eastern edge of the city where the ruler of the Majapahit empire, King Wikramawardhana, indulged himself with bathing rituals that involved prayers and holy water. The complex was entered through another impressive structure, the elegant sixteen-metre-high red-brick Bajang Ratu gate, but there was no sign of royalty that day. He saw a dozen priests and several women dressed in white and yellow robes who were busy preparing holy water ready for the king's next spa session. The temple has an interesting back story. In 1914, the town was plagued by rats, so the local population dug into a hill thought to be at the centre of the infestation. To their surprise, they unearthed the ruins of the long-lost temple, which they predictably called Candi Tikus (Temple of the Rats).

He was growing weary, so he sat in the shade of a *tanjung* cherry tree, its blossom spread on the ground like a white cloth. No sooner had he started making notes, he was approached by a man who asked him what he was doing. By now, the sharp-eared Ma Huan had started to pick up a little of the local tongue and, with the help of some sign language, he explained his most unusual mission.

His new acquaintance was thrilled – he had never met anyone like Ma Huan before – and introduced himself as the local *hulu air*, the man in charge of water irrigation in the neighbourhood. This meant he was responsible for the royal bath house, and he was very keen to share this information with the inquisitive Chinese visitor. There was an elaborate system of pipes that allowed water to enter a replica of the holy Mount Semeru which, complete with water spouts, had been built in the middle of a pond at the centre of the temple. From there, the water was funnelled back into a small canal that supplied nearby paddy fields. As the rice was continuously being nourished with holy water, only the king and his family were allowed to eat it. All very ingenuous, thought Ma Huan.

A musical walk in the moonlight

The late afternoon was when the people of Majapahit came out to enjoy themselves. The heat of the day was gone, and it was the time to see friends and also be seen. Women – bathed, powdered and scented – gathered at the *catuspatha* crossing and strolled around the square. A group of excited young girls watched a dance competition, and some were persuaded to take part. In a corner of the *alun-alun* a group of people were placing wagers on a tug-of-war match, while others competed to see who had the hardest nut, with players taking it in turns to take a swing until one of them broke.[495] And all around, men sat in the shade to chat and chew betel nuts.

As dusk fell, the evening sky turned from bright blue to red-orange and dark purple in a matter of minutes. Thousands of oil lamps and campfires were lit, creating a vaguely decadent atmosphere laced with the smell of camphor and aloe. Soldiers often spent the night in the open, gathering to drink, sing, and cook meat on big open fires.[496] At the holy crossroads an old man told of ancient battles illustrated by drawings he made on large sheets of paper. Ma Huan understood little of what was said but the audience lapped up every word.[497]

A few days later there was a full moon and he once again found himself drawn to the *alun-alun* field, the centre of so much of the city's social activity. He was not disappointed. A group of twenty young women arrived, all dressed in white, their arms on the shoulder of another to form an unbroken chain. Singing quietly in harmony, they walked through the town before returning to the square. People sat along the road to watch the girls pass and toss them a few coins. This, he was told, was a 'musical moonlight walk', a spectacular sight that left him totally enchanted.

Not everything he saw and heard was so edifying. He was interested in law and order in the countries he visited, so he asked about crime and punishment. That was the job of the *dharmadyaksas*, the religious leaders and judges, after consulting with the village heads. For some crimes, usually those involving debts, people could be sentenced to become a bondsman, essentially little more than slaves. In the most serious cases, the accused were sentenced to death. The master of the guard[498] tied the offender's hands behind his back with fine rattan and then stabbed him in the ribs. Ma Huan had witnessed far more barbarous ways of killing a man.

He had also asked Pakararas how people were buried in Majapahit. The bodies were either thrown into the river, burned at cremation grounds or left to be eaten by wild dogs on the hillsides outside the city; for widows, an agonizing death awaited as they had to accompany their husbands into the afterlife. He was lucky, Pakararas said jauntily, because today was an auspicious day for funerals. That evening he witnessed a *sati,* or widow burning:

'*On the day of the funeral, they build a high wooden framework, under which they pile a heap of firewood and they set fire to this and burn the coffin. The two or three serving girls and concubines who originally took an oath, wait till the moment when the blaze is at its height. Then, wearing grasses and flowers all over their heads, their bodies clad in kerchiefs with designs of the five colours, they mount the framework and dance about,*

*wailing, and after a considerable time they cast themselves down
into the flames and are consumed in the fire with the corpse of
their lord in accordance with their rite of sacrificing the living
with the dead.'* [499]

Although shaken by this gruesome spectacle, Ma Huan
mused that there was great tolerance for different religious beliefs
in Majapahit. The majority of the people were clearly either
Buddhists, the religion he followed back home, or Hindus, who
he had first come across in India. There also were a few Muslims
among the foreign trading community – he had seen several in the
market at Tuban – and he had encountered many more followers
of Allah on previous maritime expeditions. But there were also
other small groups of men and women who he couldn't place.
They had a wild-eyed, mildly deranged look about them, with
long tangled hair and a minimum of clothing, if any at all. He had
heard stories of ancient animist spirits and gods but in his mind
it was more likely that they were involved in some sort of devil
worship. [500]

A visit to the palace

The Chinese armada would soon be leaving Tuban and Ma Huan
had yet to visit the royal palace. Perhaps Pakararas could help.
As the man was soon to be a palace guard, he must have some
clout. Happy to show off his connections, Pakararas said he could
arrange access to at least the outer courtyards. [501] Two days later,
Ma Huan approached the entrance to the palace and passed

through the impressive double gates made of iron – 'very well kept and clean' he noted somewhat lamely – where two elephants and some guards were on duty.[502]

He noticed someone looking down from a watch tower.[503] Pakararas said that it could be anybody but the king sometimes watched the sport and entertainment taking place in the *alun-alun* from up there. The view was perfect and it meant the king did not need to leave the palace[504] and deal with the tiresome protocol involved. The two men walked on and entered a large courtyard enclosed by brick walls and passed elegant pavilions hung with cages for royal fighting cocks.

At the centre of the courtyard was a great hall, the *witana*,[505] supported by red pillars. Ma Huan soon worked out that this was the first point of contact for people who wanted to make an appointment with senior court officials, religious leaders or even the king himself. It was busy and noisy. The hall was full of messengers delivering news and requests from other parts of the kingdom, commoners with complaints and petitions, *bujanggas* – religious clerks – and plenty of palace guards to keep order. The more important supplicants sat in shaded pavilions nearby.

To the left were guard houses, little more than elevated bamboo platforms with a simple roof. Further on, he saw three altars attended by Hindu and Buddhist monks[506] and a large pond with its own shrine. Ma Huan then moved on to a smaller, slightly elevated inner courtyard and that was as far as he got. Pakararas pointed to a small gate and told him only senior officials, members of the royal court, and important foreign dignitaries were permitted to enter.

Pakararas had already proved himself to be an excellent tour guide but what he said next astounded him. The inner sanctum of the palace was protected by an elite female guard, the *bhayangkari*. Ma Huan, a man who had travelled to most of the known world, had never heard of such a thing. He pressed his friend for more details but Pakararas shrugged and was surprised by his interest. He was no expert but what he did know was that women had always played an important role in life at court in Majapahit ever since the days of Queen Tribhuwanatunggadewi and Queen Gayatri more than a century ago.

Thanks to Pakararas, he was allowed to take a quick peek when the gate was being opened. He saw a wide courtyard[507] with a central, roofed platform – the Amazing Pavilion – for the lucky few granted an appointment to meet the king.[508] The royal residences were shielded from his view but Pakararas described two special compounds – one for the Singasari branch of the family and one for the Kediri clan (some things never changed). These compounds were an oasis of calm, with their own gardens and fountains. Again, Ma Huan was impressed. The royal family lived in great style and comfort, even if the standards of luxury could not possibly meet those of the emperor back home, for that was of course impossible.

Then he got lucky. Just before he was about to leave for Tuban to meet up with the fleet, he finally got a glimpse of King Wikramawardhana during one of his rare public appearances: *'His head is unkempt, or else he wears a crown of gold leaves and flowers; he has no robe on his person; around the lower part he has one or two embroidered kerchiefs of silk. In addition, he uses a piece of figured silk-gauze or hemp-silk to bind the kerchiefs around his waist. This is called a "waist band" and in it he thrusts one or two short knives. He goes about bare-footed, and either rides on an elephant or sits in a carriage drawn by oxen.'[509]*

We don't know for sure how long Ma Huan stayed in Majapahit but it was long enough for him to become very fond of the place. It was a lively and inviting city, full of commerce, entertainment and ritual. The streets were safe, the king was popular, and people seemed content and relatively prosperous. Majapahit was also beautifully proportioned. It was not too big and at the edges merged into emerald green paddy fields that surrounded the whole town. While it was true that its people looked a little scruffy, they were friendly and welcoming, they knew what good food was and how to entertain themselves and were 'constantly busy with ceremonies'.[510]

Ma Huan returned to Tuban and sailed onwards to Sumatra, India and Arabia and never returned to Java. Years later, back in China, he wrote a book about the places he had visited, titled '*The Overall Survey of the Ocean's Shores*'.[511] It was a bestseller. The book is considered to be a primary source on Ming dynasty naval exploration and the histories of Southeast Asia and India. To this day, China still celebrates the Ming Treasure Voyages on National Maritime Day, which takes place every year on July 11th.

14

Suhita

(1430 – 1450 CE)

A diminutive queen with a radical vision

Queen Suhita had a small, round mouth, a tight waist, prominent breasts, and a weakness for jewellery. She was fond of enormous necklaces and wore three at a time; her index fingers glittered with large, red rubies and her big toes were adorned with rings.[512] She was short, so much so that when she sat on the throne built for her father and grandfather, her feet dangled like a small child. As that did not look particularly regal she tried sitting cross-legged on the throne; in the end, a special royal pedestal had to be made.

What the queen lacked in height she made up for in spirit. She was progressive in mind and assertive in style. While most royals had little time for the views of others, the queen loved debates, discussions, and hearing different opinions about most things, including sex. No wonder some of the more traditional forces at court, especially the priests, disliked her intensely.

Suhita was also a sensitive young woman. At the age of nine she had witnessed the cremation of her adored grandfather, King

Hayam Wuruk, and she remembered how the concubines died in agony with fire spouting from their eyes. The gruesome scene was chiselled into her memory. And years later, when Prince Elephant arrived at the palace and displayed the head of rebel Prince Wirabumi for all to see,[513] most people cheered, her father included. But Suhita thought it abhorrent, unworthy of royalty, even if it had signalled the end of the civil war.

Queen Suhita, National Museum, Jakarta.
[Photo: Lesley Pullen]

She was also a quick learner. The very next day her father, King Wikramawardhana, had claimed that now the war was over and the great days of Majapahit had returned. She knew better. The empire was weak, vassal states openly flirted with the Chinese, and rice stocks in the royal warehouses would soon dwindle to an alarmingly low level.

Early in life, Suhita was on centre stage. Still not yet twenty, her parents' mental illness meant she was the only royal to sit on the council of ministers, very much to the chagrin of the treacherous Prince Wirabumi, the son of Hayam Wuruk by a concubine, who saw her as a threat to the throne. What appealed to her was not the position of power but rather the chance to be involved with the day-to-day affairs of the kingdom. She listened intensely when the digging of canals, rice harvests, or the restoration of a temple were discussed; endless blather about the seating arrangements for religious ceremonies was of little interest.

The strange story of Damar Wulan[514]

Queen Suhita, ever the non-conformist, had some radical ideas about courtship, marriage and what she looked for in a man. 'Handy with a dagger, preferably good looking' pretty much covered it (she would have loved social media and online dating sites).

When she was the co-ruler with her father and still unmarried, the region of Blambangan in the easternmost part of Java from where the neighbouring island of Bali could be seen in the distance, was causing trouble. The ruler, a district governor named Kebo Marcuet – 'the Buffalo from Marcuet' – was a man with an expansive girth and, so it was said, two horns on his head. He was Balinese, ambitious and wanted more. In his mind, the king was weak and young Suhita would be a pushover.

Suhita came up with an unusual solution – a contest. She would marry the man who defeated the Buffalo from Blambangan in combat. Word spread quickly and men were soon lining up to challenge the rebel with the generous waistline. But to no avail. They all lost.

Aside from his physical strength, Kebo Marcuet had a secret weapon, a magic *keris* which was a family heirloom. With that dagger in hand, he could win any fight or contest. The only man who knew about this was Menak Jingga, whose grandfather was Kebo Marcuet's teacher. He stole the dagger and made a challenge but even without it the buffalo was a formidable opponent. Menak Jingga eventually triumphed but at huge personal cost. The fight left him with a hideously disfigured face and many broken bones. He was essentially a cripple.

Initially, Suhita was delighted to hear the news but her enthusiasm soon evaporated when she heard about the less than edifying physical condition of the winner. She politely declined Menak Jingga's marriage proposal and pondered her next move. She was in a difficult situation. The rejected and enraged Menak Jingga was now ruling Blambangan and she was still single, a most unsatisfactory state of affairs. Solution? The first plan had worked (sort of), so she would marry the man who could dispose of the troublesome Menak Jingga.

The word went out again and many were up for the challenge. But again, despite Menak Jingga's diminished strength, they all failed because of the magic dagger. Then, a handsome young stable boy whose noble family had fallen on hard times during the famine arrived on the scene. His name was Damar Wulan. When Suhita first set eyes on him, she knew instantly that this was the right man. But to both his and her surprise, Damar Wulan's challenge ended in failure and he was left rotting in one of Menak Jingga's filthy jail cells.

But word of his physical charms spread rapidly. Two of Menak Jingga's concubines, less than thrilled with what was currently on offer in the palace bedroom, came to see for themselves. After visiting the strapping young man in prison, they were completely smitten and offered to help. They first explained to the handsome prisoner how he had lost to a cripple – the magic dagger, of course – and then promised to steal it. Damar Wulan then challenged Menak Jingga to a second fight before his opponent could discover the dagger was missing. The result was a foregone conclusion and, after returning to Majapahit in triumph, he married Suhita. The course of true love never runs smooth.

Finding answers to the famine

By the time her father died in 1429, Queen Suhita was happily married and a skilled, experienced politician, respected at court and across the land. She was ready to run the empire by herself, following in the footsteps of Queen Tribhuwannatunggadewi, the daughter of Gayatri and first female ruler of Majapahit, who lived exactly a century earlier.[515] Her handsome husband seemed happy to remain in her shadow, perhaps an early example of royal arm candy. It was good for the brand.

After the trials of her traumatic childhood, spirituality was important to Suhita. Every morning, she sought solace by meditating in a simple pavilion surrounded by tamarind trees. She sat cross-legged, with her eyes closed, her arms resting on her knees, with thumbs and index fingers joined. Here, Queen Suhita was at peace with herself and the world.

She then washed her face, said her prayers, and ate some rice with water spinach, chicken and shrimp crackers while she listened to her daily horoscope. When the reading was done, it was time to go to work. She walked to the Amazing Pavilion, where the kingdom's problems fell like a heavy cloak on her shoulders; there were disputes over land, requests for tax exemptions, the approval of marriages between noble families, and military promotions to be attended to.

But it soon became clear to her that these were relatively trivial matters. Disturbing reports from across Java warned of much a bigger problem – famine had returned. In some areas, people were starving to death. The only businesses that flourished were cremation services. 'The people,' one informant said, 'are forced to live in the present. If they needed to think about any day other than today, then that is tomorrow.'

Queen Suhita quickly grasped the urgency of the situation. Just as her grandfather had done in happier times, she set out on an extensive tour of her kingdom to see for herself what needed to be done. To the astonishment of the priests and ladies at court, she regularly descended from her palanquin to converse with commoners. 'Unheard off,' sniffed the critics. This odd behaviour merely confirmed judgements made earlier, that this eccentric queen had little regard for court protocol. 'Perhaps,' some gossiped, 'it is because she is barren.' And that was true, at least in the sense that she remained childless.[516]

To the queen, these conversations with farmers and traders were invaluable. She heard first hand of the lack of food, crumbling roads and bridges, and broken dams and irrigation systems; many had been forced to sell land or become bondsmen to repay debt. Quarrels over access to paddy fields had broken out between villages and cattle theft was on the rise.

This confirmed the stories she had heard at the palace. Alarmed priests reported that they were presiding over weddings of impoverished nobles and commoners alike. 'Shameful,' was the view of one of the priests at the palace. Disquieting too were reports that village elders were returning to the traditions of their ancestors. They were offering gifts to water spirits and forest nymphs, slaughtering animals in ritual sacrifices, and worshipping phalluses and vulvas in the hope of plentiful harvests and healthy babies. 'For sure, the gods will punish such folk,' another priest predicted.

Suhita knew what to do. She told the *patih* to use her royal bondsmen to repair paddy fields, roads, bridges and canals. To secure a steady supply of fresh water to the city, a large reservoir, Kolam Segaran, was dug just north of Majapahit.[517] It was a great success and soon became a popular addition to the city's amenities. Traders and merchants set up stalls and pavilions by the edge of the water, in turn attracting families out for an evening stroll and a spot of shopping and al fresco dining.

The irrigation works even put the powerful navy in its place. If the work meant that funding for building the ships that had for so long helped Majapahit rule the waves had to be cut, so be it. Suhita regularly left the palace to inspect the digging of a new canal or repairs to a bridge and to talk to commoners. The queen also visited Candi Tikus on the outskirts of the city, not just for a ceremonial bath but to hear from the *hulu air* water managers about irrigation problems.

It worked. In the years that followed, the paddy fields were restored to health, the harvest grew bigger by the year, businesses flourished, and nobles once again carried bulging bags of rice to the annual Caitra festival. The worst, it seemed, was over.

The Ming Gap

In 1425, the Yongle emperor, Zhu Di, was the most powerful and extravagant – and one of the cruellest – rulers of the Ming dynasty. He undertook numerous military campaigns and sponsored maritime expeditions led by the famed Admiral Zhen He, but when he died in 1424 the empire changed. China looked inwards. His successor burned the giant fleet or left what remained to fall into disrepair. All foreign traders were banned from China's ports. The country was closed for business.

Imagine the confusion in Majapahit when the message arrived

saying that China had closed its ports. Not even ships loaded with precious tribute for the emperor were permitted to make land. Instead, the message continued, Majapahit should now send tribute to the Ryukyus, a chain of islands stretching from present-day Kyushu to Taiwan and including Okinawa. From there, it would be sent on to China.[518]

It was all rather odd, but merchants had heard that Siam and Malacca had received similar messages. For the wealthy and powerful in Majapahit this was a bitter pill to swallow. They were cut off from their regular supply of favourite luxury goods, including status symbols such as blue-and-white Ming vases. Later, historians would call this period the 'Ming Gap'.[519]

Although the loss of trade was the last thing she needed, Queen Suhita complied without complaint. As soon as one ship returned from the Ryukyus, a new one was dispatched. She did not want the Chinese complaining about irregular shipments, as they had in her father's days.[520] There were more than enough issues to be dealt with at home, without adding a diplomatic crisis. The new system continued uninterrupted for many years.

Then in 1442, completely out of the blue, a Chinese ship laden with precious porcelain, silk and swords sailed into the port of Tuban carrying good news. China was open again – the new emperor had reversed the closed port policy. Eager to do business, the captain of the Chinese vessel put in a large order for pepper and sandalwood.[521]

Suhita welcomed this surprising development. The resumption of trade with China was very good news, but it was a reminder of how impermanent her world had become. She was also receiving reports from her diplomats that tensions between Siam and the arrogant upstart Malacca were rising. In 1445, the Siamese sent an army to Malacca but the expedition went horribly wrong. Malacca, with support from a sultan in nearby Klang, had chased the Siamese away. To Suhita, the message was clear – Malacca was now a major power.[522] Change was everywhere, not just in Java, but also throughout the region.

Bracing for change

One day, around the start of the rainy season when pungent durians were aplenty, a group of Chinese traders from Gresik and Tuban asked for a meeting with the queen and her *patih*. After the usual pleasantries they got to the point:

'We Chinese merchants are plentiful in the ports and our businesses are flourishing. The Chinese ports are open again. We are also very grateful to the current harbour masters. They are not Chinese but nonetheless sometimes helpful. We hope for their rebirth in an even more bountiful incarnation.'

Suhita smiled to herself. She knew that the harbour masters had become complacent, lazy and corrupt, as the Chinese merchants were making it very clear in their own way. 'You want me to replace them?' she asked. The Chinese delegation remained silent but they had indeed come to seek replacements. After some small talk, they were told to wait in the courtyard outside.

The queen then summoned her friend Jayeswari, a trusted advisor, and the wife of her half-brother Kertawijaya. She, too, was a strong-willed woman who was well informed about matters of state and a keen student of the political terrain. The harbour masters were powerful men, she said, as they controlled all port traffic and customs payments. Making replacements would meet with considerable resistance as these positions had been controlled by the same families for years. And for all that time, they had been lining their own pockets at the expense of Majapahit. The *patih* agreed. Replacing them could also keep the peace with China. Best not to ignore this request, they concurred.[523]

The Chinese delegates sat in the courtyard, devouring durians, when the *patih* approached to ask if the pungent fruit was to their satisfaction. He had news, good news. There were indeed some sudden vacancies in the ports. And their men had got the jobs.[524] Of course, there would be a steep monthly payment to the palace. The merchants smiled, bowed, made a *sembah* and finished their durians.

Next to seek a royal audience was a group of Muslims. They wanted permission to build mosques in several towns on the north coast. For decades, there had been a Muslim quarter in Majapahit and Suhita had observed how these people prayed five times a day and on Fridays gathered in their mosques. She judged them disciplined and devout, attributes she appreciated, and approved their request on the spot.

A few days later the *patih* reported that the decision had proved unpopular with the more traditional Hindu priests at court. 'If they have an issue with that,' she told him, 'they can come and talk to me.' This was precisely what the priests wanted to avoid. The *patih*, they judged, was much more approachable than the strong-willed queen. But they had little choice, so off they went to the palace. They complained about the growing number of Muslims on the coast and the rising influence of the Chinese. Even worse, people in the villages had lost their way and were turning to all sorts of foolish and despicable superstitious practices. Some were even worshipping the devil.

To make their point, they brought to the queen's attention the resurgence of a ritual that was taking place on Mount Kemukus in central Java. Some fools believed that long ago a prince had fled to the mountain with his lover, who also happened to be his stepmother. Both were killed in the middle of the act of union. Now these dimwits believed that if they finished the sexual act with a stranger, they would become rich. People were arriving on the mountain every day in search of a counterparty.[525] Horror of horrors, dogging had come to Java.

Queen Suhita surely understood, the priests continued, that such repugnant rituals were clear evidence of the lamentable state of the kingdom. Many Buddhist sanctuaries were in a wretched state and had been abandoned. Hindu temples could be next.[526] On the holy mountain of Penanggungan, small temples for the worship of ancestors were being built, with reliefs depicting not the noble old Hindu stories but bawdy contemporary tales of Prince Panji going in search of Princess Candra Kirana.[527] The solution was obvious, the priests advised – build more Hindu temples.

Suhita had heard enough. She considered the Hindu priests to be narrow-minded bigots. They wanted nothing to change, and their ceremonies and rituals, including the burning of women, to be eternal. But that's not what she said. 'You are right,' she declared. 'We have to confront these changes.' As part of her building programme, two spectacular new temples, Candi Sukuh and Candi Ceto, would be constructed on the cool western slopes of Mount Lawu in central Java.

The priests knew the place very well. It was a hotbed of animist worshippers, a perfect site for building temples so people could return to the true, traditional Hindu path. They applauded her for her infinite wisdom. She was truly (and surprisingly) enlightened, they murmured among themselves, and went home.

But Suhita had very different ideas. New times required new temples, she told her *patih,* and this should be reflected in their design, which should appeal to common folk. She wanted the new temples to depict magnificent erotic bas-relief portraits featuring men and women indulging in the act of sexual union described in tantric texts.

The priests were furious. They had been hoodwinked. This was clear evidence that the queen paid far too much attention to what people of no station thought. It was well known that many women in central Java were little more than prostitutes willing to contort themselves into all sorts of positions for a few coins.

They asked for another audience. It was a disaster. The queen's response was to double down on her ideas for the temples. She was recruiting talented female designers to work with the stonemasons, 'because women have more interesting ideas about what is erotic than men'. With that, she told them to leave. Some of the older priests were now in a state of panic.

What they didn't know, of course, was that this was a kind of retribution. The queen had watched priests supervise the burning of the king's concubines at her grandfather's funeral when she was still a child. The terrible images had stayed with her and the queen had long ago decided that some of Majapahit's time-honoured customs had to change.

Meanwhile, the architects got on with the project. Elephants pushed massive boulders up the mountain where an army of stone masons were hard at work. The larger of the two temples, Candi Sukuh, high on the mountain with sweeping views over central Java, was adorned with statues of men grasping their penises and people gathering in a womb. A large phallus (lingga) and vulva (yoni) were built at the entrance. After the temple's consecration they were used as a test of virtue and virginity; ladies had to put on a sarong waist cloth and walk over the phallus. Infidelity was proven if the skirt ripped.[528] Neither Candi Sukuh nor Candi Ceto bear any resemblance to other Javanese Hindu and Buddhist temples. They are the legacy of an extraordinary woman who had her own ideas about just about everything.

The start of the final chapter

Queen Suhita would not live to see the temples finished. A decade before the architects made their final inspection, she died peacefully in 1446 at the age of about sixty-seven. She had no children, something she always regretted.

Before her death it was announced that her half-brother, Kertawijaya would sit on the throne. He did so for only four years before he passed away in 1451.[529] In his brief tenure, he ensured that Queen Suhita's work at the Sukuh and Ceto temples continued and he dispatched several diplomatic missions to China.

He also made an important contribution to Javan literature by becoming a patron to a writer called Tanakung. Tanakung completed an epic poem in praise of Hinduism, the Siwartrikalpa,[530] that was considered a masterpiece. Some scholars believe this was a response to the emergence of the powerful Malacca sultanate, through which Islam had been making gains in Java.

After Suhita's death, her trusted advisor and ally, Jayeswari, remained a figure of some influence, the grand old lady at court. She presided over the *shraddus* for Queen Suhita in 1459 and her husband, King Kertawijaya, in 1463. She died the following year.[531]

It was the start of the beginning of the end for the Majapahit kingdom, which would decay and crumble before finally disintegrating in 1527.

15

The Final Blow

(1450 – 1527 CE)

A kingdom crumbles

1486, inside the Majapahit palace.

These were troubled times, so the two stonemasons were grateful for the job, even if they were widely considered to be the best in the land. The customer was a good payer too. Over the years, they had done plenty of work for the royal family.

Shirtless and barefooted but far from humble, they sat patiently beneath a shady pavilion inside the palace, their sarongs tucked between their legs with their backs resting against a pillar. The older of the two complained as he rubbed his aching knee with oil and herbs; pain came with the job. Before them lay a banana leaf containing the remnants of breakfast: a few grains of rice, a half-eaten vegetable stalk or two, and some chicken bones, picked clean. They sat close to their precious tools, chisels and hammers of different sizes, some cloth, brushes and paint, and bowls for water to wash the dust away. Facing the pavilion on a large patch of grass stood the task in hand – three large, pristine stones, waiting to be engraved.

Two days earlier a royal courtier had walked into their workshop on the outskirts of the city. The new king wanted a stone inscription, and quickly. It was a special job, so they should be honoured; best to keep their mouths shut, too. When they reported to the iron gates at the palace a guard led them to a pavilion at the back of the royal complex, not far from where the royal beekeepers kept their colonies. 'Better get breakfast first,' mumbled the guard, 'because this is going to take some time. The king and his advisors are still working on the exact wording.'

As the two men chatted, the palm trees rustled gently in the breeze and the conversation soon turned to idle gossip. There were rumours going around town about a wise old woman – a sorceress, some said – who could make herself invisible by chanting secret incantations and putting ash on her eyelids for a month.[532] That would be handy, they both chuckled, especially when their wives were angry after they staggered home from their favourite *kedai* greatly impaired by the effects of palm wine.

The sun was already climbing when one of the assistants to the *patih* finally arrived. After hours of discussions, the wording of the inscription had been confirmed. The men studied the text and made their way to the three virgin stones. They were far more than humble masons; they were calligraphers, artists in stone. And they knew it.

The first task was to paint the outline of the words on the stone, which required exquisite brushwork. The assistant was fascinated and squatted down nearby to admire their work. Once the first letters appeared on the stone, the brushes were put to one side and the men picked up their hammers and chisels. 'It's best to have a rhythm,' the senior mason explained, delighted to have an audience. 'The cuts must be the same depth and all at the same angle.'

The chisel would cut one side, then the other, until the edge of the brushstroke was reached. When a letter was completed, it was checked for quality and the dust was rinsed off with water. Then the men moved on to the next letter. It was a delicate, painstaking, not to mention backbreaking task. Over the next few weeks, the masons became intimately familiar with the narrative. The inscription told a familiar Majapahit story: one of misdeeds, division and royal family feuds.

During their lifetime, the two craftsmen had witnessed the death of Queen Suhita and her brother and seen the rise of Jayeswari, the wife of Kertawijaya and the grand old dowager queen. She had made sure that her three sons were heirs to the throne but they were so young that Jayeswari simply ruled the kingdom herself. But no strong ruler had emerged and in the chaotic generation that followed, two brothers – Girindrawardhana and Wirabumi – both claimed the throne. A series of skirmishes followed and both attempted to have the other poisoned.[533] Things came to a head in 1478 when Girindrawardhana's army breached Majapahit's defences and his brother was killed.

The inscription began with King Girindrawardhana honouring a priest named Ganggadara for presiding over the *shraddu* ceremonies for his father, who had been forced to flee to Kediri[534] after a rebellion in the 1470s. Then came the most important part – a celebration of King Girindrawardhana's great victory which had united the mighty kingdom once again. The king would now be known as Brawijaya of Majapahit.[535]

The last words chiselled into stone were a stern warning to those who failed to pay proper respect to the new man in charge:

'They will end up in the realm of Yama, the king of the dead, they will be beaten by Yama's army for years innumerable. They will fall in the cauldron of hell, they will not be reborn. So not only will they end up in hell, but they will stay there, as there is no escape from there, because they will not be reborn and will not get a second chance in a new life. And even if they are reborn, they will be reborn under miserable circumstances.'[536]

And with that damnation – some said it wreaked of insecurity – the masons' work was done. A small crowd gathered around the stones as a priest slit a chicken's throat and cursed the king's enemies in a loud voice, instantly rendering the stones sacred objects, testimony to the power of the new ruler.

The truth was rather different. Nearly a century had passed since the cremation of the great King Hayam Wuruk. Since his death, the Majapahit empire had gone into a slow, irreversible decline. Over time, the power of the mighty navy had dwindled, as had the piles of gold in the treasury, and the kingdom's influence around the region. The majesty of the royal court was much diminished and many a government official and temple priest had decided that the future lay in farming.

This is not to say that Majapahit had completely imploded. Foreign diplomats still paid courtesy visits to the king, and tribute from vassal states arrived by ship every year, if in ever-decreasing quantities. But across Java the world of god-kings and Hindu and Buddhist priests was slowly being displaced by mosques, koranic scholars and Muslim traders. On the northern coast, the city of Demak was on the rise. The founder of the city, Prince Patah, was a charismatic and devout Muslim,[537] and most inhabitants of the city followed Islam.

Although the Majapahit world was shrinking, it still attracted some interesting visitors.

The story of Bujangga Manik.

C. 1490, Pakuan, near present-day Bogor.
Prince Bujangga Manik[538] was raised in luxury at the Pajajaran court in the town of Pakuan on the cool slopes of Mount Salak in western Java. To the north lay Kelapa (which became Batavia and then Jakarta), the harbour town from where his Sundanese ancestors had set off for Majapahit in 1357 for a doomed royal wedding which would lead to centuries of bitterness.

Bujangga Manik was slightly built, a Buddhist scholar and strong-willed. Women found him attractive and not just because he was of royal blood. Unusually, he had an interest in geography and the lands that lay to the east. In short, he was a restless soul. In that sense, he resembled Prapanca, the poet and royal scribe who lived a century earlier in the heyday of King Hayam Wuruk.

The similarity ended there. Prapanca had always yearned for female company but his amorous advances never led anywhere. Bujangga Manik steered clear of all such temptations. On one occasion at court, a princess offered him a betel nut and rolled the leaves over her thighs and breasts. She then tied them with a thread from her dress 'to excite a bachelor's desire'. The prince did not indulge.

One evening, he had an epiphany and announced that he wanted to retreat from this world of earthly excess. He told his parents: 'Away with the lavish meals, the women, the jewels, and the rich garments. I want to live the life of a monk.' Some wondered if he was cursed, others thought he had gone crazy. But it was no surprise to the ladies at court. To them, the prince had always been different, a loner, a prince without mistresses. He was a real oddball.

At first, the king and queen commended his decision. Young men did this sort of thing all the time and soon returned when they became bored. But what alarmed them was this: rather than seeking the solitude and solace of a local temple, the prince wanted to wander western Java alone. That was downright dangerous. But Bujangga Manik would not be deterred and in the years that followed, he made two journeys, both on foot and each covering well over a thousand kilometres.

It is through his writings that we get a rare first-hand glimpse of life in Java in the fifteenth century.[539] Bujangga Manik detailed the mountains he saw, the rivers he crossed, and the temples and villages he visited. He travelled all over Java and also crossed the sea to Bali, which he judged to be a dreadfully busy place even in those days.

Along the way, he continued to resist the temptations of the flesh. When approached by a female hermit in search of a mentor, he raised a stack of lontar leaves in the air and declared: 'Just like fire when it comes near to palm fibre, it will surely inflame, thus it is with men and women.'[540]

The eccentric monk was also one of the last men to describe a visit to Majapahit. His immediate destination was not the city or the palace, but Penataran, the magnificent state temple complex further south, near the town of Blitar, where he intended to learn Javanese – he spoke Sundanese – and contemplate the meaning of life.

Before going to Penataran, he approached Majapahit on foot from the west, passing through Kediri and the inland port of Canggu, which he found to be much too crowded for his taste. But the days when the quays were filled with ships and traders from across the region were long gone; most had moved to the bustling coastal town Demak, where Muslim merchants ran the market.

He continued south to Bubat, where over a century ago his Sundanese ancestors had been slaughtered in the Battle of Bubat,[541] fighting over a royal wedding that never took place. From there, he walked along the *rajamarga*, the royal highway, towards the capital. The prince arrived at the *alun-alun,* the main square outside the palace,[542] where he admired Buddhist and Hindu shrines and sheltered from an afternoon downpour in one of the old pavilions, which he noted was in need of some repair. Once in the city, he strolled around and recorded the names of the areas he visited – Dharma Anyer, Karang Jaka and Palintahan.[543] The wandering prince then left Majapahit to climb the holy Mount Penanggungan.[544]

He stayed at Penataran, the state temple near Blitar, for more than a year to study Javanese and was soon fluent enough to be able to translate ancient texts. But even this hallowed ground was too much for him: '*I did not stay long there, one year and some more. I could not stand the continuous noise of those who came to worship and offer gold, who paid homage without interruption, travelling around from the capital.*'[545]

Bujangga Manik eventually returned home to Pakuan. The queen was delighted to see her son again but was shocked by his appearance. With bushy, ungroomed hair and ragged clothes, he looked, and smelled, more like a starving pauper than a pampered prince. He did not stay long. After writing down on thick palm leaf what he had seen on his travels, Bujangga Manik lived out the rest of his life as a hermit on a mountain in western Java.

The arrival of the Portuguese

1511, Malacca.

The Portuguese arrived in Southeast Asia in the early 1500s and no sooner had they sailed into the Strait of Malacca, it became clear that they were not welcome. One day, one of their ships had a chance encounter with a Sumatran *jong*, which was looking for a fight. As the two vessels drew closer, the Portuguese were shocked by the size of the ship confronting them – the deck of the *jong* was taller than that of their fleet's flagship, the *Flor de la Mar*. Despite being experienced mariners, they had never seen anything like it.

They fired their cannons at the hull but to little effect. They shot at the masts, but the Sumatrans simply lowered the sails.

For two days and nights the two ships were locked in battle. It was only when the Portuguese managed to damage the *jong's* two rudders that the Sumatrans surrendered.[546] The Europeans were more than a little impressed by the scale and sophistication of the ships sailed by their latest seafaring adversaries.

In the years that followed, the Portuguese focused their attention on Malacca, already an important port in the region's maritime trade network because of its strategic location. They understood that whoever controlled Malacca, controlled the quickest route between the Indian and Pacific oceans. The Portuguese apothecary, colonial administrator and diplomat, Tome Pires, wrote around 1512 that: '*Whoever is lord of Malacca has his hand on the throat of Venice. As far as from Malacca, and from Malacca to China, and from China to the Moluccas, and from the Moluccas to Java, and from Java to Malacca and Sumatra, all is in our power.*'[547] To this day, it remains one of the most important shipping lanes in the world.

At the time, Portugal was in the process of expanding the business interests of its empire. The Portuguese already controlled Cochin and Goa in India and were looking for a base to establish a presence further east in Asia. They were attracted to Malacca by its natural harbour and captured the port in 1511, giving the local population a taste of their superior naval firepower.

The victorious captain in this battle for Malacca, Antonio d'Abreus, then sailed all the way to the Moluccas in the east of the archipelago in search of nutmeg, mace and cloves. This was very bad for business for the rulers of Majapahit. As the Portuguese had decided it was time to cut out the Javanese middleman, there was no need to stop in the ports of Tuban or Canggu.

However, there was still contact between the two powers, most of it positive. One of the first Portuguese ships carrying spices from the Moluccas to Malacca was blown off course by a storm and was forced to beach at Tuban. The local people helped to rescue the sailors and pulled the ship to shore. A message was sent to Malacca that the Portuguese could come and pick their cargo up in Tuban, where it was stored safely.

The Portuguese were impressed by what they saw and how they were received.

One official described in great detail a gift he received from the King of Java (probably the ruler of Majapahit):

'A *very long piece of cloth, whereon was painted a representation of the manner in which the king goes to battle, with his carriages, horses, and elephants armed with their wooden castles, and a figure of the king therein painted, riding in certain wooden erections placed above the carriages and all this very beautifully depicted; and he sent him also twenty little bells, of which their music consists, and players who could play upon them with carved sticks, and they harmonised very well and gave a very pleasant sound; and he sent him two very large bells, which they strike in battle, for they can be heard a long way off.'*[548]

Another stayed in Tuban, where a nobleman from Majapahit came to see him.

'I saw a heathen in Tuban who came there from the court to see us. They said he was a nobleman. He had three handsomely caparisoned genets (horses), with stirrups all inlaid, with cloths all adorned with richly worked gold, with beautiful caparisons;*

he brought with him about ten men with rich lances. He was robust, tall, freckled, with his hair curly on the top and frizzy; and they all did him obeisance. And he only came to see what sort of men we were, and he lodged outside the town and did not go out except once during the day, towards afternoon; and I talked to him many times.'[549]

And Jorge de Brito, Governor of Malacca, wrote to King Manuel in January 1514, saying:

'Java is a large island. It has two infidel kings: the one is king of Sunda, the other king of Java ... The coasts are controlled by Moors and powerful merchants are called governors. They have many junks, in abundance.'[550]

Antonio Pigafetta, a Venetian explorer who was part of Ferdinand Magellan's expedition to circumnavigate the world, was one of the last to make reference to Majapahit. He was wounded during the fighting in the Philippines that Magellan did not survive. The Venetian recovered and was among the eighteen of Magellan's original crew who returned to Spain on board another vessel, *Victoria*.

Along the way he heard of many strange stories, including one from a sea captain about an island near Java where women could become pregnant just by standing in the breeze. He dismissed this as nonsense, but in 1522 wrote of more prosaic matters:

'The largest town in Java is called Magepaher, whose king is the greatest of any on the island and is called Raia Patimus.'
Magepaher is, of course, Majapahit.

This is the last description we have of the city of Majapahit. The Portuguese clearly admired much about Java, but what impressed them most were the maps.

Back in 1293, Prince Widjaya had offered the Mongol invaders a detailed map of eastern Java in exchange for their support. In the fifteenth century, the Portuguese, master explorers and traders, were still marvelling at the accuracy of maps made by Javanese cartographers. In a letter to his king, Portuguese commander Afonso de Albuquerque (1453–1515) described a Javanese map which showed the Cape of Good Hope, Portugal, Brazil, the Red Sea and the Persian Gulf, the Spice Islands and the Ryukyu island chain as 'the finest piece of work I ever saw.'

The end of the city of Majapahit, 1527

It is often said that when it comes to how people go bankrupt there are two ways: gradually, then suddenly. And so it was with the fall of Majapahit.

Tensions with the rising Muslim power of Demak on the northern coast of Java had been simmering for some time. For months, the faithful had been gathering in the city's mosques in ever larger numbers to discuss what should be done about the infidels.[551] To make matters worse, Majapahit had sent envoys to seek support from the Portuguese in Malacca, their nemesis. It was time to act.

A large group of men, more of a mob really, set out from Demak to erase the last vestiges of Hindu-Buddhist power in Java. The plan, if they had one, was simple: pray, and charge towards the iron gates of the Majapahit palace waving their swords. They were no match for the Majapahit forces, who pelted them with rocks and poured boiling oil on them from the palace walls. The kingdom had survived, for now at least.

But defeat drove the imams of Demak into a frenzy. They promptly declared a holy war on Majapahit and persuaded Prince Tranggana, the ruler of Demak, to convert to Islam and renounce his loyalty to Majapahit. In 1524, he adopted the Islamic title of sultan[552] and in 1527 ordered an assault on Majapahit.

The final blow was a two-pronged punch. An assault group arrived from the west, overland from Demak. A second battle group sailed to Tuban, which soon fell. Weapons were then unloaded at the inland port of Canggu, just a short walk along the royal highway to Bubat. The enemy forces were now camped on Majapahit's doorstep.

The battle started early in the morning. By the time the signal to attack was given, the city was virtually deserted. Most of the inhabitants had already fled south, towards Blitar, or into the mountains. Once mighty officials deserted their posts and members of the royal family started to melt away. Some had left for Kediri, while others joined an exodus of noblemen to Bali. There were reports that one prince ran off to Mount Bromo to become a hermit under a new name. In some narratives, the king remained in the palace.

The invasion force advanced under blue and yellow banners, the mark of mighty Demak. The soldiers met almost no resistance and within an hour they had taken control of the royal palace. It was a massacre. Priests were drowned in lotus ponds, stable boys were stabbed as they tried to protect the king's horses, and the few remaining ladies of the court were violated and slaughtered. Everything was burned to the ground – the royal residences, the watchtower, the Amazing Pavilion with its intricate wood carvings, the army barracks, the elephant stalls and the library. By noon, all that was left of Majapahit was a heap of rubble and a pile of dead bodies.[553]

The story goes that the moment the last king, Brawijaya, a descendant of the man who liked grandiose inscriptions, was killed, a thunderclap was heard across the land and a beam of light shot into the sky.[554] The kingdom was gone.

In the years that followed, Demak armies ravaged the Majapahit lands. They took control of Kediri two years later, and soon after, Surabaya recognised Demak's authority. Mount Penanggungan, the Hindu holy of holies, fell in 1543.[555] By then, the core of the Majapahit kingdom in Java was under Demak's control.

Later that year, the same soldiers who burned down Majapahit marched to western Java to conquer Banten. Demak's sultan, Trenggana, was hostile to any Portuguese settlements in Java and decided to prevent them at all costs. In his view, Banten was too open to Portuguese settlements on west Java so he had his commander, Fatahillah, and two thousand men conquer the port city.[556] On the way back they overran a small town near the sea, Kelapa, and renamed it Jayakarta: City of Victory. By the end of the century, the Dutch sailed into the archipelago, set up a trading network and, in search for a place to build warehouses, set their eyes on Jayakarta. But soon conflicts between the Dutch, Javanese and the English, who had now also arrived in the region, broke out and after a clash the Dutch burned down large parts of the city, kicked the English out and re-named it Batavia. More than three centuries later, in 1942, it became Jakarta.[557]

It is no small irony that the Demak soldiers who destroyed the legendary city of Majapahit, the centre of the largest empire Southeast Asia has ever seen, were the same men who founded Jayakarta, now Jakarta, the multi-tentacled metropolis that gave rise to modern Indonesia.

Epilogue

Majapahit's Legacy

(1527 CE – the present)

Majapahit's footprints and the rise of Indonesia

In 1527, the year the last Demak soldier left the smouldering ruin that was Majapahit, the capital came under the control of a new ruler: Mother Nature. Tree roots forced their way through the cracks of crumbling walls, fallen pillars and flattened pavilions. Statues and shrines lay scattered across the jungle floor, smothered in a shimmering sea of green moss. As time passed, the ruins disappeared as nature had its way and farmers put the bricks that remained to good use on their land.

Immediately following the city's devastation and the royal family's demise, Majapahit was immortalized in legend. Sultan Trenggana, the man who destroyed the city, proclaimed that the founder of the Demak sultanate, Raden Patah, was a son of Majapahit. Soon, any Javanese noble of serious standing was claiming to be a descendant of the rulers of the great kingdom. Palaces were designed in Majapahit style, even though nobody could say exactly what that was. In the 1600s, by the time the Dutch arrived in the region, the Mataram sultanate in Java that lasted until the 18th century claimed that its roots went all the way back to Majapahit. As it is with all legends, the more distant the memory, the greater the reverence, and the sketchier the detail.

The truth is that neither dubious legends nor over-imaginative dynastic family trees were needed to eulogise the dynasty. Majapahit didn't disappear, it simply moved to the next island. By the time the final blow was struck, the elite had long fled to Bali. Knowing the end was nigh, scribes had loaded the contents of the royal library, ceremonial costumes, drums and bronze bells onto bull carts and carried them to the coast for the short crossing by boat. It changed the small island forever. Soon, statues of the Hindu god Ganesha adorned Balinese roads, familiar-looking temples appeared, and priests wandered the roads and villages. Bali became the reincarnation of Majapahit.

Prapanca's lifetime's work, the *Desawarnana* or *Depiction of the Districts*, was stored safely in a camphor box in a Balinese palace. Decades later, scribes opened the box to inspect the fragile leaves. They admired the descriptions of everyday life across Java that Prapanca's contemporaries had considered dull and stodgy. Eager to link their own traditions to those of their forefathers, they made a copy on thick lontar leaves. A new *Desawarnana* was born.

The *Pararaton* (*Book of Kings*), the history of the kings of Singasari and Majapahit, was also copied but was completed much later, on 3 August 1613. A Balinese scribe finished the enormous task with the words: '*May the reader not forget to improve on the mistakes I have made because this work was copied by a dimwit who just started to learn writing. Hail to those that read this book and a hail to the copyist too.'*[558]

Years later, in the early 1800s, intrigued by the legends and rumours of long-lost treasure, a handful of Dutchmen hacked their way through dense forests to uncover fragments of the ruins of Singasari, the original capital which was destroyed in 1292. They weren't very sure what they had stumbled upon and left disappointed. Instead of treasure, they had to make do with a few statues that would take pride of place in their gardens. Soon afterwards, in 1815, Sir Stamford Raffles and his men would make what would be recorded as a more official discovery, complete with notes and sketches of what they had found.

Deep in a teak forest, they uncovered the overgrown ruins of the Singasari temple, square at the base, tall and slender and about ten metres high, and a number of Hindu statues, many of exquisite quality. Tree roots reached through crevices and cracks in the ramparts of what, centuries ago, was a palace. Ruins of buildings and temples appeared at irregular intervals across the forest floor. A bigger picture began to emerge – they had discovered the remains the city of Singasari, the abode of famed King Kertanegara, assassinated inside those very walls more than five hundred years ago.

Meanwhile, a copy of Prapanca's eyewitness account of life in Java during the early reign of King Hayam Wuruk, who ruled from 1350 to 1389, found its way from Bali to the neighbouring island of Lombok. That is where, on a November morning in 1894, Dutch philologist Jan Laurens Andries Brandes snatched the manuscript from a fire raging inside a palace being overrun by Dutch soldiers. If it weren't for his quick response, perhaps the best primary historical source for the Majapahit empire at its peak, would have been lost forever.

Brandes translated the text, introducing the Majapahit world to a broad European audience for the first time. Then, in 1941, Dutch archaeologist Willem Stutterheim, using his knowledge of Balinese temples and Prapanca's tales, was the first to identify the exact location of the royal palace. However, his timing could not have been worse. At that time, the last thing Dutch officials wanted was the celebration of a great power which early Indonesian nationalists considered a glorious, pre-colonial past. Later, in 2008, archaeologists and engineers, using advanced mapping technology, found that Stutterheim's descriptions of the 14th-century Majapahit royal palace were extraordinarily accurate.

The echoes of the great empire simply refused to fade away.

Footprints

The majestic Wat Suthat is located a stone's throw from the Grand Palace in Bangkok. Commissioned by King Rama I the Great in 1807, the Buddhist temple was completed during the reign of King Rama III in 1847.

Behind the main temple, stands the gigantic Ordination Hall, or *Ubosot*, supported by massive white pillars, its walls covered from floor to ceiling with spectacular murals.

One depicts a couple dressed in shining royal garments, lighting up the temple interior. This is a scene from *Inao and*

Bussaba in the Cave, a classical royal dance drama which most Thais know from school plays, television series and a popular song.[559]

The story of Inao, the handsome prince, and Bussaba, his beautiful fiancée, has been retold for centuries throughout Indonesia, Malaysia, Thailand and Cambodia.

This story originated in Majapahit with the popular tale of Prince Panji going in search of his beloved Princess Kirana. Children were raised on these stories from an early age, *wayang* plays were performed across the land, the royal family enjoyed Panji dance performances, and the legend was engraved on the walls of temples.

When Thai carpenters arrived at Majapahit to learn how to build ships that could carry elephants, or when Malay merchants stayed in the river port of Canggu, they listened to these Panji stories and saw the shadow puppet plays being performed on the streets. When they sailed home, they took the stories back with them.

It is just one of the ways the Majapahit legacy lives on.

Wrapping up

In 1945, free of Dutch rule, Indonesia was in search of an identity. It had to look no further than Majapahit which the country's first president, Sukarno, considered a precursor to modern Indonesia. Indeed, the colours of the Indonesian flag, red and white, are the same as those displayed on the banners borne by Kediri forces during the attack on King Kertanegara in Singasari in 1292. These 'Malay' red-and-white colours are also found on the national flags of Malaysia and Singapore.

Bhinneka Tunggal Ika – Unity in Diversity – is the official national motto of Indonesia. The phrase is used in the national constitution to celebrate the nation's different cultures, languages and religions. Its origins lie in a poem written by a contemporary of Prapanca during the reign of King Hayam Wuruk in the fourteenth century. The motto was later incorporated into the state emblem, the Garuda, the half eagle half human creature that is the Hindu god Visnu's preferred means of travel.

In typical Majapahit style, Sukarno was pushed aside by Suharto, Indonesia's second president. He, too, saw Majapahit as a basis for nation building. And when Indonesia launched its first extra-orbital satellite, Palapa I, it was named after Gajah Mada's *palapa,* the powerful official's bold plan to unify the archipelago during the fourteenth century.

And our old friend Prapanca also had an important role to play. His lifetime's work, the *Desawarnana*, was an inspiration for the Indonesian independence movement. And in 1970 during the state visit of President Suharto to the Netherlands in 1970, the manuscript was returned to Indonesia, where it is on display at the National Library of Indonesia. Later, when Indonesia was searching for a suitable name for the new capital city being constructed on the island of Kalimantan, it chose *Nusantara*, a Majapahit term for the entire Indonesian archipelago.

There are also signs that modern Indonesia is replicating some of the triumphs of the past. After a blood-soaked first encounter, the Majapahit empire found a way to come to an accommodation with the mighty emperors who ruled China. The same applies today, with Jakarta navigating a careful diplomatic path to match its own interests with those of Beijing.

Less visible elements of heritage are also discernible. The Majapahit court was a place of political intrigue where power was perpetually in flux, influential women pulled strings and ruled behind the scenes, and it was easy to tell different social groups apart. Some of this, too, is preserved in Indonesia today.

Attitudes to the legacy are as diverse as the dynasty itself. To many, the empire represents a glorious past when Majapahit commanded respect across the region, particularly from those who wished to trade with this rich Javanese power. Rulers across Southeast Asia were eager to gain its favour.[560] In this narrative, Gajah Mada, the legendary *patih*, is the 'hero of national identity'. To others, such as some Acehnese and Sulawesian separatist figures, he was nothing but a Javanese aggressor in search of imperial glory at any cost.[561]

As for Majapahit's reputation for diversity and tolerance, there are many different truths, depending on which side of the sword or dagger people found themselves. Despite the kingdom's enormous contributions to everything from art, literature, drama and architecture, to rice cultivation and ship building, there are even those who still ignore that Hinduism and Buddhism created a distinct culture across Indonesia.[562]

But for all Majapahit's strengths and weaknesses – every empire had them, after all – there can be no doubt that its rise and fall remains a story worthy of a broader audience. It is one of intrigue, murder, secrets, suspense, revenge and war in a land filled with beautiful temples and imposing palaces. The streets were crowded with Brahmins with matted hair, hermits in bark cloth, widows dressed all in white, and Chinese, Persian and Arab traders. Bustling markets offered an astonishing range of goods from home and afar.

In the mornings, farmers walked their buffalos to rice paddies, and priests chanted ancient verses written in Sanskrit. And spirits were everywhere – in trees, bushes, temples, houses and on mountaintops. In the evenings, the city was lit up by thousands of torches and campfires as if the sun had never set. There were mass cremations and huge religious celebrations, with palm wine consumed in great quantities whenever an opportunity presented itself. Majapahit was a glorious medley of customs and beliefs, as indeed Indonesia to a lesser extent is today.

Perhaps the same can be said of societies as it can be for people. However much they may change, the essential nature of their character is set when they are in the process of forming. In Indonesia, and large parts of Southeast Asia, this was the glorious civilisation that spawned the Majapahit.

Endnotes

1 Technically, he discovered what was left of the Singasari empire, the precursor to Majapahit. There were three broad periods of empire – Kediri, Singasari and Majapahit – that spanned the 13th-15th centuries. Few statues or literature survived from the Kediri period (pre-1222). Some statues from the Singasari period survived but not much of its literature. But from the Majapahit empire (post 1292), a range of statues and literature are available to modern scholars.

2 See van der Linde, 2020.

3 *A Journal of a Tour in the Island of Java*, p126.

4 This comes from a report of this journey titled 'A Journal of a Tour in the Island of Java (By a Gentlemen resident at Batavia)' in the The Asiatic Journal and Monthly Register for British India and its Dependencies, 1816.

5 Raffles, 1830, Vol 2, p44. One of the earlier visitors was Engelhard.

6 Raffles, 1830, Vol 2, p44.

7 Also called Supit Urang, on the mountain of Arjuna, western Java.

8 Dumarcay 1985, p95.

9 While Raffles notes it was a golden statue, there is none such item in his collection in the British Museum. It was most likely a bronze lingam. A lingam (or linga) is an abstract representation of the Hindu god Shiva.

10 Although in later letters from Engelhard it appears he was not aware of *Candi* Jago in 1803. See Krom 1920, p446.

11 Jordaan 2016, p55. Krom 1920 mentions this too.

12 There was a growing interest in the archipelago's history. A Batavian society was established to discuss matters of history and art and in the Netherlands, museums with art and artifacts opened their doors (the Teyler Museum in Haarlem opened in 1778). But most Dutch who arrived in the region were there to make money and trade.

13 Jordaan, 2016 p42 and Krom 1920.

14 Blom 1939 p9-11.

15 Krom 1920.

16 The Prajnaparamita statue was discovered in 1818 by the assistant resident of Malang, D. Monnereau. In 1822, it was shipped to the Netherlands by Prof. C.G.C Reinward. For long it was part of the collection of museums – the Museum of Antiquities in Leiden and, from 1903, the Rijksmuseum voor Volkenkunde – until in 1978 it was returned to Indonesia. It is now in the National Museum in Jakarta. Local tradition links the statue to the first queen of Singasari (Ken Dedes) while others have suggested it is Queen Gayatri, wife of the first king of

Majapahit. See Keputusan Mentri Pendidikan dan Kebudayaan Republik Indonesia 2013 or Fontein, 1992, p24.

17 This vignette appears on page 134 of the first edition of *History of Java* in 1816.

18 Raffles, 1816, p54.

19 Wardenaar's plan of Majapahit was later found in the Drake Collection of the British Museum in March 2008. Wardenaar's survey proved to be remarkably accurate. See Carey 2018 or Gomperts et al, 2008.

20 Bataviaasch Genootschap van Kunsten en Wetenschappen. This happened in 1879.

21 Carey 2018, p7.

22 Hendrik Jacob Domis (1781 – 1842) was the Semarang resident from 1822-1827 and in Surabaya from 1831 to 1834.

23 Van Hoëvell, 1849, p173-175 (free translation by the author).

24 Wallace, p102-103.

25 Cool, De Lombok expeditie, pages 440 onwards.

26 Hagen, 2018, p363.

27 Eerde, p9.

28 Hagen 2018, p370.

29 Cool, De Lombok expeditie and Vanvught, 1994, p48.

30 Vanvught, 1994, p46.

31 'De Kraton van Majapahit', Stutterheim, 1948. See page 1, footnote 4.

32 Stutterheim, 1948, p7. It would be entirely convenient to ascribe Stutterheim's 'enigma' to the looming Japanese invasion of which Stutterheim had inside information as a high-ranking member of the colonial civil service. But Stutterheim's enigma was a deliberate colonial policy since 1924. The two gentlemen, who published Stutterheim's July 1941 manuscript in 1948, knew both the hidden ground truth in the monograph and chose to leave it as such. What they did not know is that Stutterheim ordered an excavation in July 1941-December 1941 with the explicit intent to date the site. Arnoud Haag discovered the excavation reports in 2016 which were published in Gomperts et. al, 2018.

33 Gomperts et.al, 2008.

34 We are unsure who Prapanca really was. The name was probably the pseudonym of a young courtier and an aspiring poet who was associated with the superintendent of Buddhist affairs; he was possibly his son. See Sastrawan, Sydney 2021, p113. Assuming he was the son, a decree, the Jaya Song, mentions a bishop called Kanakamuni and in another charter of 1365, the bishop is named Nadendra. This is likely Prapanca's father and Kanakamuni was his grandfather. Prapanca mentions that he was about the same age as Hayam Wuruk – they had played together as children. In 1358, Hayam Wuruk was about 24 years old, so Prapanca

was most likely also in his mid-twenties.

35 Gomperts et al., 2018.

36 Although, by 1448, what is now Beijing, was the largest city on earth and had 950,000 inhabitants.

37 A Mandala empire is a loose confederation of states or territories centred around a powerful kingdom or city-state, which acted as a kind of hub. This centre would exert influence over the surrounding territories, but not necessarily through direct control or domination. Instead, relationships between the centre and the surrounding states were often mediated by alliances, patronage, tribute, and diplomacy.

38 See 'Early research on Sivaic Hinduism during the Majapahit Era' by Hariani Santiko in Miksic, 1995, p69

39 It is from this work where Indonesia's motto, 'Bhinneka Tunggal Ika', usually translated as 'unity in diversity' is taken.

40 See O'Brien 2008, p9-10, for a discussion about the identity of Mpu Tantular and his relationship with Prince Ranamanggala (probably a son in law of one of Hayam Wuruk's sisters) at the Majapahit court. The Sutasoma was probably written around the same time or a little later than Prapanca's *Desawarnana*, probably somewhere between 1365-1389.

41 It was believed that an aesthetic experience should arise from specific 'flavours' or '*rasa*'. These were love, heroism, disgust, loathing, anger or fury, mirth, terror, pity and wonder. Some scripts, such as the Bhomataka, have all of this with some philosophical ideas thrown in for good measure. The *Nagarakertagama* lacks nearly all of these elements. See intro into the Bhomantaka, Teeuw and Robson, 2005, page 2.

42 The location of the monestary in Darbaru remains a mystery. Sidomulyo suggests that Hujung is now Ngujung, a small town about 10 km from Pasaruan If so, it would be about a 3 hour walk from Pasaruan. Sidomulyo 2007, p77

43 Pigeaud, Volkvertoningen, 1938, par 303

44 Indigo was a major source of the blue dyes that were popular in the day. Red dye was made, amongst others, from sappan wood. The colours worn by the Javanese in the early part of the second millenium must have been closer to more recent Nusa Tenggara Timur than 19th or 20th century Java. See Jan Wisseman Christie, 1993, p186.

45 The Borobudur shows pictures of millet, not rice. So rice was probably introduced to Java in the later Hindu-Buddhist period. Irrigated rice came in the medieval times, perhaps before the rise of the Majapahit empire. See Bray 1994, p10/11.

46 Later in the twelfth century a new term, *desa*, borrowed from the Sanskrit, began to slowly replace other terms for the community as a whole, while in the fourteenth century, the term *dapur* ('cluster') appears to have emerged Christie, 1991, p34

47 Pigeaud 1962, IV, p494-504.

48 The population of east Javanese states appears to have risen fairly consistently from the early tenth century through the fourteenth, despite wars and internal strife. By 1300, the population of Java could have reached nearly five million. (McDonald's estimates quoted in J.W Christies 1991, p29.) These days, it is over 120 million.

49 The Sivaitic character of many of the *maṇḍala* communities is apparent from the Tantu Panggelaran tales.

50 For example, much later, at the height of Majapahit, King Hayam Wuruk grants the estate of Madakaripura, just north of Singasari, to Gajah Madah, the vizir of the kingdom.

51 Pigeaud 1962, IV, p470.

52 Bondsmen were called *bhertya*.

53 Des 49:5.

54 Based on Jakl 2021, p175.

55 The Pararaton can be translated as 'The Monarchs'. The word is formed from pa-(ra)ratu-an, with the base word 'ratu', monarch.

56 Prapanca, the author of the *Desawarnana*, seems to have seen documents that 'gave him insight' (Des 35:2) and that it 'aroused him' (Des 35:3) and shortly thereafter, on an auspicious day, he goes to visit Kagenengan, where Ken Arok was buried (Des 36:1). Perhaps this was because, for the first time, it became clear to him how the Rajasa dynasty was founded after reading a sort of proto-Pararaton version. At least, that is what C.C.Berg argued, although not all historians are convinced about this. See Moens (1954) and Bosch (1965).

57 The story of Aji Saka is probably a stereotyped tale of the risk-seeking Indian sailor who arrived on their shores (Munoz p52). Majapahit temples follow a Saka date count. Saka 1200 = 1278CE.

58 I-Tsing is the older romanization of Yijing, a monk who lived from 635 to 713CE and travelled from China to Sumatra and onwards to India.

59 Wolters 1974, p123. Translation from Wolters.

60 Its is specifically the Daemonorphps Blume.

61 Buzurg ibn Shahriyār, 1883, p125. Translation from French by the author.

62 Wolters 1974, p1195.

63 This was in AD928.

64 This is from Zhou Qufe's Lingwai Daida, as quoted in Wolters 1974, p 251.

65 Sidomulyo 2011. The site of the tamarind tree where the sage failed to divide the lands was later the cemetery of Wurare, near the palace of Majapahit. These days it's a Buddhest center with a giant reclining Buddha.

66 The full title of the book is 'Pararaton: The Book of Kings of Tumapel and Majapahit'. It is a compilation of different writers and stories, a

'conglomerate text', and was finished between 1478 and 1486. The oldest surviving copy was discovered in Bali in 1600. This chronicle narrates the mythical beginnings of the Majapahit empire, describing a man named Ken Arok, for long considered a fairy tale but his existence was later confirmed on the Mula-Malurung copper plates. The book that the abbot read to Prapanca would have been a sort of 'proto-Pararaton' version.

67 See Berg, 1928, 'Inleiding tot de studie van het Oud-Javaansch', page 135, footnote 1. The theme of a lowlife rising to become an important man, or kings having links with deities, would frequently return in Java. Much later, a similar story of robber turned saint – Kalijaga was his name – was told at the time of the rise of Islam in Java.

68 It is commonly assumed that this is the year in which Ken Arok was born. The date is mentioned in Desawarnana 40. Given the lack of dates of future kings, we can only estimate how old they were by counting forward from this date and assume that children were born some 20 years later.

69 Jiput is quite possibly the village that carries the same name today, near Blitar and close to the famed temple complex Panataran, on the western side from mount Kawi (Robson and Sidolulyo, 2021, p 175, footnote 282)

70 These 'historical' events play against a backdrop of a kingdom in Kediri in the 12th and 13th century. This is a time where the stories of the Pararaton overlap with another old Javanese script, the Tantu Panggelaran. See Robson et al 2021, p173.

71 The location of this place is uncertain but Sido Hadimulyo points at the town of Kepanjen in the southern part of the regency of Malang, see Robson 2021, p175, footnote 285.

72 Pararaton p47.

73 It is difficult not to see this as a precursor for the devastation that Ken Arok himself would inflict on so many people in his own life. See Bosch 1965 p470. And being a robber or lowlife was not a problem for men to become kings or religious leaders later. Kalijaga, a bringer of Islam to Java a few centuries later, was said to have been a robber before he converted. See Berg p20 in Stapel, Volume 2.

74 Pararaton p55.

75 It was also decided that, as king, Ken Arok would be re-named Bharata Guru.

76 *Desawarnana* p57.

77 Hall 2010, p30.

78 Aside from magical powers these forged metals had a more mundane advantage – local kings now had access to metal weapons, a useful tool in an era marked by endemic warfare (Hall 2010, p30).

79 Pararaton p59. Today, there is a district called Lumbang about 50 kilometres east of Singasari and Malang, near Probolinggo.

80 Pararaton p60.

81 He is also named Dangdang Gendis.

82 Pararaton p62.

83 The name Rajasa stuck and 70 years later, one of his descendants in 1294 called himself -'Kerta-Rajasa-Wardhana', with Rajasa as part of his name. See Berg 1958, p2.

84 There is little hard evidence that this man existed but we do know from the charter of Lawadan that Kertajaya did exist. He was defeated in 1222, by Ken Arok or not.

85 We don't know where the town of Ganter was located but Sidomulo (2010) suggests it might be identifiable with Ganter, a small village near the border of the present regencies of Malang and Kediri.

86 The Pararaton suggests that he hanged himself but in Prapanca's *Desawarnana*, canto 40:3, it says he lived his final days as a hermit.

87 Short for Sri Rajasa Sang Amurwabhumi.

88 In Desawarnana 49:5 it is suggested that this proto-Pararaton had history up to 1265.

89 There is considerable uncertainty about the exact genealogy of the Rajasa dynasty. The *Desawarnana* and Pararaton provide different dates for different kings but more recently, the Mula-Malurung copper plates shed a new light on this matter. See Sidomulyo 2010.

90 This is the year mentioned in the *Desawarnana*, which seems to be more consistent over time when it comes to dates and events. The Pararaton reads that all this happened in 1247, which is highly questionable and seems more of an attempt by the author(s) of the Pararaton, the Book of Chronicles, to skip over what would be an embarrassing part of local history – the multiple assassinations described in the next chapter.

91 Pararaton p64. The role of Ken Dedes here is rather questionable – she could have known what the consequences were of telling Anusapati about the murder of his biological father by Ken Arok. Maybe it was exactly what she wanted after being kidnapped from her father's house and later being married to her husband's murderer. Alternatively, given she was the daughter of a prominent religious leader, maybe she felt she had a responsibility to tell the truth.

92 Thursday because it was said it was the Pon day of the wuku Landep. Pararaton p64.

93 Slametmuljana, 1976, p19.

94 The remaining part of the chapter is a description of a funeral. The Pararaton stops at the death of Ken Arok.

95 This scene of the burial is not in the Pararaton but most likely kings and queens were cremated and their ashes thrown in the River Brantas. See Kwa Chong Guan, 'Shradda Sri Rajapatni: An Exploration of Majapahit Mortuary Ritual' in Miksic and Endang, 'The Legacy of Majapahit', 1995, p76. This funeral is a description of a Balinese funeral

which the author witnessed in 1991 in Bali. See also Stephen 2010, p440 onwards.

96 The description of the funeral is actually not in the Pararaton. It just states that Ken Arok dies and Ken Dedes simply disappears from the narrative. We do not know when she died nor where she is buried or if some sort of commemorative temple was constructed for her. She might have retreated to a quiet hermitage in the forests and possibly died there. A local legend (in Malang) suggests that she went to a lake and drowned herself, the act of suicide worthy of her becoming an enlightened being. But in thirteenth century Java the dramatic *sati* (widow burning) was more the norm than an exception and we can also assume that she died by fire. In pre-Islamic Java, there are only two fragments that *sati* actually was practised. One is an 880 CE inscription and the second is on a relief on temple Jago which was constructed between 1268-1280, a few decades after the death of Ken Arok. It shows a scene of a legend in which a lady named Satyawati prepares to step into the fire. Actual evidence of this gruesome death is rather fragmentary and pregnant women did not need to perform a sati, which explains why she did not have to perform the sati when Tunggula Ametung died (she was pregnant with Anusapati). 'Sati' became the origin for the Indonesian word 'setia', which means loyalty.

97 It remains unclear where Kagenengan is but there are suggestions it is near a small town just south of Malang. Kagenengan does re-appear in the *Desawarnana* in the description of King Hayam Wuruk's visits to the shrine. That was in conjunction with a visit to two other temples – Candi Kidal and Candi Jago – suggesting that Kagenengan should be near to or south of today's Malang. This is also what Blom 1939, p150 writes ('6km south of Malang').

98 Cross swords in the sense of conflict. The two men never met.

99 Kasurangganan or 'Abode of the Heavenly Nymphs' is located at Kedung Biru; the name is still used today. See Robson et.al 2023 (Margasmara), p4.

100 Zhu Fan Zhi, Hirth and Rockhill, Chao Ju-kua, p35-37. See also Yang's 2023 'A Chinese Gazetteer of Foreign Lands – A new translation of Part 1 of the Zhu Fan Zhi 諸蕃志 (1225)'.

101 Later, Tumapel was re-named Singasari.

102 In 13th century Tumapel/Singasari, mortar was not available but masons were able to place bricks on top of each other with great skill and accuracy.

103 For these Chinese sources, see Yang 2023 under the heading 'Java'. Tax rates for the professional traders differed from the locals. Taxes would, eventually, become a particular important source of income for the king. Future kings took to this new concept and it was in Ken Arok's days 'when the *dapur* (village tax), *kuwu* (manor tax) and *juru* (it is

uncertain what this is) were first introduced' (Des 40:4). See also Kern, Hindoe-Javaansche Geschiedenis, p317.

104 This is an actual description in the 12th century Bhomantaka 1:9. That is written well before Ken Arok's days but gives an idea of what these places looked like. See Bhomantaka 1:11: 1-3.

105 Translation Yang 2023 under 'Java'. See also Zhu Fan Zhi, Hirth and Rockhill, Chao Ju-kua, p77, Gelman, p43.

106 Bhomantaka 1:13:2-3.

107 For example, see Galestin, 1936, p162. Galestin's book on Javanese wood-constructions, founded on a study of illustrative reliefs on the walls of East Javanese temples, sheds much light on housing in the 14th century.

108 Translation Yang 2023 under 'Java'. See also Zhu Fan Zhi, Hirth and Rockhill, Chao Ju-kua, p77.

109 Translation from Yang 2023. See also Zhu Fan Zhi, Hirth and Rockhill, Chao Ju-kua, p76.

110 Zhu Fan Zhi, Hirth and Rockhill, Chao Ju-kua, p77.

111 Zhu Fan Zhi, Hirth and Rockhill, Chao Ju-kua, p83. For mushrooms and alcohol, see Jakl, 2021, p103-104.

112 Translation by Yang 2023 under 'Java'. See also Zhu Fan Zhi, Hirth and Rockhill, Chao Ju-kua, p77.

113 Zhu Fan Zhi, Hirth and Rockhill, Chao Ju-kua, p77-78.

114 We don't know when Wisnuwardhana was born, but he was a mature king and died in 1270 or 1272. Assuming he was over 50 years old at the end of his life, he was born around 1220, when Anusapati was around 20 years old.

115 A so-called shraddu ceremony marked the departure of the soul from the world of mortals. See Kwa Chong Guan, 'Shradda Sri Rajapatni: An Exploration of Majapahit Mortuary Ritual' in Miksic and Endang, 'The Legacy of Majapahit', 1995, p76.

116 Kinney, p30.

117 What exactly happened is still unclear but the recent discovery of inscribed copper plates gives the impression that there was a rapid succession of kings, all brothers. In 1975, 10 copper plates displaying Old Javanese script were discovered in the regency of Kediri. The charter of Mula-Malurung, as it has since been named, is dated 1255 and is an official document confirming a royal grant to a loyal servant in the form of an area of land in the villages of Mula and Malurung. This charter will return in a later chapter. On one of the plates is a list of the reigning king – Wisnuwardhana at the time – and his close relatives. While the Pararaton suggests that there was a period of about 20 years of peace under Anusapati's rule, this is refuted by these copper plates. It seems the authors of the Pararaton conveniently skipped over some of the more violent details, glossing over an otherwise embarrassing period in the

history of the dynasty. The same can be said of Prapanca's *Desawarnana*, who in *Desawarnana* 41-5 stated only that Anusapati's rule brought stability to Java. See Sidomulyo 2010 for details. The copper plates suggest that this was the order of kings (dates are added, but were not on the copper plates):

Ken Arok, murdered by Anuspati in 1227

Anusapati is succeeded (probably killed) by Mahisa, Ken Arok's oldest son. Date unknown

Mahisa was succeeded by his younger brother Narayya Guning Bhaya). Date unknown

Narayya Guning Bahaya is succeeded by Toh Jaya, the son of Ken Arok from a concubine

Toh Jaya is killed by the guards loyal to the sons of Mahisa and Narayya, the two cousins – Wisnuwardhana (son of Anusapati) and Narasinghamurti. This is in the year 1250.

118 This is an odd statement and Nihon 1986, p488-489 suggests that Wisnuwardhana was quite possibly physically impaired. If correct, Toh Jaya's comment about the boys being beautiful was ironic and puts this response by Pranaraja – he could scarcely have permitted himself to compare two royal princes in this way – in a different light.

119 It was quite possibly *patih* Pranaraja who is later rewarded with land for protecting the boys. This returns in a later chapter.

120 There appears to have been two dominant factions – the Rajasa's and the Sinelirs. See Krom Geschiedenis p322, footnote 1 on p323. These two groups are also mentioned in the Nawatnya, a charter that explains the functions at court. See Pigeaud p125.

121 It is unclear where he wanted to run to; perhaps Bali or on the island of Madura.

122 It is uncertain where this is but this place is named again in *Desawarnana* 73:3. See Krom, Geschiedenis , p322 Some have pointed to a village named Ketonggo in Lumbang, near Pasaruan (Krom p322, footnote 3). If so, it is a 10 hour walk from Singasari (Tumapel) where Toh Jaya's palace was located. Berg 1938 disputes this though.

123 In the Mula-Mulurung plates (3b:4) it is mentioned that Sang Apanji Patipati presided over Wisnuwardhana's consecration.

124 The relationship between the two cousins, Wisnuwardhana and Narasingamurti, remains one of the major outstanding issues in ancient Javanese history. Some suggest that the two cousins got along well and that they ruled together peacefully, 'like Visnu and Indra' (*Desawarnana* 41:2) or 'two snakes in one hole' (Pararaton p77). But the name Narasingamurti never appears on any of the stone reliefs – *prasasti* – from this period, casting this view into doubt. However, what the prasasti do illustrate is that there was a tier of 'secondary kings' (called 'raja angabhaya'). In another book, the Kidung Harsawijaya – a story

first translated into Dutch 1928 and published in 1931 by C.C. Berg – it is Narasingamurti who takes a prominent role and Wisnuwardhana is a secondary character. This seems rather at odds with other evidence we have. See Berg 1931, p23). Nihon 1986, p488-489 suggests that this unique arrangement was possibly because Wisnuwardhana was physically impaired or disabled in some way. It is also possible that Narasingamurti left Singasari and went to Bali – there is a temple dedicated to him near Singaraja in north Bali (source: conversation with Dwi Cahyono).

125 Narasingamurti disappears from the texts. There is a Balinese legend that he went to Singaraja in north Bali and that a temple was erected in his name. See I Kadek Sudana Wira Darma, April 2019, p52.

126 The quotes 'like Visnu and Indra' come from Des 41:2 and 'two snakes in one hole' comes from the Pararaton, p77.

127 This description is from a Shiva statue, now in the Tropenmuseum (inventory nr TM-A-5950), which might be his father Anusapati. See also Pullen 2021, p134-135.

128 This is stated in plates VIb and VIIa-b of the Mula-Malurung inscription. See Sidomulyo2010, p87.

129 In 1255 the land of Wurawan was under the control of Turuk Bali (a daughter of Wisnuwardhana) and her consort Sri Jayakatyeng, Sidomulyo 2010, p92.

130 There is no evidence of this but it seems rather likely.

131 This is mentioned in the Mula-Mularung copper plates. See Sidomulyo 2010.

132 This was their second trip. The first was in 1260 to Karakorum on the Mongolian grasslands.

133 Aung-Thwin, 1985, p196.

134 Sun 2014, p204-205.

135 These attacks were in 1257-1258, 1284-1285 and 1287-1288. See Anderson, 2014, p120 and Sun 2014, p216.

136 Anderson, 2014, p122-123.

137 It is unknown when this took place, but it was probably in the early 1250s. Prapanca mentions Linggapati (Des 41:2) and in the Pararaton he is named Lingganingpati of Mahibit (Pararaton p77).

138 Krom 1931, p325.

139 We don't know when Kertanegara was born. Some assumed 1254. Others (like Moens 1954, p 405) suggest he was already fifty years old by then. The Pararaton, however, informs us that he was still young at the time. While he was probably still young at the time of his coronation, he acts as a very mature man twenty years later.

140 *Desawarnana* 41:3-2.

141 See Krom 1931 p325.

142 Paraton 74.

143 By that time he went under the name of Mpu Kupat.

144 This is from the Sukharta inscription. This was given to Pati-Pati in 1296. By then Kertanegara was dead, so this was provided to him by the next king, Prince Widjaya ('Raden Widjaya' or Vijaya), still a young boy when Kertanegara received training at court. See Poerbatjaraka 1940. Translation from Jakl, 2020, p35-36.

145 See the inscription of Penampihan, 1269. See Brandes 1913, inscription 79.

146 It is assumed here that he was born around 1246, but his birth date is unknown. It explains why his father was still an active ruler after Kertanegara was crowned king in 1254, at the age of six.

147 It seems his father still ruled while he was younger. See Krom 1911, p17 onwards.

148 Krom, Geschiedenis 1931 p327 and Oudheidkundig Verslag 1918, p109.

149 That's what the Kidul Harsa Widjajya says, see also Berg 1931, p4.

150 It actually mentions Janggala (near Singasari) and Kediri.

151 This is where the king was to become a Buddha (in Jago) and as Shiva in another shrine in Maleri near Blitar.

152 It is unknown when Candi Jago was constructed, but most likely it was in full use by 1280, twelve years after Wisnuwardhana's death when his sharddu ceremony would been conducted. Stutterheim has suggested that large parts of it were modified a century later. An analysis of reliefs at Candi Jago – see Klokke (1993:81-2) – argues that based on stylistic comparison, the sculptures date from the end of the thirteenth century, while for the reliefs she agrees with the dating of the mid fourteenth century. The original construction of Candi Jago was thus prior to the Majapahit period, but the extension or rebuilding and the decoration of the temple was conducted in the time prior to or around the beginning of the reign of Hayam Wuruk. Candi Jago served both the Hindu and Buddhist communities, and is a major example of the special blend of these two religions in the Majapahit period. See also Kieven 2013..

153 It is a bothisatvva, the six-armed Amoghapasa, a redeemer – with a noose in hand to reach out to Buddhists – and whose powers of salvation are infallible. The statue is at Candi Jago, but unfortunately the head is long gone.

154 Krom, 1931, p328

155 The Kidung Harsawijaya tells a different story in that Kertanegara was only allowed to become king after Narasingamurti had died. See Berg 1931 p4 and p23). Elsewhere, the Pakis inscription suggests that he started his rule somewhere around 1266 (Slametmuljana, 1976, p22 and Krom, 1931, p325).

156 Acri and Wenta, 2022, footnote 10. See also Sinclair 2022.

157 Malawani et al, 2022. The latest findings suggest that the Samalas eruption had a close connection to the climatic disruption that led to the

apocalyptic plague: the Black Death (Fell et al., 2020). In the long term, the Samalas eruption in 1257 CE was one of the significant triggers that contributed to the 'Little Ice Age' in late medieval times.

158 The Harihara Ardhanari, a deification of a god, possibly resembles King Kertanegara. The statue is currently in the State Hermitage Museum, St. Petersburg. Inventory nr. BD-543. See also Pullen 2021, p203. Later, when he is older, statues that most likely depict Kertanegara, such as the Joko Dolog, show him as a slightly bulky, plump man with bright, round eyes, and a small mouth with full, chubby fingers.

159 Shaw 1994, p81.

160 Prapanca describes Kertanegara as being involved in some rituals but does not provide details. However, an important central ritual to gain power, or *sekti*, was the *ganacakra*. At least, that is what Moens (1924) argues. Nihon (1986) argues that this is a mistake and that there is no evidence that this particular ceremony was actively in use. The description in this chapter of a ganacakra is loosely based on Shaw 1994. See also Santiko 1997, p217-218 and Miksic 1995, p65. It is not clear in how far this ritual was performed but tantric feasts, or communal assemblies such as the *ganacakra*, centered around the use of madya (alcohol), maṃsa (meat), matsya (fish), mudra (pound grain), and maithuna (sexual intercourse). See Shaw 1994, p80-81.

161 This Bhairava statue is in the Leiden Museum voor Volkenkunde in The Netherlands.

162 Over time, these religious foundations were divided into three classes: *dharma dalem/haji, dharma lepas*, and *karshyan*. See Kieven 2013 Chapter 4. The first class, *dharma dalem,* included all religious foundations reserved for the royal family, amongst them the Singasari temples for King Kertanagara and Candi Jago for King Wishnuwardhana.

163 Sarwadharma inscription plate 4, line 7 as in Pigaud 1960. This could well have happened at the annual Caitra festival in March or April.

164 These are the Sarwadharma inscriptions from 1269. See Plate 3, line 4,5 as in Pigaud Vol 3 1960. The Sarwadharma ceremony marks a turning point in Kertanegara's policies, which become more assertive afterwards. In the arts it was a turning point too and new styles started to develop. See Pullen, 2021, p162-163. It's unclear where his monestary of dharma was located, but the plates were found on Mount Willis, to the west of Kediri.

165 Sarwadharma plate 5, line 5-7, Pigaud 1960.

166 Sarwadharma plate 7, line 4-6.

167 *Desawarnana* 41:5.

168 *Desawarnana* 42:1.

169 This is from the 1296 Sukamerta inscription, issued after the death of Kertanegara in which lands are bestowed to Pati-Pati. See Poerbatjaraka 1940. Translation from Jakl 2020 p35-36. We do not know if this

inscription refers to this particular uprising, but there were a few other occasions where Kertanegara was able to crush his adversary's troops himself.

170 Pararaton p79.

171 We meet him later again in Kertanegara's company when they are killed in a tantric ritual in 1292.

172 Poerbatjaraka 1940. It's not clear if he also created that role for the Buddhists at the same time as the Shivaist bishop position. But a few decades later, in 1294, there was such a Buddhist bishop (See Krom 1931 p329) which, years later, was a function occupied by Nadendra, possibly Prapanca's father. Also, by then, Pati-Pati had changed his name to Mpu Kupat.

173 The inscription of Rameswarapura mentions Aragani as *patih* in 1275, so Kertanagara's replacement of senior officials had already begun before the year 1275.

174 See Hunter 2007, p40 and Ringpapontsan, 2016. He writes that this took place in 1253 and for a second time before 1263.

175 This was the assessment of an Arab traveller, Ibn Said, who mentions Sriwijaya in 1286. Chinese annals mention this too. See Reid 2001, p297.

176 The date for the beginning of Kertanagara's campaign to subdue Sumatra is widely accepted as 1275, except for Berg (1950), who suggested that the decision to conquer Sumatra was made in 1275 but the army was not actually sent until 1292.

177 Slametmuljana 1976, p24.

178 See Berg 1950, p15. Also in Des 41:5-3. A lot depends on the interpretation of this verse in the *Desawarnana* – some argue the preparation of this naval expedition began in 1275, others suggest it is the year when the actual military expedition left.

179 Pamelayu is actually 'towards Melayu', which was southern Sumatra at the time.

180 In the Kidung Harsawijaya there seem to have been many more changes of top officials. One leaves out of discontent and lives as a hermit on Mt. Meru. See Berg 1931 p5. This is the head of religious affairs, Santasmreti. See also Slametmuljana, 1976, p24.

181 This is mentioned in the Kidung Harsawijaya. This is the head of religious affairs, Santasmreti. See also Slametmuljana, 1976, p24

182 The inscription of Rameswarapura mentions Aragani as *patih* in 1275, so Kertanagara's replacement of senior officials had already begun before the year 1275.

183 Pullen 2021, p53

184 See Des 42:3.

185 There is no evidence that his father Wishnuwardhana already had Madura under control (nor does the opposite appear to be the case) but if one concludes that the possession of Madura was a prerequisite for

Kertanagara, the assumption that the addition of Madura to the realm of Singasari took place under Kertanagara seems justified. See also Berg 1950.

186 Liebner 2014, p227.

187 For details see Manguin 1980 and Manguin 1993.

188 Acri and Wenta, 2022

189 This is the so-called Padang Roco inscription of 1286, discovered in Sumatra in 1906. The invasion must therefore have occurred on or before 1286 but after 1275, when the *Desawarnana* first mentions the expedition against South Sumatra.

190 Desawarnana 42:2

191 This was the statue that Raffles and Engelhard missed when they visited Singasari in the early 1800s. It was discovered later by an assistant-resident, shipped to The Netherlands and in 1978 returned to Indonesia. It's unclear if and when Kertenegara ordered this statue to be carved.

192 At least, that's what the inscription on the statue mentions. The statue might also have been brought over after the expedition to Sumatra.

193 Kertanegara wanted to control access to the archipelago through the narrow strait between Sumatra and Kalimantan (Borneo), with the islands of Bangka and Belitung at the centre. It is quite possible that these two princesses came from two different locations; one from Sumatra – that would have been Dara Petak as her son, Adityawarman, later returns to Dharmasraya in Sumatra – while Dara Jingga came from Kalimantan.

194 Groeneveldt 1880, Book 210 on p44

195 Rockwell, T'oung Pao 15 p439). By 1279, missions from India had presented him with a live elephant and a rhinoceros (Rockwell, T'oung Pao 15, p430). It is likely that a desire for trade figured in Kublai Khan's decision to attack Java.

196 *Desawarnana* 42: 1:3

197 Nothing is mentioned about this queen. We do not know her name, nor her fate. There are no reports on this expedition into western Java. Neither are we sure whether Sunda was independent at this time, or whether it still belonged to the territory of Sriwijaja, the state which for centuries had been the great power of the Straits of Malacca. But we can assume that Sunda must have created a threat to Kertanegara's troops in case of an attack on Sumatra, as they could be attacked by the Sundanese in the rear.

198 One argument (Berg 1950) is that the Joko Dolog ceremony in 1289 would not have been useful if at that time the entire Java unification program had already been completed (and Sundanese in West Java were subjugated). However, according to the *Desawarnana* (42:2), Sunda was incorporated into his realm before Kertanagara's death in 1292. Hence, Berg argues, in 1289, Kertanegara was on the verge of launching a campaign against Sunda. The subjugation of Sunda in West Java must

then have occurred in that same year or in 1290-1291 at the latest.

199 See also Pullen 2021, p17 for more details

200 Kublai Khan's missions to Java in 1279,1280, 1281 and 1286 are mentioned and dated in Books 10-14 of the Yuan Shi. The mission of Meng Qi is mentioned in Book 210 but nowhere is mentioned when it occurred. Many believe it was in 1289 but there is no evidence for this.

201 Des 46. Also in the Penanggungan inscription as quoted in Slametmuljana, 1976, p48

202 That is what Chinese reports state. The 'History of the Yuan dynasty', a serious doorstopper with 240 chapters compiled in 1370 by the 'Bureau of History' of the Ming Dynasty (which followed the Yuan), writes that the Chinese rulers had good relations with the rulers of Java but 'they have cut the face of imperial envoy Meng Chi and that you have come to punish them for that' (Groeneveldt p22). What exactly happened to Meng Qi, when and why this happened is not clear; whether he was actually branded in the face, slashed, cut, beaten, or merely treated in a rude or hostile manner has been debated. Whatever happened, his treatment was condemned by Kublai Khan.

203 An inscription of 1306 mentions a queen-daughter from Yavadhipa – that is, Java – named Queen Tapasi. This might have been a family member, a sister, or daughter of Kertanegara, further supported by the fact that when things got tight in Champa, her son Che Nang fled to Java in 1318. Its unclear when she left for Champa. See Krom 1931, p333 and Griffiths Lepoutre, 2016, p206.

204 Bade 2013, p20

205 Rossabi p219-220, Stapel vol 1, p253-257

206 His birth date is unknown, but it appears he was younger than Kertanegara. Later we will see that he was old enough to command an army in 1292 and probably born anywhere between 1250 and 1270. Later, when he became king, he is generally referred to as Kertarajasa Jayawardhana. While Prince Widjaya is used throughout this chapter, in the literature he is most often called 'Raden Widjaya'.

207 The story of the fall of Singasari and the invasion of Chinese troops has survived history in various forms. Most reliable is a 1294 inscription from Butak in which Kertarajasa Jayawardhanna, also known as Raden Wijaya (Prince Widjaya), had the main points of the history etched on copper plates. Other sources are the Pararaton and scripts such as Kidung Harsa-Wijaya and the Panji Wijayakrama, which were written down centuries later. Schrieke (1957, v. 2, p. 11) argues that the Kidung Harsa-Wijaya is the Kediri version of the history of the fall of Kertanegara, and the Kidung Panji Wijayakrama presents the Madurese version of those events. With the inscription of Kudadu and the Pararaton offering the Majapahit version of these events, we have a wonderful chorus of

complementary narratives describing the same actors and events. A first copy of the Kidung Harsa-Wijaya was written in 1843 in Bali. In the Kidung Harsa-Wijaya, the author seems to have had access to the Pararaton and writes 'it would be too much to relate it here, its whole charm is to be found in the Pararaton'. In this chapter a combination of all these sources is used. But these stories cannot be accepted as history as it stands — it is more in the nature of legend, but largely based on historical events. See Robson (2000)

208 The Pararaton writes that he had fallen out with Kertanegara years earlier. See also Kidung Harsawijaya, Berg 1931, p7.

209 Brandes' Pararaton p79

210 In the Kidung Harsa-Wijaya, he was the chamberlain at Kertanegara's court before he was assigned to Madura, presumably a step down. It is quite possible that he held a grudge against Kertanegara, possibly because he was aligned with Narasingamurti, the deputy king (it is uncertain what happened to him).

211 Berg 1950

212 Slametmulyana 1976 p28

213 It's surprising that Raganata does this – remember, he resigned from his role as key advisor years earlier when he was not in support of the expedition to Melayu and Kertanegara re-assigned him to a religious role.

214 The name of the location suggests a place near the sea, a bay. If so, this place is much further north east and suggests Jayakatwang's forces were initially forced back.

215 These dharwapalas are still there.

216 An inscription of 1351 that says a temple was erected to remember the place where the murder took place. Oudheidkundig verslag 1928, p32

217 The siblings were Tribhuwana the oldest, Prajnaparamita, Narendra Duhita, and Gayatri Rajapatni the youngest. The *Desawarnana* (canto 46) confirms this, showing that this information was known at the Majapahit court in the mid-fourteenth century. See Sastrawan 2021, p170. In the Pararaton and the Kidul Rangga and the Kidul Harsa-wijaya, the daughters of Kertanegara who marry Wijaya are two rather than four in number.

218 Krom 1931 p349

219 Krom 1931 p347. The Kudadu inscription says something about this battle – 'from the east of Hanyiru, the enemy hoisted red and white coloured flags. Seeing them, Ardaraja (the son of Jayakatwang) laid his weapons and ran to Kapulungan in treason, which caused the destruction of his majesty's troops, but his majesty remained loyal to King Kertanegara'. Her majesty here is Prince Wijaya. see Slametmuljana, 1976, p36

220 Kidung Harsawijaya, Berg 1931, p11

221 Pararaton p85

222 Kidung Harsawijaya, Berg 1931, p12

223 At the hermitage, legend has it that Raden Wijaya had a rather odd experience. He asked for a coconut to be cut open but, to his amazement, it was not filled with juice but with cooked white rice. The female hermit Santamurti promptly proclaimed that this wonder was a sign that he would become king.

224 Brandes Pararaton p99, Krom 1931 p348

225 Slametmuljana 1976, p37, based on the Panji Wijayakrama.

226 The *Desawarnana* mentions Sagala and Wairosana but the locations are unclear. One of the places is probably in the centre of Singasari. Some (Moens, 1934, p554) suggest the other place is the Jawi temple some thirty kilometres from Singasari between Mount Arjuna and Mount Penanggungan.

227 Brandes Pararaton p88, Berg 1931 p13

228 Slametmuljana, 1976, p38.

229 The Galangan festival is still celebrated in Bali. These days, Galangan is celebrated every 210 days according to the Hindu Saka Calendar and it is the time when all the gods descent to earth and join the festivities. The spirits of ancestors and deceased relatives return to visit their homes, and for this reason a variety of rituals are conducted to welcome them. During Galungan, a 'barong' – the divine protector in the form of a mythical beast – is invited into homes as he makes his way through the village and its presence is meant to restore the balance between good and evil in the house. At the closure of the festival, the gods and ancestors return to their own realm.

230 This is a romantic episode in the Panji Wijayakrama. See also Slametmuljana, 1976, p38/39

231 This is based on the Kidung Harsawijaya, Berg 1931, p15. This story was probably written down in the mid-19th century in Bali and was discovered there by C.C. Berg in 1928. It's unclear on what this kidung is based but it provides an interesting narrative which should, however, be taken with a grain of salt.

232 This is a bit odd in many ways as it is highly unlikely that Jakakatong would give such a strategically located place to Prince Wijaya. Although the narrative suggests that the prince established the town of Majapahit, some sort of small community might have already been there. Indeed, it is the very close to the place where Kertanegara was deified, at the cemetery of Wurare. Archaeologists have also found evidence that there was already a settlement before 1292. See Gompert 2014, p94. The Majapahit is a fruit tree that grows luxuriantly in the Brantas Valley and that the name of Majapahit is based on the maja fruit is also confirmed in the shape of a crown of a Ganesha statue found in Singasari. The maja fruit was also painted on the carriages of future kings, such as Hayam

Wuruk while travelling around his realm in 1359.

233 Slametmuljana, 1976, p40

234 This is where Lawe is given the title Rangga – head of the guards – and from thereon he was known as Rangga Lawe (Slametmuljana, 1976, p41)

235 Much of the chapter is based on the Kidung Rangga Lawe, a script translated into Dutch by C.C. Berg in 1930.

236 The construction of Majapahit probably happened somewhere in the last months of 1292, so Sagara Winotan's visit actually took place in February or early March 1293 (Slametmuljana, 1976, p43), a few weeks before the Chinese armada arrived in Tuban.

237 Slametmuljana, 1976, p41-42

238 Book 2010 of the Yuan Shi (Groeneveld, p22): 'In the first month of the year 1293 they arrived at the island Ko-Ian (Billiton) and there deliberated on their plan of campaign'. The Chinese language 'Pasir Kapal' inscription on the tiny island of Serutu, just off the coast of Kalimantan, near Karimata, reads: 'Five hundred boats, Zhiyuan year 30, 1st month, 18th day, park here, 10 days have passed, going to conquer the king of Java, writing on this standing rock, to commemorate the glory of copper column.' This corresponds with February 25, 1293. See Hung et. al 2022. Hence, add a few days sailing from there to java and we conclude that the Chinese Armada arrived in Java in March 1293.

239 Groeneveldt, 1880, p. 25

240 Krom 1931 p357

241 Rockwell, T'oung Pao 15, p439

242 Rickleffs 2001 p4

243 See Hung et. al, 2022. On Serutu island, near Karimata, off the coast of west Kalimantan, a Chinese language inscription was found dated 25 February 1293.

244 What kind of ships they used for the expedition is not noted in the Chinese records, the Yuan Shi, but they were apparently large since smaller boats had to be constructed for entering the rivers of Java.

245 Krom 1931 p358

246 The existence of a bridge indicates that Sedayu was an important commercial centre for the Singasari kingdom. This floating bridge is mentioned several times in Chinese sources. Apparently trade was conducted on this bridge, as it was on a similar bridge in Melaka in the 15th century where, for a long time, the Javanese were one of the largest groups of traders (Groeneveldt 1960: 22-23).

247 Groeneveld 1880, p23

248 This description is based on the Harihara sculpture of the prince. See https://heritage.asean.org/view/MNI/MNI_CB1390 and is part of the collection of National Museum of Indonesia, inventory number 256/103a/2082.

249 Different sources give different narratives. The Chinese report – in book 210 of the Yuan Shi – reads that Prince Wijaya offered his submission but would not leave his army. The Pararaton makes no mention of submission at this early date; rather Wijaya waits until the arrival of the Mongol messengers before attacking Kediri in a three-pronged attack by his own army together with Wiraraja's men from Madura in the east and the Mongol army in the north. The Panji Wijayakrama offers a slightly different account in which Wiraraja's and the Chinese armies attack Kediri from the north and Wijaya's army from the south. For details on what the differences are, see Bade 2013, part 1.
250 Krom 1931 p361
251 Groeneveldt, 1880 p. 26.
252 The Kidung Harsawijaya
253 For a detailed comparison of the various sources on the Mongol invasion, see Bade 2013, p43 onwards.
254 There is no mention of a mass suicide by the palace ladies in the Chinese texts or the Pararaton. This is only mentioned in the Kidung Harsawijaya, the same account that also tells us that King Jayakatwang suddenly vanished into the heavens.
255 Rockhill p446
256 Pararaton p92
257 Slametmuljana 1976, p70.
258 Brandes p103-106 and Vickers, 2014, p14.
259 Rockhill p446.
260 Creese, 2004, chapter 4

261 Just like Tapasi, a relative of Kertanegara who had, decades earlier, married into the royal family of Champa. This marriage with the two Sumatran princesses was the very first act of solidarity in the Indonesian archipelago.
262 Based on a description in the Sumanasantaka by Mpu Monaguna, written in the thirteenth century, possibly in the days of King Widjaya. See Monaguna et al., 2013, especially page 8 onwards (cantos 52.1-65.15 of the poem). Also see Creese 2004, especially chapter 4. There is, however, no evidence that the coronation and wedding took place at the same day.
263 Slametmuljana 1976, p44
264 The coronation took place during the full moon, according to the Kidung Harshawijyaya, although this date is debated and not particularly relevant in terms of the course of history.
265 *Desawarnana* 45:1
266 *Desawarnana* 45:2
267 Years later, in 1305, Wijaya again publicly announced that he founded the Rajasa dynasty (Poetbatjarakan, 1936, p 373 and p378

268 The bath was called the 'tawur'.

269 It is unclear how many daughters Kertanegara had. There are reports there were four and, to add to the confusion, they also had personal names and titles, which were (titles in brackets) – Tribhuwana (Paramesvari), Narendraduhita (Mahadevi), Prajnaparamita (Jayendradevi) and Gayatri (Rajapatni). Piguad (Vol IV, p138) lists them as Tribhuwana, Duhita, Prajnaparamita and Gayatri. Raden Widjaya married four wives, which in some accounts (Pararaton) includes the two princesses from Melayu. That implies that Kertanegara had only two daughters – Tribhuwana and Gayatri – and this is a view held by some historians. It is also possible that there were four but two did not survive the Kediri war. One of them was possibly married to the son of Jayakatwang and it is unclear what happened to the other princess. But this is based on secondary sources, such as the Pararaton or Kidung Harshawidjaya. Primary sources such as charters issued in Wijaya's name between 1294 and 1305 strongly emphasise the importance of his four wives – all Kertanegara's daughters – by mentioning them at length and giving them elaborate epithets. It is unusual for a king's wife, especially multiple wives, to be included in Old Javanese charters. The reason for the special prominence of Widjaya's wives is that they are stated to be daughters of Kertanegara. It seems that Wijaya's status as the husband of Kertanegara's daughters was an important basis for his claim to legitimacy as his successor. The Kudadu charter (1294) describes Widjaya as 'having union with the daughters of Kertanagara'. The Sukhamrta charter (1296) provides more detail: 'all four siblings were his wives [...] all of them daughters of Kertanegara'. The Desawarṇana confirms these identifications in canto 46, showing that this information was accurately known at the Majapahit court in the mid-fourteenth century. See Pigaud (1960), Vol IV, p137-138, Sastrawan 2021, p170 and Krom 1931, p364. This would suggest that we only know of the Melayu princesses from secondary sources and thus, quite possibly, the whole story of the Malayu princesses is a legend, embedded in a historical context by the Pararaton's compilers and kidung poets much later. In the narrative of this book we assume they were married off to Majapahit noblemen.

270 Senior positions were patih (vizir), demung (chamberlain), kanuhuran (master of ceremonies), rangga (head of the guards) and a tummenggung (a commander in chief).

271 Slametmuljana, 1976, p47, based on the Pananggungan dated 1296

272 We do not know exactly when he came into power. It is often assumed that he was crowned as king upon the death of his grandmother Gayatri in 1350, but some inscriptions suggest it was probably a few years later. We assume it to be around 1353.

273 Kudadu charter (1294)

274 It's uncertain when Gajah Mada was born but it is generally assumed

to be 1293 or 1294, just after the fall of Singasari, based on his position in the military nearly twenty years later.

275 At least we do not hear anything of his father, possibly because he lost his life in these wars.

276 As for his name, in the historical texts the elephant is also the mode of transport of the God Indra and thus, this part of his name can refer to the man being a conduit for kings.

277 He is the son of Dara Jingga, one of the Sumatran princess who was brought over, initially as a gift to Kertanegara. His father appears to have been Majapahit nobleman Adwayawarman. See Kern 1913.

278 Pararaton p125.

279 There is some confusion about the year this happened but Brandes (Pararaton, p125) and Berg in 'Opmerkingen over de Chronologie van de Oudste Geschiedenis van Maja Pahit en over Krtarajarasajayawardhana's Regeering', Bijdragen tot de Taal-, Land- en Volkenkunde van Nederlandsch Indië 97 (1938): 152 suggest this timeline.

280 We only have the Pararaton and the Kidung Rangga Lawe as sources, which means that there is not a good foundation for what exactly happened in this rebellion, or if it actually took place. The *Desawarnana* jumps over this period rather quickly in a few sentences and does not mention Lawe at all. See Berg 1930 and Berg 1931 p372

281 Sorandaka, van den Berg, 1939. Translation into English by the author.

282 Ibid.

283 In the Kidung Rangga this makes more sense as there Lawe is described as the son of Wiraraja.

284 The machinations of Mahapati, the influential intriguer, is the main part of the Kidul Sorandaka.

285 This is the 1296 inscription of Penanggungan, see also Slametmuljana 1976, p51.

286 Statement in Sumenep kraton in Madura

287 See Wright 1977 and Nicholl 1983

288 The charters issued in Wijaya's name between 1294 and 1305 strongly emphasize the importance of his wives by mentioning them at length and giving them elaborate epithets. It is unusual for a king's wives, especially multiple wives, to be included in Old Javanese charters. The reason for the special prominence of Wijaya's wives is that they are the daughters of Kertanegara so perhaps Wijaya's struggled to maintain the loyalty of his subordinates. He felt the need to stress that he, husband of Kertanegara's daughters, was the legitimate ruler. See also Sastrawan 2021, p170.

289 Adityawarman was born around in 1294 in Majapahit, around the same time at Gajah Mada and Jayanegara. According to the Kuburajo inscription discovered in Limo Kaum, West Sumatra, Adityawarman's

father was Majapahit nobleman Adwayawarman and according to the Pararaton his mother was Dara Jingga, one of the two princesses from Sumatra. He might have visited China on a diplomatic expedition in 1325 if, as some historians believe, he is the envoy whom Chinese source calls Sengk'ia-lie-yu-lan. See Kern (1913), 'Grafsteenopschrift van Koeboer Radja', Bijdragen tot de Taal-, Land- en Volkenkunde van Nederlands-Indië, p. 401–404.

290 The Pararaton p123 suggests he was sick, but it is not known from what.

291 *Desawarnana* 48:1. These two daughters were the queens of Kahuripan and Daha. Kahuripan was near Singasari while Daha was the old name for Kediri.

292 While the Kidul Rangga Lawe and Sorandaka (in Berg 1939, p1) place these rebellions in the reign of Widjaya, the Pararaton alone puts them all in the reign of his son Jayanegara. See also Sastrawan 2021, p176 and van den Berg 1939. The fall of Sora is taken from the Sorandaka, a poem (*kidung*) written in Bali years after the fall of Majapahit, in 1754 AD. For details, see van den Berg 1939.

293 Sorandaka I: 20-65. The conversation with Mahapati that follows.

294 The Sorandaka writes it was a *kemuning* tree, which is the murraya paniculata, commonly known as orange jasmine, orange jessamine or China box.

295 Sorandaka I: 32 as in van den Berg 1939.

296 Sorandaka I: 33-34.

297 Sorandaka I: 62

298 Sorandaka I: 69

299 Sorandaka I: 92

300 Sorandaka I: 122

301 Sorandaka I: 127

302 Sorandaka II: 25

303 Sorandaka II:32

304 Sorandaka II:64

305 Sorandaka II: 103-118

306 Sorandaka II: 121-130

307 Sorandaka II:152-153

308 Slametmuljana 1976, p54

309 This is also confirmed in the *Desawarnana* 48:2

310 The Majapahit army followed and razed the town of Gending – close to Probolinggo – to the ground, which suggests that Nambi and his forces were moving south into the mountains to look for shelter.

311 In a town called Rabut Buhayabang. See Stapel Vol 1, p267.

312 This is in Pajarakan. See Krom 1931 p375, Pararaton p127 or Stapel Vol 1, p267.

313 The fall of Nambi in or near Lumajang happened in 1316.

314 At least that is what a Balinese edicts from 1304, 1324 and 1328 seem to suggest. See van Stein Callenfels in Oudheidkundig verslag 1924, p31.

315 There is no clear evidence of this, but it is not unreasonable to assume.

316 Pararaton p127. This is the first time that Gajah Mada is mentioned in the records. Assuming he was born around 1294, he must have been 24 or 25 years old at the time of the Kuti rebellion in 1318 or 1319.

317 It is unknown where Badander is but perhaps this is where Gajah Mada grew up. The whole escape shows how dangerous the whole situation was for Jayanegara.

318 We do not know how he was put to death and the Pararaton p127 is the only source for this. Nowhere else is the death of Mahapati confirmed.

319 In Balinese texts it seems the wife was actually Gajah Mada's, which would give more credence to his murder of Jayanegara. See Oudheidkundig Verslag, 1924, p146-152.

320 The item of clothing was a 'kemitan', which seems to have given him some sort of protection. Maybe it was an amulet.

321 We only know what happened from Gajah Mada's words. The assassination of Jayanegara was in 1328. Whatever happened between Gayatri and Gajah Mada remains a mystery, but we see that they both benefited from pushing Jayanegara from the throne. There have also been suggestions that Jayanegara had a fling with Gajah Madah's wife (Berg 1951, p221). It is remarkable that Gajah Madah, who would have been the king's favourite after he saved his life during the Kuti rebellion, turned against the king so soon.

322 *Desawarnana* 48:3. It suggests he had links with Kediri where the adoration of Visnu was (probably) stronger. See also Pigaud 1962 Vol IV, p140/141). Later, the Prince of Wengker, who also originated from Kediri, was a Visnuite, as referred to in the Bililuk charter.

323 It is unknown where that is. But given his links with Kediri, its makes sense to start looking near this city.

324 Immediately after Jayanegara's death there are two people with a strong claim to the throne. These are Gayatri Rajapatni herself and her young daughter Tribhuwanatungadewi. But Gayatri chose not to sit on the throne, allowing her daughter to become queen with herself as regent. The added benefit was that if there were any future claims on the throne – given that Gayatri might have been involved with the assassination of Jayanegara – these claims could not be made against her daughter.

325 Later, the religious pendulum swung again and Hayam Wuruk, the first born son of Tribhuwanatunggadewi, would reverse this and assign Shivaists. He also installed officials to oversee the holy places of the *rshi*, the Shivaist seers.

326 Sadeng was, according to the *Desawarnana*, on the south coast of

eastern Java. Berg points at Bali, based on similarities to other stories, such as the Usana Jawa, but this is very unlikely. See Berg, De Sadeng-oorlog, 1951. In his book Suma Oriental (p198), Tome Pires also mentions a 'Chamda' in the eastern part of Java and de Graaf and Pigeaud wondered if this was Sadeng (see De Graaf and Pigeaud, 1974, p192-194).

327 His name was Raden Kembar. 'Raden' means prince, so he was a noble and possibly part of the royal family.

328 Berg (1939) questions the whole story of Sadeng. When the Sadeng story is over in the Pararaton (page 139-140), it is followed by a sort of announcement: a certain Tuhan Wuruju was a son of Pamelekahan (possibly 'Melaka') and a comment – 'when he clapped the whip, it was heard everywhere and it alarmed at Majapahit'. According to Rouffaer, that may be the oldest entry of the name of Malaka in the history books, which had already begun to spread terror even in the Javanese capital.

329 All this happened in 1331 and straight after the conquest of Sadeng, Gajah Mada was appointed *patih* of the whole empire. It must have been an heroic victory because even on Gajah Mada's funeral references are made to his victory in Sadeng (see Stapel 1, p270) and a statue erected in 1332 recorded that 'at the time that the Queen was victorious in Sa...', with the last letters unreadable, but probably referring to Sadeng..

330 The head of the delegation was the same man who made a similar trip in 1325 (see Rockhill 1914 p 447). As gifts they planned to carry exotic birds, jewellery and a golden letter.

331 It is unclear if West Java was a unified part of Java at the time, although Berg assumed it was.

332 What 'palapa' exactly is, we do not know. Some have argued it is a fruit or food, others believe it is sexual abstinence or maybe even a sort of break from religious rites. But Gajah Mada meant not to retire until the whole archipelago – what is called Indonesia today as well as parts of Malaysia and southern Thailand – submitted to Majapahit.

333 See Pararaton p141. Prapanca lists the places as Gurun (Gorong), Seran (Seram in the Moluccas), Tajungpura (Kalimantan), Haru, Pahang (Malaysian peninsula), Dompo, Bali, Sunda, Palembang and Tumasik (Singapore).

334 Prapanca and Hayam Wuruk were about the same age.

335 The Majapahit nine-decked 'jong' ships were larger than the Portuguese ship of the 15th century, but as no shipwrecks have been discovered their exact size is unknown. It is believed they carried up to 1,000 people. See Averoes 2022. Javanese cartography must have been well developed by the time. But many old Javanese charts have disappeared through sheer neglect. Others may have been deliberately destroyed by the Portuguese by Royal Decree of 13th November 1504 with respect to all maps, charts and logbooks connected with navigation south of the equator. Not a single indigenous specimen is known to

have been preserved, which presumably explains why pre-Portuguese Indonesian cartography has never been the subject of any specific study. See also Gelpke 1994 and Gelpke 1995.

336 This paragraph is based on an inscription on the back of a Amoghapaca statue that year. See Krom 1931 p392 and Slametmuljana, 1976, p61.

337 Des 49 and 79. The 'nefarious and vile' attributes assigned to the Balinese leaders were because of their unwillingness to subject to Majapahit rulers. Bali is the only island where Buddhist shrines were erected and inscriptions in 1386 suggest that Bali continued to be closely aligned with Java. In the following centuries, when Majapahit was in decline, Bali would become the centre of Javanese literature. Even today, much of Bali's culture and heritage – its temples, ceremonies, dress code – has its origins in Majapahit. See also Stutterheim 1929.

338 While the remains at Trowulan give us an idea of what urban life in Majapahit was like, Panataran, located just north of Blitar, offers a glimpse of religious life in those days. It is the only east Javanese site where the full extent of the complex is revealed today. For a full description of the temple see Kinney 2003, p179 onwards. Penataran was constructed over 250 years and the first reference is from 1197, with extensions between 1319 and 1454, so mostly during the reigns of Jayanegara and Hayam Wuruk when Gajah Mada was the *patih*.

339 Much like the *bale agung* in Balinese temples of today.

340 It is uncertain if this was capped with a *meru*, as this wooden material has perished. But similar temples in Bali do have such a meru.

341 The term 'nusantara' came into use much later in Majapahit's history.

342 Probably Boyolangu, as this is where later temples were built for her.

343 Stutterheim 1931.

344 Kwa Chong Guan, 'Sradda Sri Rajapatni: An Exploration of Majapahit Mortuary Ritual' in Miksic and Endang, 'The Legacy of Majapahit', 1995, p78.

345 Stutterheim 1931.

346 'Cakrawarti prabu'. See Desawarnarna 68.5 and Vickers 2014, p53. Many assume that Hayam Wuruk became king after the death of Gayatri, but The Gajah Mada inscription of 23 April 1351 states that the paramount ruler was still Hayam Wuruk's mother. He must therefore have been crowned after that date. On the other hand, a large pavilion was constructed nearby Penataran – that is Situs Umpak Balekambang -in 1350 and this might well have been constructed for the inauguration ceremony of Hayam Wuruk at Penataran.

347 Krom 1931 p420.

348 That we know from the 1375 inscription of Singasari. This is also where we find a reference to the royal council that advises the new king.

349 Pigeaud, 1962, IV, p403.

350 Plate 9, line 3-4 of the ferry charter of 1358. In Pigeaud 1962.

351 The festival was in the months Phalguna and Caitra, which are February, March, and April.

352 See also Pigaud 1962, IV, p273.

353 This was the *angastreni* (consecration) and the four religious dominions were Visnuists, Shivaists, Buddhists and frairs (*reshi*)) while officials would come to make a flower-homage (*Desawarnana* 84 and Pigaud 1962, IV, p284/5).

354 On Caitra, see See Pigaud, 1962, IV, p277. Bubat was around 4 ha. It was probably located north of Majapahit, not far from Cancggu, where the Kali Brangkal and Kali Gunting meet.

355 Bubat was a more appropriate location for all this than the sanctified court. Hall 2000 p81.

356 Chili's only arrived centuries later when the Portuguese brought them to Java's shores, but there were pastes – 'sambals'– of Javanese and Balinese long pepper and ginger. See Surya and Tedjakusuma, 202.

357 See also Bhimantoka 81.35-38

358 On this day, land use and ownership was to be clearly delineated. The status of villages claimed by religious establishments was to be investigated, and subsequently inscriptions were to be issued that would define and document jurisdiction. Hall 2000 p92.

359 This would continue every day and each day, a new shrine was added. This was also accompanied by fire-offering ceremonies performed by Buddhist and Shivaist priests. See Pigaud 1962, IV, p276.

360 Pigaud 1962, IV, p279 onwards.

361 The great hall was called the *witana*. It was considered an insult if a regional governor did not show up, as Wiraraja did when Wijaya was king.

362 Over-population had clearly not yet set in, that would only come in the 19th century.

363 In a sense, the royals benefitted from more land being cultivated as it meant more tribute to the king but on the other hand, the rural Majapahit economy also benefited from royal rule. See Pigaud 1962, IV, p301.

364 *Desawarnana* 88:5-3

365 Although it is difficult to believe that many had the courage to do so.

366 *Desawarnana* 91:9.

367 Timekeeping in the day was probably done by the position of the sun and the length of the shadow of a stick, a relatively accurate way of measuring time for any location close to the equator.

368 *Desawarnana* 90:2-1

369 This suggests it was the custom for the king, for one day, to waive his rights to divine worship and mix with people on an equal footing. See

Desawarnana 90:5-6, Pigaid 1962, IV, p314.

370 The 'Juru i Angin' in *Desawarnana* 91:1

371 Pigaud 1962, IV, p316

372 For details, see Pigaud, 1938, paragraph 464, page 501. All based on *Desawarnana* 91.

373 *Desawarnana* 91:9-2. This bowing ritual is still common in Java today.

374 A Batu Tulis inscription from 1333 suggests that in that year, or maybe a little earlier, a new kingdom arose in what is now Bogor in west Java. This is the Sundanese Pajajaran kingdom and the inscription is evidence that this kingdom established itself in the mountainous parts of west Java despite Majapahit's dominant influence across Java. See also Stapel 1, p277

375 There is no evidence of this but such attempts were mentioned in the Kidung Sunda, a book of probable Balinese provenance. This kidung narrates the story of King Hayam Wuruk of Majapahit who was looking for a bride.

376 Prabhu means 'king'. Actually, the Sunda king was re-named Prabu Wangi ('King with a pleasant scent') after he died. His descendants, the people of Sunda, came to be known as Siliwangi ('the successors of Wangi').

377 Her name is mentioned in the Pararaton as Dyah Pitaloka Citraresmi or Citra Rashmi; born in 1340 she was seventeen years old.

378 The nine-decked 'jong' ships were larger than the Portuguese ships of the 15th century, but as no shipwrecks have been discovered, their exact size is unknown. It is believed they carried up to 1,000 people. See Averoes 2022. There is also a reference to a jong in Bujangga Manik's travelogue (Noorduyn 2008). Another jong's dimensions are described in Bujangga Manik (Noorduyn 2006, p262, verse 996-997): 'a jong eight fathoms wide, its length twenty-five fathoms.' That puts it at about 46 metres long and 15 metres wide. See West 2020, p243 although he suggests we must thus allow for some exaggeration on Bujangga Manik's part.

379 Kidul Sundayana, Berg, 1927, p79.

380 Kidul Sundayana, Berg, 1927, p78.

381 Kidul Sundayana, Berg, 1927, p82.

382 Kidul Sundayana 58b.

383 This is the Kidul Sunda, translated by Berg into Dutch in 1927. It represents the Sundanese view of what happened afterwards, so has to be taken with a pinch of salt.

384 Kidul Sundayana 65a.

385 Kidul Sundayana, Berg, 1927, p96

386 For an example, see such a cannon at the Metropolitan Museum in New York. It is almost one metre long and had a clear Majapahit

'surya' sun emblem on it. See https://www.metmuseum.org/art/collection/search/37742

387 Kidul Sunadayana, Berg, 1927, p105 and Krom 1931 p404.

388 Kidul Sundayana, berg, 1927, p115.

389 Brandes p158.

390 Whether the princess died that day is questionable. On a ferry charter issued a year later, in 1358, there is a reference to a matrimonial alliance that might refer to the Sundanese princess (Ferry Charter, Plate 1, line 4 as in Pigeaud 1962, III, p156). But there are no other accounts of what happened to her.

391 Kidung Sunda, part 3, canto 74 (Berg 1927, p132)

392 Japer 1928, p9 suggests that Gajah Mada ran off to Sengguruh, near Malang.

393 The Battle of Bubat led to a schism between Majapahit and the Sundanese that never healed; even today Sunda has its own language and identity separate from the rest of Java. In Sundanese poems and stories, the death of the Sundanese king and the princess are commemorated as noble acts. Even today, it's hard to find a road named after Gajah Mada or Hayam Wuruk in most cities in West Java and it is equally difficult to find a road named Siliwangi in eastern or Central Java. In August 2017, nearly seven centuries after the Battle of Bubat, the central Java city of Yogyakarta tried to address this issue. Two new ring roads surrounding the city, located in the former Majapahit territories, were named *Siliwangi* and *Pajajaran* (Nurmansyah, Suara.com, 2017) in an attempt to end generations of bitterness between the Sundanese and the rest of Java.

394 And there were no more conquests in Gajah Mada's second term as *patih*.

395 Krom 1931 p404.

396 In the Pararaton she is known as Bhre Lasem.

397 The Hikayat Raja Pasai, a 14th-century Aceh chronicle, describes this Majapahit naval invasion on Samudra Pasai in 1350. See Hill, 1960, p157 onwards.

398 See Ludivico and Jones, 1863, page 250-251. A footnote on page 251 adds that it is improbable the Javanese (Malay) sailed this far but that they knew of Australia: 'This sentence is very important if it should point to latitudes on a line with or south of Australia. The point where the shortest day would only last four hours would be 15° south of the southern point of Van Diemen's Land (Tasmania). It is most improbable that the Malay skipper should have been so far south; yet his statements indicate a knowledge of countries as far south, at least, as Australia.'

399 Archaeologists at Flinders University have identified rare images of Moluccan vessels from Indonesia's eastern islands in rock art paintings that may provide the first archaeological evidence of visitors from

Southeast Asia from somewhere other than Makassar in Sulawesi. These were not people from Majapahit. But there were contacts between the Indonesian archipelago and Australia and therefore we cannot rule out that there was contact between Australia and Majapahit. See also Flinders University 2023.

400 The description of the trip starts in *Desawarnana* 17.

401 Pigaud 1962, IV, p161.

402 Candi Rimbi is located south of Trowulan, in the foothills or Arjuna and Welirang. The temple is unusual as it features a multitude of creatures with floppy ears. There is also a depiction of two people in a cauldron, possibly a rather terrible punishment. Kinney 2003, p216-219.

403 *Desawarnana* 18:3, Pigaud 1962, IV, p54.

404 It is unknown when the caravan started this year, but it was in the dry season month of September and on that day, Sirius was at its zenith and geomancers may have decided that was a good time.

405 *Desawarnana* 18:2

406 Pigaud 1962 IV, p59.

407 *Desawarnana* 18:6.

408 Pigaud 1962, IV, p55.

409 Pigaud 1962, IV, p62.

410 It is not confirmed where Gajah Mada hid after the disaster at Bubat, but this might well have been a place where he had a loyal following and where he felt safe.

411 Pigaud, 1962, IV, p65 states that this place was near today's Sengguruh, just south of Malang; Hadi Sidomulyo (Bullough 2007) puts the town further north.

412 *Desawarnana* 22:1.

413 Making salt on ponds near the sea was only possible in the dry season; in the wet season these ponds would not dry. A saline spring would provide a supply of salt throughout the year.

414 Pigaud 1962, IV, p79.

415 This is also a town that was conquered in 1331, some 28 years earlier, by Gajah Mada.

416 This is possibly the reason for the issue of the so-called Batur Charter (Pigaud 1962, IV, p100. See also p145). It is a copper plate of which only fragments now remain.

417 *Desawarnana* 32:3 and Pigaud 1962, IV, p98. He also notes the palm-fibre roofs, only used for temples in Majapahit, but seen everywhere in Segara.

418 A total of seven in the next ten years. The first one was in 1353, the last one in 1363 (Pigaud 1962, IV, p161).

419 It is also called a *puspasarira*. In Bali it is today it is a *puspa* or *sekar*. See Kwa Chong Guan, 'Sradda Sri Rajapatni: An Exploration of Majapahit Mortuary Ritual' in Miksic and Endang, 'The Legacy of

Majapahit', 1995, p78.

420 See also Galestin, Houtbouw, p53.

421 Pigaud 1962, IV, P196.

422 It is also called Kutaramanawa (Krom 1931 p421).

423 This is Candi Sumber Jati, now in the city of Blitar.

424 An interesting observation is that at this new location, the entrance to this temple lines up with the entrance to the temple dedicated to Gayatri (Candi Gayatri), far from the temple.

425 CC Berg suggested once that perhaps Gajah Mada was poisoned by the royal family, but this seems unlikely. Old age is a more likely explanation.

426 For the royal council, see *Desawarnana* 71: 2 and Krom, 1910, p158-168). These were Hayam Wuruk, his uncle Bhre Wengker, his mother Trubhuwana (Bhre Kahuripan), his aunt Rajadewi Maharajasa (Bhre Daha), and his two younger sisters Bhre Pajang and Indudewi. The husband of Bhre Pajang was also in attendance, a man called Singhawardhanna. There were seven, so this meant that one of the sisters was not married yet.

427 Pigaud 1962, IV, p251.

428 Pigaud 1962, p215.

429 This is also suggested in *Desawarnana* 73:1

430 It is also possible that another local ruler in southeast Sumatra, perhaps in Palembang, was responsible for sending the mission in around 1379. Majapahit: inspiration, Vickers, 2014, p17. Adityawarman was the son of a Melayu princess brought over in Kertanegara's days. He lived to a great age and might have visited the Yuan court in the capacity as a diplomatic envoy as early as 1325 and 1332. In 1327, the Javanese sent a gold spotted leopard and a white parrot over to China. A group of 83 people who arrived in China in 1331 with a golden letter and other presents, led by a man called Kala, also led an expedition to China in 1325 (see Rockhill T'oung Pao 15, 1914, p446/447). In short, there was peace between China's Yuan dynasty and Majapahit. He was devoted to Buddhism, deeply interested in demonic, tantric, and Buddhist rituals, which decades ago had enchanted King Kertanegara so much. We know this of the so-called Manjusri inscription which was destroyed by fire later. See 'Early research on Sivaic Hinduism during the Majapahit Era' by Hariani Santiko in Miksic, 1995, p58. This would explain the 70 year gap between the temple itself and some of the dates on statues inside the temple. The temple contains statues of the devilish Hayagriwa and a dagger-and-skull-equipped god. See Kinney, 2007, p124.

431 An inscription of 1356 discovered in Sumatra carries a list of kings including those from Majapahit. But it is a local king, Adityawarman, not the kings of Majapahit, who is listed first; in the previous inscription it was the other way around, Krom 1931, p413. See also the inscription

of Soeroaso of 1375 (Moens, 1924, p571).

432 One wonders what the Javanese did with the paper money; perhaps they spent it in China to buy goods to take back to Java? See Majapahit inspiration, Vickers, 2014, p16-17.

433 Sang Nila Utama, a prince from Palembang in south Sumatra, attracted initially by its white sands, landed on an island known then as Temasek. Chancing upon a fast and ferocious looking animal, Sang Nila Utama was told that it was a 'singa', a lion. Seeing it as a good omen, he called the place the Lion City – Singapura. He ruled Singapura for 48 years until his death in 1347.

434 According to the Pararaton, which is not always accurate in dating events, Hayam Wuruk died in 1389. But the last discovered copper plates that mention Hayam Wuruk as king are the Karang Bosem plates, carved in 1368. In another plate from 1405, the Walandit inscription, Hayam Wuruk is mentioned with his name given to him after his death ––Hyang Wekasing Suka. Hence, it is likely that Hayam Wuruk died somewhere in between, possibly in 1389. He died relatively young at the age of fifty-five. It's unknown why he died, but it was probably from natural causes (a murder or an illness would probably have been mentioned in the Pararaton).

435 The description of his funeral is based on the Kidung Sunda, starting in part III, canto 48 as in Berg 1927, p126.

436 In the Pararaton she is referred to as Bhre Lasem 'the beautiful'. Bhre Lasem is a title – Princess of Lasem – and there are more people who are referred to in these terms, such as 'Bhre Lasem, the fat one', the wife of Wirabumi. Over the generations, the Rajasa dynasty produced fewer children. It started to die out because repeated marriages inside the family became increasingly risky. Inbreeding or consanguinity is a cause of low fertility rates, birth defects, abnormalities and decreased cognitive abilities in children with weaker immune systems. See also Fareed et. al, 2017

437 She was born after the Battle of Bubat in 1357 (it is only after that battle that Hayam Wuruk married her mother). By the time of Hayam Wuruk's death in 1389, she would have been at most 32 years old, possibly a few years younger.

438 Her fondness for arts over statecraft is drawn from the fact that while she was the heir to the crown, it is her husband that is mentioned when it comes to matters of state.

439 He would die soon and we only know his name after death, which was similar to that of Hayam Wuruk's final name – Hyang Wekas ing Sukha.

440 It is unclear where Hyam Wuruk's shrine is located. It is assumed to be Candi Cetos (Krom 1929, p25-27, Kinnay et al, 2003, p285), near Kediri, right at the heart of the empire.

441 This we don't know for certain. After he finished his book, the *Desawarnana*, in 1365, he left the scene and he was not heard of again.

442 We do not know when Prapanca died.

443 It was only in 1397 that the whole region was subject to Majapahit control again. After the conquest, the capital of Sumatra (also named Suwarnabhumi) was moved from Jambi to Palembang, on the coast.

444 Vickers, 2014, p18.

445 Rentse 1936, p303.

446 The Pararaton says that the boy was given a shrine in Paramasukhapura. It is unclear where this is but presumably a place close to the shrine of Hayam Wuruk.

447 The Paraton tells us that in 1400 the king decided to become a 'bhagawan'. Brandes translated this as a 'hermit' even though the king did return to his duties some years later. But King Wikramawardhana might also simply have given himself a spiritual title and did not actually retreat to a hermitage. For a discussion, see Krom, 1923, II, p428.

448 Pigeaud, 1960, IV, p172.

449 It is actually very unclear what exactly happened in 1400 and how tensions grew between Wikramawardhana and Wirabumi. Perhaps Suhita was already seen as the next in line if Wikramawardhana died and that was possibly unacceptable to Wirabumi.

450 The word 'Regreg' means slowly, with halts and jerks and this is how this civil war started. It is usually referred to as the Paregreg, but that term is based on a linguistic misunderstanding. In the Pararaton, events are labelled by adding the prefix pa- to one or more keywords. For example, the Javanese attack on Malayu in Sumatra in 1275 is called Pamalayu. Hence the better translation of Paregreg is 'the Regreg event'. Sastrawan 2021, p119.

451 Actually, the new emperor wanted to confirm relations between China and other countries and on 3 October 1402 he issued a proclamation ordering missions to Annam, Siam, Java, Ryukyu, Japan, Xi-yang, Samudera (Aceh) and Champa. The envoys to Java were Wen Liangfu, an Investigative Commissioner, and Ning Shan, an ambassador. In October 1403, just before the Paregreg war started, they arrived on the island. It is unsure what message they brought back to China but they must have noticed the tensions in the land.

452 It was long believed that Wirabumi's son, Bhre Daha (Prince Daha) was still a little boy during the civil war and was captured and brought to Majapahit, where he was raised. When he was about thirty years old, in 1437, he wanted to avenge his father's death and rebelled against Majapahit. This tale seems, however, to be based on a mistaken reading of dates and titles. See Noorduyn 1979, p216-217.

453 The bathing places were finished in 1415 and they might have been installed to celebrate Wikramawardhana's victory in the war of succession

over his brother-in-law. See Kinney 2003, p209. It is interesting that there were no large building projects in these years, no major new temples, but just additions to existing ones. Perhaps there was a lack of funds or uncertainty about what was to come.

454 This was 'Pu Ni', Brunei. See Krom 1931, p432.

455 In the 1370s, in the days of Hayam Wuruk, Brunei was attacked by Sulu raiders. Majapahit helped but did not seem to care much that Brunei was looted.

456 A kati is a measure of weight of 760 grams. Forty kati of wood is not a lot. Possibly this forty kati is a value measurement and is the amount of silver that is equivalent to their camphor shipments. A tahil, another measurement of weight, is 38 grams. Twenty tahil is one kati.

457 We do now know how Java responded to this Chinese order to send camphor from Brunei to China instead of Majapahit, but they could not have been pleased about it.

458 Groeneveldt, 1880, p69.

459 Groeneveldt, 1880, p36.

460 Groeneveldt, 1880, p36.

461 Krom, 1931, p435.

462 Pigaud en de Graaf 176, p7.

463 The Pararaton mentions a 'lantaran' in 1416, although its unknown what that exactly is. Here it is assumed to be a landslide. See Pararaton p152.

464 The Pararaton mentions an earthquake in Julung-puput in 1411. See Pararaton p152.

465 The Brantas river started to narrow, slowly cutting off access to the rest of the archipelago. See 'The Destruction of Majapahit from the Perspective of Geology by S. Sartono and Bandono in Micsik, and Endang, 1995, especially p49-53.

466 It is actually unknown if irrigation problems caused a famine later in 1426.

467 Originally named Ma He, Zheng He was born to a Muslim family in Yunnan. The family had migrated to China from Central Asia and had served in the Mongol administration in this region. Both Zheng He's father and grandfather bore the title of haji, indicating that they had completed pilgrimages to Mecca. In 1381, when the Ming army invaded Yunnan to subdue the Mongol remnants there, eleven-year-old Ma He was captured. The young prisoner of war was castrated and given, as a servant, to the court of Prince Yan, Zhu Di. The intimate company with the young prince bred a lifetime trust. See also Wei 2014.

468 Ma Huan p 91

469 Ma Huan p 90

470 They are mentioned in the *Desawarnana* 83

471 Ma Huan did not write it down but this might have been the case

and is something recorded in Bhomantaka 40.5.1.

472 Ma Yuen p 88

473 Ma Yuen p 88

474 The well-forested mountain slopes in the region regulated water supply and thus, the 14th century rivers would have a much higher water mark then today and this explains why Canggu and, further inland, Bubat were accessible by sea-craft of the time. At least large river-vessels could be brought up from the coast by paddling or poling. At the end of the monsoon season, Canggu and Bubat were in a frenzy, full of all sorts of ships that had recently arrived. See Pigaud, 1962, IV, p291

475 Foreigners, both Indians and Chinese, were frequent visitors at the East Javanese seaports. The existence of foreign trading quarters in Canggu, the Majapahit port on the river Brantas, is referred to in the *Desawarnana* 86. The Chinese and Moorish kampungs still extant in modern Javanese towns and partly dating from the 17th century are indications of the existence of foreigners' quarters in several mercantile towns of the 14th century Majapahit realm. Note also that the first Muslim sultanate in the archipelago was founded in Aceh in north Sumatra even before the founding of the Majapahit empire by Hayam Wuruk's grandfather. See Pigaud 1962, IV, p291/2.

476 Bubat was situated at some distance from the royal court, outside the town of Majapahit. It was around 6 soccer pitches in size, 4ha. See also *Desawarnana* 86:2.

477 Chili's only arrived centuries later when the Portuguese brought them to Java's shores, but there were pastes –'sambals'– of Javanese and Balinese long pepper and ginger. See Surya and Tedjakusuma, 2022

478 See also Bhimantoka 81.35-38.

479 According to archaeologist Agus Munandar, the settlement in Trowulan is based on a geographical division between the settlements of the common people, the nobility or people of wealth and the courtiers. Some have, in the past, suggested that there was a large network of canals criss-crossing the city. This idea is rejected by most archaeologists but the Trowulan museum has a large Majapahit city map with large canals on it.

480 Even today, the word 'piggybank' or 'savings' in Javanese is still *celengan*, which means wild boar.

481 These are so-called 'makara', sea monsters that were the vehicle of Baruna, God of the Sea. See Damais p70 and p73 and p145. On Majapahit ceramics, see also Miksic 2009, p68-69 or Muller 1978.

482 Some, such as Dyvendak, have argued that the number of 200-300 foreign families is too high. See Ma Huan p 91, footnote 3

483 Bhimantoka 81.35-38

484 To facilitate easy decapitation, the head and the body of a figurine were made separately and then superficially attached to each other. This

decapitation rite was fashionable in Southeast Asia. See Muller 1978, p63-64.

485 Stutterheim 1948, p9-10.

486 It was a strange looking fruit and he described it in detail, a kind of pomegranate, but the skin inside looked like the case of an orange and it has four white lumps of flesh that have a delicious sweet-sour taste. This is the oldest ever mention of a mangosteen. Ma Huan p92

487 In the *Desawarnana*, Prapanca makes a distinction between the *pura* (palace compound) and the *Nagara*, or city. The Nagara should be interpreted essentially to mean all those inhabitants whose occupations tied them directly to the palace compound.

488 The eastern boundary of the city was most likely marked by the course of the present-day River Brangkal, which flows northwards from the foothills of Mt Anjasmoro and separates the district of Trowulan from neighbouring Puri. This eastern boundary, moreover, finds perfect accordance with Prapanca's description of King Hayam Wuruk's eastern progress of 1359. If the eastern boundary of the city can be determined with some confidence, not so the western limit, about which the literature is silent. Even so, given the probability that this boundary was also formed by a river, a reasonable choice would be the Kali Gunting, which likewise flows northwards from the mountains, passing through the town of Mojoagung, before turning eastwards to join the Brantas at Mojokerto. The latter section of the Kali Gunting might well be the river forming the northern boundary of the plain of Bubat, as referred to in *Desawarnana* 86:2. Source: email conversation with Hadi Sidomulyo

489 Pigeaud 1962, IV, p516-520

490 From here on, the description of the city follows the map of Stutterheim (1948) and the later geographical surveys described as in Gomperts et. al (2008).

491 The description of the area and royal palace is based on Sutterheim's 1948 account of the kraton of Majapahit. see also Gompert et al, 2008, p423. As an aside, Tantular's Sutasoma (written circa AD 1385) confirms that the crossroads is situated to the east of the watchtower and the crossroads is to the south of the army mustering field that coincides with the southeastern area of the *alun-alun*.

492 Ma Huan p 172

493 Ma Huan page 92

494 At the heart of the royal city was a crossroads and a nearby *alun-alun* (open field or great square in front of the court). Prapanca refers to the sacred crossroads with the Sanskrit word *catuspatha* which literally means 'a place where four roads meet'. See Gompert et al, 2008, p420

495 Pigeaud 1962, IV, p516-520.

496 From Bhomantaka 5: 1

497 This was a *wayang baber* performance Ma Huan saw. See Ma Huan

p 93.

498 Called the *juru pangalasan*

499 Ma Huan p 95

500 Ma Huan p 93

501 Guards seem to have received some pay in cash out of the treasury of their master, and for the rest they subsisted upon the revenue of their family's estates. In time of peace they were not permanently in attendance but served by turns, every man for some days a week. In a scripture, the Nawanatya, the functions of the superior royal servants at court are described with full particulars and their incomes are mentioned. The incomes in cash are stated in hundreds and thousands *per diem*; they came from the market.

502 Ma Yuan Page 87. The wall of the royal compound was made of large red bricks (no mortar was used, Sutterheim 1948, p13), thick and high (*Desawarnana* 8:1), with one side of the compound about a kilometre long. This is based on archaeological excavations, mapping and confirmed by a description of Chinese traveller Ma Huan. The kraton was about 1,000 metres x 1,800 metres. The wall was about 8-11 metres high. See Sutterheim, 1948, p8 with an iron entrance door gate in the north.

503 The *panggung,* about 20 metres from the gate, Gomperts 2010, p73

504 An Islamic shrine with tombs now stands on this site. It is built over ancient brick remains and still bears the name Panggung. See Gomperts et al, 2008, p413.

505 *Desawarnana* 8. Some have argued that the *wanguntur* was outside the royal walls.

506 There was possibly some competition between the two groups. See Pigeaud 1962, IV, p14

507 About half the size of a soccer field. The dimensions of the terrace are 70 metres in length on a north-south directional axis, 55 metres wide and two metres high. See Gompert et al, 2008, p420.

508 Some remnants of this 'Amazing Pavilion' pavilion are still visible today. For a picture, see Gomparts et. al (2014), figure 9. The Amazing Pavilion (*witanabhinawa* in Prapanca's *Desawarnana* 9.4b) was 13 metres long, 9 metres wide and 1.6 metres high, oriented north-south. Its westward-facing stairs were the northeastern corner of a terrace. See also Pigeaud, 1962, IV, p26-28.

509 This is based on Ma Huan's description of Wikramawardhana, who lived in the 15th century. Ma Yuen p87.

510 Pigeaud, 1962, IV, P11/12.

511 The Overall Survey of the Ocean's Shores' ' Ying Ya Sheng la.

512 This description is based on a statue, presumed to represent Queen Suhita, housed in the National Museum, Jakarta, inventory number 6058. Assuming she was born 5 years before Hayam Wuruk's death (in

1389), she was born in 1384. That meant she was 20 years old when the Paregreg civil war broke out and 46 when she became queen in 1430 and she died at the age of 62 in 1446.

513 Note the similarity with the Damar Wulan legend, that is included elsewhere in the chapter.

514 This is a shortened and adjusted version of the Damar Wulan legend. It is a story of her marriage but might also be related to the end of Paregreg war (when a king in the eastern part of the land loses and a winner comes to claim his trophy in Majapahit). The Damar Wulan (MSS.Jav.89) manuscript is currently in the British Library. The book is from 1815 and reads: 'This book is said to be two hundred years old'. However, it is written on Dutch paper and probably a late 18th-century dating is perhaps most likely for this manuscript. Given its similarities to Paregreg, it might be based on that war. See Gallup, 2013.

515 The Pararaton says she became queen in 1402, when her father had a breakdown. But he came back afterwards, so her role might have been ceremonial for some time. She ruled as the foremost royal after her father's death in 1329.

516 Over time, the fertility of the Rajasa dynasty, possibly because of inter-family marriages, appears to have fallen significantly.

517 It is unknown when the Segaran, an enormous pool (375m x 175m, nearly 3 metres deep) just north of Majapahit, was constructed. It is not mentioned in the Pararaton or in the *Desawarnana* and hence, it is most likely it was constructed after 1365. Given a famine and silting up of the river, perhaps the pool was constructed to ensure water supply into the city. Excavations and large numbers of ceramics found at the bottom suggest that the pool was also used for traders to sit on pavilions over the water and discuss deals.

518 This started in 1424 when China stopped trading and that all communication was cut off.

519 Roxanna Brown (2004) confirmed the existence of the Ming Gap, that is, a lack of blue-white ceramics supply in southeast Asia. She listed 15 shipwrecks with Chinese and Southeast Asia ceramics in the region and identified two types of shortages. The first is a general shortage of Chinese ceramics during 1325-1380. The second is a specific severe shortage of blue and white porcelain, which she called the Ming Gap, during 1352-1487. She has proven that China had a 100% share of ceramics market before 1325, but the market share decreased to 50% from 1368 to 1424-1430, and further to 5% from 1424-1430 to 1487. It rebounded from 1488 to 1505 and decreased again for the next 60 years. China regained its monopoly in the ceramic trade after 1573.

520 Queen Suhita reigned from 1429-1446 and during those years, she sent nine missions to China (1430, 1436, two in 1437, 1438, 1440, 1443, 1446 and a last one that arrived in China in 1447).

521 Ryukyu records confirm the 1442 voyage, and add other earlier voyages to Java in 1430, 1440, and 1441. Their cargoes included textiles, swords, and porcelain (Kobata and Matsuda 1969: 156-161; see also Wade 2007). See Vickers 2014, p23.

522 According to the Sejarah Melayu, Siam attacked Malacca twice, in 1445 and in 1456.

523 Maybe she was going with the times or maybe she was too weak to resist pressure from the Chinese traders, a view taken by Slametmuljana (See Slametmuljana 1976, p193).

524 This might have happened earlier, around 1423, when a Chinese man, Gan Eng Chou, was appointed in Tuban. His half-brother was appointed to the position in 1443. See Slametmulyana, 1976, p188 and p193.

525 Indeed, this continues until today. In 2014, it became an affront to the more conservative parts of Indonesian society and doctors warned of diseases while Muslim organizations and members of parliament called for a ban. Mount Kemukus was promptly closed that year although it seems pilgrims are still visiting. There is however, no clear evidence that this was the custom in the days of Majapahit. But we know that there were a host of tantric rituals that involved sexual practices. In fact, there are a couple of striking similarities between tantric practices and what happened on Mount Kemukus – the sexual act is preferably performed with a person to whom one is not married, under the free sky (before the eyes of the gods), at a sacred site (if possible, on a grave or in a cemetery) and – last but not least – as an integral part of ritual practices (and not for reproduction purposes or even out of lust or love).

526 That the search for religious knowledge had become more important during the late Majapahit period is reflected in the large number of sanctuaries and hermitages on Mount Penanggungan. To a certain degree this was probably due to the chaotic political situation of the time, and perhaps also a revival of the Hindu-Buddhist beliefs against the influences of Islam. The hermitages were centres for retreat from the world and for religious teaching. Kieven 2013, p325.

527 The increasing number of sanctuaries on Mount Penanggungan during the fifteenth century may reflect the political instability of this late phase of Majapahit, when many members of the aristocracy sought the advice of hermits or even withdrew from daily life to remote areas on mountains. The story of Prince Panji, who struggles to become an accomplished noble (kshatriya), was a model for these royals. See Kieven 2013, p309. Since sculptures were usually only erected to depict deities, a large Panji statue shows how far this story had risen in status.

528 Candi Sukuh, constructed between 1437 and 1457, is a unique and beautiful Hindu temple and takes visitors on a journey through the

sexual tantra practised in Java in the 15th century. Nearby is Candi Ceto, which has similar figures. Both seem to have nothing in common with other Javanese Hindu and Buddhist temples and are more reminiscent of a Mayan monument. This is possibly because of a re-appearance of the pre-Hindu animism that existed centuries earlier. It's an isolated place with a strange, potent atmosphere. It is assumed that both temples suggest a resurgence of pre-Hindu Javanese religious practices. See also Kinney 2003, p265-281.

529 Over the generations, there is a remarkable fall in fertility in the Rajasa dynasty, possibly the result of consanguineous marriages. For general comments on such marriages and fertility, see Fareed et. al, 2017.

530 Kertawijaya reigned from 1447 to 1451. A mission from Java reached China in September 1447, but we do not know whether it was sent by Suhita or Kertawijaya. Other than this one mission, no others came to China from Java during his reign. See also Vickers, 2014, p21 .

531 She probably reached the age of 64, and possibly lived a good many years longer (according to the charter of Bungur of 1367, her parents were already married in that year).

532 Based on Shaw 1994, p79-80.

533 There is a reference to this in the Trailokyapuri charter.

534 There was also an eruption of Mount Kelud somewhere around 1450-1460. This might also have caused part of the royal house of Majapahit to move to Kediri. See Sastrawan 2022.

535 It is very unclear what happened after 1450 in Majapahit. In either case the conquest of Majapahit which is mentioned in 1486, and which must have taken place sometime between 1478 and 1486, was probably a reconquest of the palace by a branch of the legitimate Rajasa royal line. It is often assumed that this was a turbulent time. This conquest of Majapahit possibly marked the end of a civil war between these two branches of the royal line. The end of this kingdom did not come until some forty years later, in 1527. But there is little evidence of this, and one could argue that the last stone engraving from 1486 also marked the last year of Majapahit.

This is a list of kings from Hayam Wuruk onwards:

King Rajasanagara (Hayam Wuruk) 1350-89

King Wikramawardhana 1389-1429

Queen Suhita 1429-47

King Wijayaparakramawardhana (Kertawijaya) 1447-51

King Rajasawardhana (Wijayakumara) 1451-53

An interval of three kingless years. It is unclear why this was the case. The reign dates of two further kings are known:

King Girisawardhana (Suryawikrama) 1456-66

King Singhawikramawardhana (Suraprabhawa) 1466-78

From Ricklefs 2001, p21-22. Noordyn also concludes that

Rajasawardhana, Girisawardhana and Singhawikramawardhana (Suraprabhawa) were sons of Kertawijaya. Their mother was Jayeswari, the grand old lady. See Noorduyn 1978, p235. Lastly, the name Brawijaya only is mentioned in other Javanese sources, not in the inscription of Trailokyapuri.

536 The Trailokyapuri inscriptions (also called the Jiyu inscriptions, there are three of them) as by Van den Veerdonk, 2001, p108-109.

537 Raden Patah led the Demak Kingdom from 1500 to 1518. We do not know exactly when Bujangga Manik walked around Java, and this might well have been a few years before Prince Patah founded the city. Under Patah's leadership, the Demak sultanate became the centre of power for the spread of Islam. This period was the initial phase of the development of Islamic teachings in Java.

538 His name is Jaya Pakuan but in his own writings he uses the name Bujangga Manik. 'Bujangga' is a bachelor and a priest or sage. West (2020, p8) translates it as 'jewel serpent'.

539 Bujangga Manik made two journeys across Java, both on foot and each covering well over a thousand kilometres We know of this monk because of the existence of his writings on old palm leaves, presented to the Bodleian Library in Oxford, England in 1627 by a merchant called Andrew James. A Dutch scholar of Sundanese languages, Dr J. Noorduyn, rediscovered these palm leaves in 1968 and started translating them, bringing back to life the story of the wandering prince-monk from Pakuan. It was written in the late 1400s or early 1500s, but it does not mention the Portuguese, who took Melaka in 1511, so the book and the journeys were most probably finished before that happened.

540 Noorduyn, 2006, p 258-259.

541 In his book, he does not mention anything about it.

542 He calls the alun-alun square of the city the Manguntur (Noorduyn 2006, p258 (800-803 in the poem). It is referred to as Wanguntur in the *Desawarnana* 8. See also Pigeaud 1960-63 IV: 14.

543 Perhaps these were nearby villages.

544 Noorduyn, 2006, p 258. The mountain was named Pawitra in those days and had four smaller hills surrounding it, one of them being Gajah Mungkur, which he also ascended.

545 Noorduyn 2008, p 265 (sentences 1065-1069).

546 On board the Portuguese ship was a writer, who recorded the encounter. See Gaspar Carrea, 1510, p216 onwards. Translation and description from Manguin, 1980, p267.

547 Tome Pires, Book II, p287.

548 This painting has never been recorded since, but this description might be a 'Wayang Beber' scroll . See Vickers, 2014, p24.

549 Pires, 1512-1515, p191-192.

550 Freely translated by the author from Krom 1931, p458

551 Some gravestones suggest that perhaps, in the fifteenth century, there were a few high-ranking Muslim officials at the Majapahit court. Sidomulyo, however, argues that it is uncertain what the purpose of these stones were and their original provenance, and thus suggests that such a thesis remains highly hypothetical. Sidomulyo, 2012.

552 This was probably around 1524. See Pigaud en de Graaf 176, p7.

553 The date for the fall of Majapahit is generally given as 1527 but this is open to question. The last Portuguese source that mentions Majapahit is Pigafetta and this suggests that the kingdom was still in existence in 1522. This is also confirmed in Barros IV, Liv I, Cap XIV where we see a mission from the city of Panarukan arrive in Melaka on 10 August 1528. That would not have happened if Majapahit was still around. See also Krom 1931, p461. Thus, the end of Majapahit probably took place between 1522 and 1528. Javanese sources, such as the Babad Sangkala and Chinese chronicles of Semarang, place the final assault on Majapahit in 1527. See Slametmuljana, 1976, p259. But in many Javanese texts the fall of Majapahit is placed at the end of the fourteenth Javanese century, which is Saka 1400 or 1478 AD. The turn of the century was later regarded as a time when changes of dynasties or courts normally occurred. Despite their lack of accuracy in portraying actual events, these tales reveal much about the desire of subsequent rulers to establish a dynastic lineage with Majapahit as some sort of legal recognition of their power.

554 Remmelink 2022, Babad Tanah Jawa verse 88. Babad are traditional Javanese chronicles written in verse. The 'mother' of all Babads is the text known as the Major Babad Tanah Jawi. The latest version of it dates from 1836, although the events described end around the year 1770. It describes the history of Java, or rather the kings of Java, until about 1770.

555 Ricklefs p41-42.

556 See Herald van der Linde, 2020, especially page 19 and 20. It is assumed that Kelapa was taken on 22 June 1527, and this is now the birthday of Jakarta.

557 Herald van der Linde, 2020, p162-163.

558 Pararaton, last words, freely translated. The year given is Saka 1536, that is 1613 AD.

559 Robson and Changchit, 1999.

560 Vickers, 2014, p57.

561 Muslim separatist figures such as the Acehnese Daud Beureu'eh and the South Sulawesi Kahar Muzakar reframed the term 'Majapahit' with anti-Islamic, imperialist notions, pointing to the early Indonesian government's reliance on (and legitimisation through) the kingdom. See van Dijk, 1981, page 313-314 and Druce, S., 2020, p163..

562 This is what some historians call a shift from 'Indonesia-centred'

to 'Islam-centred' history in Indonesia. See Agus Suwignyo's (2014). On page 125, he writes that some historical publications 'the period of Islam is discussed with an entire focus on Islam and Islamic influence while the preceding Hindus and Buddhist period is completely ignored.'

Bibliography

Acri, Andrea. 'On Birds, Ascetics, and Kings in Central Java: "Rāmāyana" Kakawin, 24.95-126 and 25.' *Bijdragen Tot de Taal-, Land- En Volkenkunde* 166, no. 4 (2010): 475–506.

Acri, Andrea, Peter D. Sharrock, and ISEAS-Yusof Ishak Institute, eds. *The Creative South: Buddhist and Hindu Art in Mediaeval Maritime Asia*. Singapore: ISEAS-Yusof Ishak Institute, 2022.

Acri, Andrea, and Aleksandra Wenta. 'A Buddhist Bhairava? Kṛtanagara's Tantric Buddhism in Transregional Perspective.' *Entangled Religions*, 2022. https://er.ceres.rub.de/index.php/ER/article/view/9653/9263.

Aelst, Arjan. 'Majapahit Picis; The Currency of a "moneyless" Society 1300-1700.' *Bijdragen Tot de Taal-, Land- En Volkenkunde / Journal of the Humanities and Social Sciences of Southeast Asia* 151, no. 3 (January 1, 1995): 357–93. https://doi.org/10.1163/22134379-90003037.

Ammarell, Gene. 'Sky Calendars of the Indo-Malay Archipelago: Regional Diversity/Local Knowledge.' *Indonesia*, no. 45 (1988): 85–104. https://doi.org/10.2307/3351177.

Ammarell, Gene, and Anna Tsing. 'Cultural Production of Skylore in Indonesia,' 2207–14, 2015. https://doi.org/10.1007/978-1-4614-6141-8_236.

Anderson, James. 'Man and Mongols: The Dali and Dai Viet Kingdoms in the Face of the Northen Invasions.' In *China's Encounters on the South and Southwest: Reforging the Fiery Frontier over Two Millennia*, edited by John K. Whitmore, 106–34. Handbook of Oriental Studies = Handbuch Der Orientalistik. Section 3, Southeast Asia, volume 22. Leiden: Brill, 2014.

Aung-Thwin, Michael. 'The Decline of Pagan.' In *Pagan*, 182–99. The Origins of Modern Burma. University of Hawai'i Press, 1985. https://doi.org/10.2307/j.ctv9zck80.17.

Averoes, Muhammad. 'Re-Estimating the Size of Javanese Jong Ship.' *Historia: Jurnal Pendidik Dan Peneliti Sejarah* 5, no. 1 (February 25, 2022): 57–64. https://doi.org/10.17509/historia.v5i1.39181.

Babad Tanah Jawi, The Chronicle of Java: The Revised Prose Version of C.F. Winter Sr. (KITLV Or 8). Leiden: Leiden University Press, 2022.

Bacus, Elisabeth A., Ian C. Glover, Peter D. Sharrock, John Guy, and

Vincent C. Pigott. *Interpreting Southeast Asia's Past*. NUS Press, 2008. https://doi.org/10.2307/j.ctv1nthr2.

Bade, David W. *Of Palm Wine, Women, and War: The Mongolian Naval Expedition to Java in the 13th Century*. Singapore: Institute of Southeast Asian Studies, 2013.

Barker, Randolph. 'The Origin and Spread of Early-Ripening Champa Rice: It's Impact on Song Dynasty China.' *Rice* 4, no. 3–4 (December 2011): 184–86. https://doi.org/10.1007/s12284-011-9079-6.

Barnhart, Edwin, and Christopher Powell. 'The Importance of Zenith Passage at Angkor, Cambodia.' Maya Exploration Centre, 2012. http://www.mayaexploration.com/pdf/angkorzenithpassage.pdf.

Bastin, John. 'Raffles' "Aides-de-Camp" in Java.' *Journal of the Malaysian Branch of the Royal Asiatic Society* 65, no. 1 (262) (1992): 1–14.

Batchelor, Robert. 'The Selden Map Rediscovered: A Chinese Map of East Asian Shipping Routes, *c.* 1619.' *Imago Mundi* 65, no. 1 (January 2013): 37–63. https://doi.org/10.1080/03085694.2013.731203.

Bennett, Anna T. N. 'Gold in Early Southeast Asia.' *ArchéoSciences*, no. 33 (December 31, 2009): 99–107. https://doi.org/10.4000/archeosciences.2072.

Bennett, James. 'Ilm or Fashion?' In *Ilm*, edited by Samer Akkach, 157–80. Science, Religion and Art in Islam. University of Adelaide Press, 2019. http://www.jstor.org/stable/j.ctvb4bt41.18.

Berg, C. C. 'Bijdragen Tot de Kennis Der Panji-Verhalen: 1. Het Prototype Der Structuurmythe.' *Bijdragen Tot de Taal-, Land- En Volkenkunde* 110, no. 3 (1954): 189–216.

———. 'De Geschiedenis van Pril Majapahit.' *Indonesie* 5, no. 3 (1951).

———. 'De Middeljavaansche Historische Traditie.' Leiden University, 1927.

———. 'De Sadeng Oorlog En de Mythe van Groot-Majapahit.' *Indonesie*, no. 5de jaargang (1951): 385–422.

———. 'Een Vleugje Licht in Een Duister Verhaal.' *Bijdragen Tot de Taal-, Land- En Volkenkunde van Nederlandsch-Indië* 98, no. 1/2 (1939): 1–74.

———. 'Eenige Opmerkingen over Het Pararaton-Verhaal Betreffende Toh-Jaya's Dood.' *Bijdragen Tot de Taal-, Land- En Volkenkunde van Nederlandsch-Indië* 97, no. 4 (1938): 443–52.

———. 'Het Javaanse Gebruik van Het Sanskrit Woord Rajasa.' *Bijdragen Tot de Taal-, Land- En Volkenkunde / Journal of the Humanities and Social Sciences of Southeast Asia* 114, no. 1–2 (1958): 1–16. https://doi.org/10.1163/22134379-90002263.

———. 'Kartanegara, de Miskende Empire-Builder.' *Orientatie*, July

1950.

————. 'Kidung Sunda. Inleiding, Tekst, Vertaling En Aantekeeningen.' *Bijdragen Tot de Taal-, Land- En Volkenkunde van Nederlandsch-Indië* 83, no. 1 (1927): 1–161.

————. 'Naar Aanleiding van Prajnaparamita's Recente Verhuizing.' *Bijdragen Tot de Taal-, Land- En Volkenkunde / Journal of the Humanities and Social Sciences of Southeast Asia* 137, no. 2–3 (1981): 191–228. https://doi.org/10.1163/22134379-90003497.

————. *Rangga Lawe, Middeljavaanse Historische Roman.* Weltevreden: Albrecht en Co., 1930. https://ia801807.us.archive. org/1/items/rangga-lawe/Rangga%20Lawe.pdf.

Berg, C. C., and Harsa-Widjaya. 'Kidung Harsa-Wijaya Middel-Javaansche Historische Roman Uitgegeven.' *Bijdragen Tot de Taal-, Land- En Volkenkunde van Nederlandsch-Indië* 88 (1931): 49–238.

Berg, C.C. 'De Arjunawiwaha, Er-Langga's Levensloop En Bruiloftslied?' *Bijdragen Tot de Taal-, Land- En Volkenkunde / Journal of the Humanities and Social Sciences of Southeast Asia* 97, no. 1 (January 1, 1938): 19–94. https://doi.org/10.1163/22134379-90001331.

————. *Inleiding Tot de Studie van Het Oud-Javaansch.* Soerakarta: De Bliksem, 1928. https://resolver.kb.nl/resolve?urn=MMKB1 8A:025289000:00009.

————. 'Opmerkingen over de Chronologie van de Oudste Geschiedenis van Maja-Pahit En over Krtarajasajayawardhana's.' *Bijdragen Tot de Taal-, Land- En Volkenkunde / Journal of the Humanities and Social Sciences of Southeast Asia* 97, no. 1 (January 1, 1938): 135–239. https://doi.org/10.1163/22134379-90001336.

Berg, E.J van den. *De Val Van Sora (Somandaka).* Brill, 1939.

Bloembergen, Marieke, and Martijn Eickhoff. 'Exchange and the Protection of Java's Antiquities: A Transnational Approach to the Problem of Heritage in Colonial Java.' *The Journal of Asian Studies* 72, no. 4 (2013): 893–916.

Blom, Jesse. *The Antiquities of Singasari.* Leiden: Burgersdijk & Niermans, Templum Salomonis, 1939.

Boechari. *Prastasi Koleksi Museum National.* Vol. 1. Jakarta: Proyek Pengembangan Museum Nasional, 1985.

Borschberg, Peter. 'The Melaka Empire, c. 1400–1528.' In *Empires of the Sea*, edited by Rolf Strootman, Floris van den Eijnde, and Roy van Wijk, 263–93. Maritime Power Networks in World History. Brill, 2020. http://www.jstor.org/stable/10.1163/j.ctv2gjx041.15.

Bosch, F. D. K. 'C.C. Berg and Ancient Javanese History.' *Bijdragen Tot de Taal-, Land- En Volkenkunde* 112, no. 1 (1956): 1–24.

————. 'De Mythische Achtergrond van de Kèn Angrok-Legende.'

Bijdragen Tot de Taal-, Land- En Volkenkunde / Journal of the Humanities and Social Sciences of Southeast Asia 121, no. 4 (1965): 468–72. https://doi.org/10.1163/22134379-90002954.

———. 'De Oorkonde van Sendang Sedati.' Oudheidkundig Verslag 1922, 1922, 22–27.

———. 'Uit de Grensgebieden Tussen Indische Invloedssfeer En Oud-Inheems Volksgeloof Op Java.' Bijdragen Tot de Taal-, Land- En Volkenkunde / Journal of the Humanities and Social Sciences of Southeast Asia 110, no. 1 (1954): 1–19. https://doi.org/10.1163/22134379-90002388.

Bosch, F. van den. 'Der Javanische Mangsakalender.' Bijdragen Tot de Taal-, Land- En Volkenkunde 136, no. 2/3 (1980): 248–82.

Bowring, Philip. Empire of the Winds: The Global Role of Asia's Great Archipelago. Place of publication not identified: BLOOMSBURY ACADEMIC, 2020.

Brandes, Dr. J.L.A. Oud-Javaansche Oorkonden; Nagelaten Inskripties van J.L.A. Brandes, Uitgegeven Door N.J Krom. Leiden: Instituut Kern, 1913.

———. Pararaton (Ken Arok) of Het Boek der Koningen van Tumapel en van Majapahit. Tweede druk. Verhandelingen van het Bataavaasch Genootschap van Kunsten en Wetenschappen, LXII. 's Gravenshage en Batavia: Martinus Nijhoff en Albrecht &Co, 1920.

Bray, Francesca. The Rice Economies: Technology and Development in Asian Societies. Berkeley: University of California Press, 1994.

Bressan, L. 'Odoric Of Pordenone (1265-1331). His Vision of China and South-East Asia and His Contribution to Relations between Asia and Europe.' Journal of the Malaysian Branch of the Royal Asiatic Society 70, no. 2 (273) (1997): 1–23.

Brook, Timothy. De Kaart van Mijnheer Selden: China, de Specerijenhandel En Een Verloren Zeekaart. Translated by Peter van der Veen and Chiel van Soelen. Amsterdam: Wereldbibliotheek, 2013.

———. The Troubled Empire: China in the Yuan and Ming Dynasties. First Harvard Univ. Press paperback ed. History of Imperial China. Cambridge, Mass.: The Belknap Press of Harvard Univ. Press, 2013.

Brown, Roxanna M. The Ceramics of South-East Asia: Their Dating and Identification. Oxford in Asia Studies in Ceramics. Kuala Lumpur; New York: Oxford University Press, 1977.

———. 'The Ming Gap and Shipwrech Ceramics in Southeast Asia.' University of california, 2004. https://www.proquest.com/openview/1d6930a781a2191ab3d80ef4a6b5684d/1?pq-origsite=gscholar&cbl=18750&diss=y.

Bullough, Nigel. Historical East Java: Remains in Stone. ADLine Communications, 1995.

———. *Napak Tilas Perjalanan Mpu Prapañca*. Jagakarsa, Jakarta: Wedatama Widya Sastra bekerja sama dengan Yayasan Nandiswara [dan] Jurusan Pendidikan Sejarah Unesa, 2007.

Buzurg ibn Shahriyār. *Kitāb 'ajāyib Al-Hind*. Translated by P.A Van der Lith and Marcel Devic. Leiden, 1883. https://archive.org/details/kitabajayibalhin00buzu/page/125/mode/1up?q=lameri.

Carey, Peter. 'Raffles, Majapahit and Wardenaar's Survey of Trowulan in October 1815 - The Case of the Dog That Didn't Bark in the Night,' 2018. https://www.academia.edu/37945098/Raffles_Majapahit_and_Wardenaars_October_1815_Survey_docx.

Chhabra, B.Ch. *Expansion of Indo-Aryan Culture*. New Delhi: Oriental Publishers and Booksellers, 1965. http://asi.nic.in/asi_books/41979.pdf.

Christie, Anthony. 'The Political Use of Imported Religion: An Historical Example from Java.' *Archives de Sociologie Des Religions* 9, no. 17 (1964): 53–62.

Christie, Jan Wisseman. 'Javanese Markets and the Asian Sea Trade Boom of the Tenth to Thirtheenth Centuries A.D.' *Journal of the Economic and Social History of the Orient* 41, no. 3 (1998): 344–81.

———. 'States without Cities: Demographic Trends in Early Java.' *Indonesia*, no. 52 (1991): 23–40. https://doi.org/10.2307/3351153.

———. 'Texts and Textiles in "Medieval' Java." *Bulletin de l'École Française d'Extrême-Orient* 80, no. 1 (1993): 181–211.

———. 'The Medieval Tamil-Language Inscriptions in Southeast Asia and China.' *Journal of Southeast Asian Studies* 29, no. 2 (1998): 239–68.

———. 'Under the Volcano.' In *Environment, Trade and Society in Southeast Asia*, edited by David Henley and Henk Schulte Nordholt, 46–61. ALongue DuréePerspective. Brill, 2015. www.jstor.org/stable/10.1163/j.ctt1w76vg1.7.

———. 'Water and Rice in Early Java and Bali.' In *A World of Water*, edited by Peter Boomgaard, 235–58. Rain, Rivers and Seas in Southeast Asian Histories. Brill, 2007. www.jstor.org/stable/10.1163/j.ctt1w76vd0.12.

Clements, Jonathan. *Brief History of Khubilai Khan*. Little, Brown Book Group Limited, 2019.

Coedès, George, Walter F. Vella, and Sue Brown Cowing. *The Indianized States of Southeast Asia*. 3. Dr. Honolulu: Univ. of Hawaii Press, 1996.

Cohen Stuart, A.B. *Kawi Oorkonden in Fascimile, Met Inleiding En Transscriptie*. Leiden: Brill, 1875.

Colenbrander, Dr. H. T. *Koloniale Geschiedenis*. Vol. 3: De Oost sinds 1816. 3 vols. 's Gravenshage: Martinus Nijhoff, 1926.

Cool, Wouter. *De Lombok Expeditie*. Batavia: Kolff en Co., 1896. https://resolver.kb.nl/resolve?urn=MMKIT03:000135823:00009.

Correa, Gaspar. *Lendas Da India*. Vol. 1. Lisboa, 1510.

Coster-Wijsman, L. M. 'Illustrations in a Javanese Manuscript (Met Platen).' *Bijdragen Tot de Taal-, Land- En Volkenkunde / Journal of the Humanities and Social Sciences of Southeast Asia* 109, no. 2 (1953): 153–63. https://doi.org/10.1163/22134379-90002412.

Creese, Helen. 'Old Javanese Legal Traditions in Pre-Colonial Bali.' *Bijdragen Tot de Taal-, Land- En Volkenkunde* 165, no. 2/3 (2009): 241–90.

———. 'Pieces In The Puzzle: The Dating of Several Kakawin from Bali and Lombok.' *Archipel*, no. 52 (1996): 143–71.

———. 'Ultimate Loyalties: The Self-Immolation of Women in Java and Bali.' *Bijdragen Tot de Taal-, Land- En Volkenkunde* 157, no. 1 (2001): 131–66.

———. *Women of the Kakawin World: Marriage and Sexuality in the Indic Courts of Java and Bali*. Armonk, N.Y.; London: M.E. Sharpe, 2004.

Cresque, Abraham. 'Catalan Atlas.' 1375. Panel V. gallica.bnf.fr / BnF.

Dalrymple, William. *The Last Mughal: The Fall of a Dynasty: Delhi, 1857*. 1st Vintage Books ed. New York: Vintage Books, 2008.

Damais, Soedarmadji J. H. *Majapahit Terracotta: The Soedarmadji Jean Henry Damais Collection*. 1st. ed. Jakarta: Bab Pub. Indonesia, 2012.

De Graaf, H. J., and Theodore G.Th. Pigeaud. 'Geschiedenis van Java's Oosthoek in de 16e Eeuw.' In *De Eerste Moslimse Vorstendommen Op Java*, 69:179–84. Studiën over de Staatkundige Geschiedenis van de 15de En 16de Eeuw. Brill, 1974. http://www.jstor.org/stable/10.1163/j.ctvbqs7vc.19.

Degroot, V.M.Y. 'Candi, Space and Landscape: A Study on the Distribution, Orientation and Spatial Organization of Central Javanese Temple Remains.' Leiden University, 2009. http://hdl.handle.net/1887/13781.

Dijk, C. van. 'Aceh, The Rebellion of the Islamic Scholars.' In *Rebellion under the Banner of Islam*, 94:269–339. The Darul Islam in Indonesia. Brill, 1981. http://www.jstor.org/stable/10.1163/j.ctvbqs6vx.12.

Dokras, Uday. *One Against Many- the Tantric Temples of Indonesia*. Indo Nordic Author's Collective, 2022.

Domis, H.J. 'Bijzonderheden Betrefende Soerabaya En Madura.' *De Oosterling*, 1836. Deutsche Digitaler Bibliothek.

Drake, Earl. *Gayatri Rajapatni: The Woman behind the Glory of Majapahit*. Penang, Malaysia: Areca Books, 2015.

Dramer, Kim. *Kublai Khan*. World Leaders Past & Present. New York: Chelsea House, 1990.

Drewes, G. W. J. 'The Struggle between Javanism and Islam as Illustrated by the Serat Dermagandul.' *Bijdragen Tot de Taal-, Land- En Volkenkunde / Journal of the Humanities and Social Sciences of Southeast Asia* 122, no. 3 (1966): 309–65. https://doi.org/10.1163/22134379-90002925.

Druce, Stephen C. 'A South Sulawesi Hero and Villain: Qahhar Mudzakkar (Kahar Muzakkar) and His Legacy.' *International Journal of Asia Pacific Studies* 16, no. 2 (2020): 151–79. https://doi.org/10.21315/ijaps2020.16.2.8.

Dubois, R. 'The Birth of the Kingdom Majapahit.' *The China Journal* 15, no. 1 (July 1931): 17–24.

Dumarçay, Jacques, and Michael Smithies. *The Temples of Java*. Singapore; New York: Oxford University Press, 1986.

Eerde, J. C. van. 'Hindu-Javaansche En Balische Eeredienst.' *Bijdragen Tot de Taal-, Land- En Volkenkunde / Journal of the Humanities and Social Sciences of Southeast Asia* 65, no. 1 (1911): 1–39. https://doi.org/10.1163/22134379-90001829.

Engelhard, Nicholas. 'Van de Landreis van Gouverneur Nicolaus Engelhard Naar de Oosthoek, 1802 September 15 - 1802 November,' n.d. 2.21.004.19, invnr 196. Nationaal Archief Den Haag.

Ensink, J. *On the Old-Javanese Cantakaparwa and Its Tale of Sutasoma*. 's-Gravenhage, Leiden: Martinus Nijhoff Brill, 2015.

Fa-hsien (ca.337-ca.422), and James (1815-1897) Legge. *A Record of Buddhistic Kingdoms; Being an Account by the Chinese Monk Fâ-Hien of His Travels in India and Ceylon, A.D. 399-414, in Search of the Buddhist Books of Discipline. Translated and Annotated with a Corean Recension of the Chinese Text*, 1886.

Falvey, Lindsay. 'History of Rice in Southeast Asia and Australia,' 2010. https://doi.org/10.13140/2.1.4005.6327.

Fareed, Mohd, Mir Kaisar Ahmad, Malik Azeem Anwar, and Mohammad Afzal. 'Impact of Consanguineous Marriages and Degrees of Inbreeding on Fertility, Child Mortality, Secondary Sex Ratio, Selection Intensity, and Genetic Load: A Cross-Sectional Study from Northern India.' *Pediatric Research* 81, no. 1 (January 1, 2017): 18–26. https://doi.org/10.1038/pr.2016.177.

Fisher, Robert E. *Buddhist Art and Architecture*. World of Art. New York: Thames and Hudson, 1993.

Flecker, Michael. 'The Thirteenth-Century Java Sea Wreck: A Chinese Cargo In An Indonesian Ship.' *The Mariner's Mirror* 89, no. 4 (January 2003): 388–404. https://doi.org/10.1080/00253359.2003.10656872.

Flinders University. 'Archaeologists Identify Moluccan Boats That May Have Visited Australia from Indonesia in Rock Art Drawings,' May

31, 2023. https://phys.org/news/2023-05-archaeologists-moluccan-boats-australia-indonesia.html.

Flood, Gavin D. *An Introduction to Hinduism*. New York, NY: Cambridge University Press, 1996.

Fontein, Jan. *Het goddelijk gezicht van Indonesie: meesterwerken der beeldhouwkunst 700 - 1600*. Zwolle: Waanders Uitgevers, 1992.

Fontein, Jan, R. Soekmono, and Satyawati Suleiman. *Ancient Indonesian Art of the Central and Eastern Javanese Periods*. New York: Asia Society; distributed by New York Graphic Society, 1971.

Foo, Shu Tieng. *Salt-Making and Prehistoric Shell Middens in the Straits of Melaka*, 2020.

Fruin-Mees, W. *Geschiedenis van Java*. Vol. 1 and 2. 2 vols. Weltevreden: Commissie voor de volkslectuur, 1919.

Galestin, T.P. *Houtbouw Op Oost-Javaansche Tempelreliefs*. 's Gravenhage, 1936.

Gallop, Annabel. 'Everyday Life in Java in the Late 18th Century: Serat Damar Wulan.' *Southeast Asia Library Group (SEALG) Blo* (blog), March 21, 2013. http://southeastasianlibrarygroup.wordpress.com/2013/03/21/everyday-life-in-java-in-the-late-18th-century-serat-damar-wulan/.

———. 'The Early Use of Seals in the Malay World.' *Bulletin de l'École Française d'Extrême-Orient* 102 (2016): 125–64.

Geertz, Clifford. *Islam Observed: Religious Development in Morocco and Indonesia*. 15th pr. Chicago: Univ. of Chicago Press, 1999.

———. *Negara: The Theatre State in Nineteenth-Century Bali*. Princeton, N.J: Princeton University Press, 1980.

———. *The Religion of Java*. The Free Press of Glencoe, Illinois, 1960.

Gelpke, J.H.F. Sollewijn. 'Afonso de Albuquerque's Pre-Portuguese "Javanese" Map, Partially Reconstructed from Francisco Rodrigues' Book.' *Bijdragen Tot de Taal-, Land- En Volkenkunde* 151, no. 1 (1995): 76–99.

———. 'The Report of Miguel Roxo de Brito of His Voyage in 1581-1582 to the Raja Ampat, the MacCluer Gulf and Seram.' *Bijdragen Tot de Taal-, Land- En Volkenkunde* 150, no. 1 (1994): 123–45.

Gentleman resident at Batavia. 'A Journal of a Tour in the Island of Java (By a Gentleman Resident at Batavia).' *The Asiatic Journal and Monthly Register for British India and Its Dependencies* I, no. 2-3 (February-March 1816) (1816): 124–29, 233–35.

Gislén, Lars, and J.C. Eade. 'The Calendars of Southeast Asia. 4: Malaysia and Indonesia.' *Journal of Astronomical History and Heritage* 22 (December 30, 2019): 447.

Gomperts, Amrit. 'In the Footsteps of Hayam Wuruk.' *IIAS Newsletter*, no. 39 (2005). https://www.iias.asia/sites/default/files/2020-11/IIAS_NL39_17.pdf.

Gomperts, Amrit, Arnoud Haag, and Peter Carey. 'De Veertiende-Eeuwse Javaanse Hofstad Majapahit Alsnog Op de Kaart Gezet.' *Caert-Thresoor -Tijdschrift van Der Geschiedenis van de Kartografie*, no. 27 (2008): 71–78.

———. 'Mapping Majapahit: Wardenaar's Archaeological Survey at Trowulan in 1815.' *Indonesia* 93 (April 1, 2012): 177–96. https://doi.org/10.1353/ind.2012.0006.

———. 'Rediscovering the Royal Capital of Majapahit.' *Newslatter of the International Institute for Asian Studies* 53 (Spring 2010): 12–13.

———. 'Stutterheim's Enigma: The Mystery of His Mapping of the Majapahit Kraton at Trowulan in 1941.' *Bijdragen Tot de Taal-, Land- En Volkenkunde* 164, no. 4 (2008): 411–30.

———. 'The Sage Who Divided Java in 1052: Maclaine Pont's Excavation of Mpu Bharaḍa's Hermitage-Cemetery at Lĕmah Tulis in 1925.' *Bijdragen Tot de Taal-, Land- En Volkenkunde* 168, no. 1 (2012): 1–25.

Gomperts, Amrit, Arnoud Haag, Peter Carey, and Djoko Umbaran. 'The Archaeological Identification Of The Majapahit Royal Palace:Prapañca's1365 Description Projected Onto Satellite Imagery.' *Journal of the Siam Society* 102 (2014): 67–118.

Gomperts, Amrit, Arnoud Haag, Djoko Umbaran, and Hari Subekti. 'New Light on the Archaeology of the Majapahit Court Capital.' *Newsletter IIAS*, no. 70 (Spring 2018). https://www.iias.asia/the-newsletter/article/new-light-archaeology-majapahit-court-capital.

Goris, R. *Ancient History of Bali*. Den Pasar: Udayana University, 1965.

Gottowik, Volker. 'Pilgrims, Prostitutes, and Ritual Seks.' *Bijdragen Tot de Taal-, Land- En Volkenkunde* 174, no. 4 (2018): 393–421.

Griffiths, Arlo, and Amandine Lepoutre. 'Études Du Corpus Des Inscriptions Du Campā, VIII.' *Bulletin de l'École Française d'Extrême-Orient* 102 (2016): 195–296.

Griffiths, Arlo, and Pauline Lunsingh Scheurleer. 'Ancient Indonesian Ritual Utensils and Their Inscriptions: Bells and Slitdrums.' *Arts Asiatiques* 69 (2014): 129–50.

Groeneveldt, Willem Pieter. *Notes on the Malay Archipelago and Malacca Compiled from Chinese Sources*. Batavia, Den Haag: W.Bruining, M. Nijhof, 1880. https://archive.org/details/notes-on-the-malay-archipelago/page/n1/mode/2up.

Guy, John. 'Ornaments of Empowerment The Kundala-Subang in Old Javanese Jewellery.' *Aziatische Kunst* 38, no. 4 (2008): 55–61. https://doi.org/10.1163/25431749-90000158.

Hagen, Piet. *Koloniale Oorlogen in Indonesië: Vijf Eeuwen Verzet Tegen Vreemde Overheersing*. Amsterdam: Uitgeverij De

Arbeiderspers, 2018.

Hall, Kenneth R. 'Indonesia's Evolving International Relationships in the Ninth to Early Eleventh Centuries: Evidence from Contemporary Shipwrecks and Epigraphy.' *Indonesia*, no. 90 (2010): 15–45.

———. *Maritime Trade and State Development in Early Southeast Asia*. University of Hawaii Press, 2019. https://doi.org/10.2307/j.ctv9zckps.

———. 'Personal Status and Ritualized Exchange in Majapahit Java.' *Archipel* 59 (2000): 51–96.

———. 'Ritual Networks and Royal Power in Majapahit Java.' *Archipel*, 1996, 95–118.

———. 'The Roots of ASEAN: Regional Identities in the Strait of Melaka Region Circa 1500 C.E.' *Asian Journal of Social Science* 29, no. 1 (2001): 87–119.

———. 'The Śailendra Era in Javanese History.' In *Maritime Trade and State Development in Early Southeast Asia*, 113–47. University of Hawai'i Press, 1985. https://doi.org/10.2307/j.ctv9zckps.12.

Hannigan, Tim. *A Brief History of Indonesia: Sultans, Spices, and Tsunamis: The Incredible Story of Southeast Asia's Largest Nation*. First edition. Tokyo; Rutland, Vermont: Tuttle Publishing, 2015.

———. *Raffles and the British Invasion of Java*. Singapore: Monsoon Books Pte Ltd, 2012.

Harrisson, Tom. 'Part 2: Gold in West Borneo.' In *Gold and Megalithic Activity in Prehistoric and Recent West Borneo*. Southeast Asia Program, Dept. of Far Eastern Studies, Cornell University, 1970. https://ecommons.cornell.edu/handle/1813/57545.

Harsani, Arsip. '"Don't Come to Kediri, Jokowi": The Myth Surrounding the City's Presidential "curse".' The Jakarta Post. Accessed June 28, 2020. https://www.thejakartapost.com/news/2020/02/20/dont-come-to-kediri-jokowi-the-myth-surrounding-the-citys-presidential-curse.html.

Hazeu, Dr. G. A J. 'Iets over de Koedri and Tjoendrik.' *Tijdschift van Het Bataviaasch Genootschap* XLVII (1904): 396–413.

Heine-Geldern, Robert. 'Conceptions of State and Kingship in Southeast Asia (Revised Version).' *The Far Eastern Quarterly* 2 (1956): 15–30.

Henley, David, and Henk Schulte Nordholt. *Environment, Trade and Society in Southeast Asia*. Brill, 2015. http://www.jstor.org/stable/10.1163/j.ctt1w76vg1.

Hill, A. H. 'Hikayat Raja-Raja Pasai.' *Journal of the Malayan Branch of the Royal Asiatic Society* 33, no. 2 (190) (1960): 1–215.

———. 'The Coming of Islam to North Sumatra.' *Journal of Southeast Asian History* 4, no. 1 (1963): 6–21.

Hinzler, H. I. R. 'Balinese Palm-Leaf Manuscripts.' *Bijdragen Tot de*

Taal-, Land- En Volkenkunde 149, no. 3 (1993): 438–73.

Hinzler, H. I. R., Pieter ter Keurs, and Marijke J. Klokke. *Boeddha En Shiva Op Java*. Leiden: Rijksmuseum voor Volkenkunde, 1992.

Hirth, F., and W.W Rockhill. *Zhufanzhi: Chau Ju-Kua: His Work on the Chinese and Arab Trade in the Twelfth and Thirteenth Centuries*. St. Petersburg: Imperial Academy of Sciences, 1911. https://archive.org/details/chaujukuahiswork00chao/page/76/mode/1up.

Ho, Ping-Ti. 'Early-Ripening Rice in Chinese History.' *The Economic History Review* 9, no. 2 (1956): 200–218. https://doi.org/10.2307/2591742.

Hoëvell, Wolter Robert van. *Reis over Java: Madura En Bali in Het Midden van 1847. I-III*. Vol. 1. III vols. Amsterdam: P.N. van Kampen, 1849. https://books.google.com.hk/books?id=e4FRAAAAcAAJ&printsec=frontcover&hl=zh-TW&source=gbs_ge_summary_r&cad=0#v=onepage&q&f=false.

Holt, Claire. *Art in Indonesia: Continuities and Change*. Ithaca, N.Y.: Cornell University Press, 1967.

Hooker, M. B. 'The Indian-Derived Law Texts of Southeast Asia.' *The Journal of Asian Studies* 37, no. 2 (1978): 201–19. https://doi.org/10.2307/2054162.

H.Th. Verstappen and J. Noorduyn. 'Purnavarman's River-Works near Tugu.' *Bijdragen Tot de Taal-, Land- En Volkenkunde / Journal of the Humanities and Social Sciences of Southeast Asia* 128, no. 2–3 (1972): 298–307. https://doi.org/10.1163/22134379-90002752.

Hung, Hsiao-chun, Hartatik, Tisna Arif Ma'rifat, and Truman Simanjuntak. 'Mongol Fleet on the Way to Java: First Archaeological Remains from the Karimata Strait in Indonesia.' *Archaeological Research in Asia* 29 (March 1, 2022): 100327. https://doi.org/10.1016/j.ara.2021.100327.

Hunter, Thomas M. 'The Body of the King: Reappraising Singhasari Period Syncretism.' *Journal of Southeast Asian Studies* 38, no. 1 (2007): 27–53.

I Kadek Sudana Wira Darma. 'Pengarcaac Dewa Wisnu Pada Masa Hindi-Buddha Di Bali (Abad VII-XIV Mahesi).' *Forum Arkeologi* 32, no. 1 (April 2019): 51–62.

Ibn Battuta, and H.A.R Gibb. *Travels in Asia and Africa 1325-1364*. London: Broadway House, 1929. https://archive.org/details/in.ernet.dli.2015.173790/page/n380/mode/1up?q=Java.

Ibn Battuta, and Samuel Lee. *Travels of Ibn Batuta*. London, 1829. https://archive.org/details/in.gov.ignca.21238/page/n7/mode/1up?q=java.

Ikehashi, Hiroshi. 'Domestication and Long-Distance Dissemination of Rice: A Revised Version.' *Rice Research: Open Access* 03, no. 01

(2014). https://doi.org/10.4172/2375-4338.1000128.

Indonesian Heritage Society, ed. *Majapahit, Trowulan*. Jakarta: Indonesian Heritage Society, 2006.

Jakl, Jiří. *Alcohol in Early Java: Its Social and Cultural Significance.* Brill's Southeast Asian Library, Volume 8. Leiden; Boston: Brill, 2021.

———. 'Alcohol in Early Java: Its Social and Cultural Significance.' KILTV, April 12, 2022.

Jakl, Jiri. 'Bhoma's Kitchen: Food Culture and Food Symbolism in Pre-Islamic Java.' *Global Food History* 1, no. 1 (September 2015): 33–57. https://doi.org/10.1080/20549547.2015.11435411.

Jakl, Jiří. 'Liquor in Glass Vessels: A Note on Glassware in Pre-Islamic Java and on Its Socio-Religious Symbolism.' *Archipel*, no. 93 (June 6, 2017): 15–29. https://doi.org/10.4000/archipel.404.

———. 'The Figure of "Pañji" in Old Javanese Sources; What Is in a Name?' *Wacana* 21 (April 9, 2020): 28. https://doi.org/10.17510/wacana.v21i1.874.

———. 'The Loincloth, Trousers, and Horse-Riders in Pre-Islamic Java: Notes on the Old Javanese Term Lañciṅan.' *Archipel*, no. 91 (May 15, 2016): 185–202. https://doi.org/10.4000/archipel.312.

Jakl, Jiri. 'Warriors Killed, Sliced as Cucumber: Food Symbolism in the Martial Arts Scenes of Old Javanese Kakawins.' Nalanda-Sriwijaya Centre, 2013. http://www.iseas.edu.sg/nsc/documents/working_papers/nscwps013.pdf.

Jakl, Jiri, and Tom Hoogervorst. 'Custom, Combat, and Ceremony: Java and the Indo-Persian Textile Trade.' *Bulletin de l'École Française d'Extrême-Orient*, no. 103 (2017): 207–35.

Jasper, J.E. *Tengger and de Tenggerezen*. Weltevreden: Kolff en Co., 1928.

Jatuthasri, T. 'Inao of King Rama II: The Transformation of the Panji Stories into a Masterpiece of Thai Court Drama Literature.' *SPAFA Journal* 2 (2018). https://doi.org/10.26721/spafajournal.v2i0.576.

Johns, Anthony H. 'The Role of Structural Organisation and Myth in Javanese Historiography.' *The Journal of Asian Studies* 24, no. 1 (1964): 91–99. https://doi.org/10.2307/2050416.

Jonker, J.C.G. *Een Oud-Javaansch Wetboek Vergeleken Met Indische Bronnen*. Leiden: Brill, 1885.

Jordaan, Roy E. 'Nicolaus Engelhard and Thomas Stamford Raffles: Brethren in Javanese Antiquities.' *Indonesia*, no. 101 (2016): 39–66. https://doi.org/10.5728/indonesia.101.0039.

Kanwa, and S. O. Robson. *Arjunawiwāha: The Marriage of Arjuna of Mpu Kaṇwa*. Bibliotheca Indonesica 34. Leiden: KITLV Press, 2008.

Kaur, Maganjeet, and Mariana Isa. *From the Bay of Bengal to the Java Sea*. Singapore: Marshall Cavendish, 2018.

Kĕmuling Rat Dyah Atapêng Raje, S. O. Robson, Nigel Bullough, Kĕmuling Rat Dyah Atapêng Raje, and Kĕmuling Rat Dyah Atapêng Raje. *Kidung Pañji Margasmara: A Middle Javanese Romance*. Bibliotheca Indonesica, volume 38. Leiden; Boston: Brill, 2023.

Keputusan Mentri Pendidikan dan Kebudayaan Republik Indonesia. Penatapan Arca Prajnyaparamita Koleksi Musium Nasional Nomor Inventaris 17774 Sebagai Benda Cagar Budaya Peringkat Nasional, Pub. L. No. 251/M/2013 (2013). http://munas.kemdikbud.go.id/ ecargarbudaya/arcaprajnyaparamita251m2013.pdf.

Kern, H. 'De Wij-Inscriptie Op Het Amoghapâça-Beeld van Padang-Tjandi, Door H. KERN (Met Een Plaat.' *Tijdschift Voor Indische Taal-,Land-En Volkenkunde* 49 (1907): 159–70.

———. 'Grafsteenopschrift van Koeboer Radja.' *Bijdragen Tot de Taal-, Land- En Volkenkunde van Nederlandsch-Indië* 67, no. 3 (1913): 401–4.

———. 'Grafsteenopschrift van Koeboer Radja.' *Bijdragen Tot de Taal-, Land- En Volkenkunde / Journal of the Humanities and Social Sciences of Southeast Asia* 67, no. 1 (1913): 401–5. https://doi. org/10.1163/22134379-90001797.

———. 'Het Opschrift van Batoe Beragong Opnieuw Onderzocht.' *Bijdragen Tot de Taal-, Land- En Volkenkunde van Nederlandsch-Indië* 25 (1877): 159–64.

———. 'Levensbericht van J.L.A. Brandes.' *Jaarboek van de Maatschappij Der Nederlandse Letterkunde*, 1906, 31–51.

Kersten, Carool. *A History of Islam in Indonesia: Unity in Diversity*. The New Edinburgh Islamic Surveys. Edinburgh: Edinburgh University Press, 2017.

———. *Islam in Indonesia: The Contest for Society, Ideas and Values*. Oxford: Oxford University Press, 2015.

Kieven, Lydia. 'Candi Jago: The Cap, a New Fashion of Headgear,' 143–59. Leiden, The Netherlands: Brill, 2013. https://doi. org/10.1163/9789004258655_007.

———. *Following the Cap-Figure in Majapahit Temple Reliefs: A New Look at the Religious Function of East Javanese Temples, Fourteenth and Fifteenth Centuries*. Verhandelingen van Het Koninklijk Instituut Voor Taal-, Land- En Volkenkunde 280. Leiden, Boston: Koninklijke Brill NV, 2013. https://brill.com/view/ title/22937.

———. 'Getting Closer to the Primordial Panji? Panji Stories Carved in Stone at Ancient Javanese Majapahit Temples – and Their Impact as Cultural Heritage Today.' *SPAFA Journal*, 2017, 2–24.

———. 'Sanctuaries on Mount Penanggungan: Candi Kendalisodo, Candi Yudha, and the Panji Statue from Candi Selokelir – the

Climax.' In *Following the Cap-Figure in Majapahit Temple Reliefs. A New Look at the Religious Function of East Javanese Temples, Fourteenth and Fifteenth Centuries.* Amsterdam: Brill, 2013. https://www.jstor.org/stable/10.1163/j.ctt1w76vm3.15.

Kinney, Ann R., Marijke J. Klokke, and Lydia Kieven. *Worshiping Siva and Buddha: The Temple Art of East Java.* Honolulu: University of Hawai'i Press, 2003.

Klokke, Marijke. *The Tantri Reliefs on Ancient Javanese Candi.* Verhandelingen van Het Koninklijk Instituut Voor Taal-, Land- En Volkenkunde 153. Leiden: KILTV Press, 1993.

Koek, E. 'Portuguese History of Malacca.' *Journal of the Straits Branch of the Royal Asiatic Society* 17 (1886): 117–49.

Kraton Yogyakarta, and Indonesia Marketing Association, eds. *Kraton Jogja: The History and Cultural Heritage.* 1st ed. [Yogyakarta: Karaton Ngayogyakarta Hadiningrat: Indonesia Marketing Association, 2002.

Krishan, Y. 'The Doctrine of Karma and Śraddhas.' *Annals of the Bhandarkar Oriental Research Institute* 66, no. 1/4 (1985): 97–115.

Krom, Dr. N.J. 'De Begraafplaats van Hayam Wuruk.' *Bijdragen Tot de Taal-, Land- En Volkenkunde van Nederlandsch-Indië* 75, no. 1/2 (1919): 25–27.

———. 'De Familie van Hayam Wuruk.' *Tijdschift van Het Bataviaasch Genootschap* 52 (1910): 158–68.

———. *De Familie van Hayam Wuruk.* Batavia: Albrecht en Co., 1910.

———. 'Eenige Opmerkingen Aangaande Den Val van Majapahit.' *Oudheidkundig Verslag 1915*, n.d., 29–32.

———. 'Engelhard over de Javaansche Oudheden.' *Bijdragen Tot de Taal-, Land- En Volkenkunde van Nederlandsch-Indië* 76, no. 3/4 (1920): 435–48.

———. 'Het Jaar van Den Val van Majapahit.' *Tijdschrift Bataviaasche Genootschap* 55 (1913): 252–58.

———. *Het Oude Java En Zijn Kunst.* 2nd ed. Haarlem: De Erven F. Bohn, N.V., 1943.

———. *Hindoe-Javaansche Geschiedenis.* 2nd-e ed. 's-Gravenhage: Martinus Nijhoff, 1931.

———. *Inleiding Hindoe-Javaansche Kunst I, II and III.* Vol. 1–3. 3 vols. 's Gravenshage: Martinus Nijhoff, 1923.

———. 'Inscripie van Krtanegara van 1188.' *Rapporten van de Commissie in Nederlandsch-Indië Voor Oudheidkundig Onderzoek Op Java En Madoera*, no. 1911 (n.d.): 117–23.

Krom, N. J. 'Oud-Javaansche Oorkonden, Nagelaten Transscripties van Wijlen Drs. J. L. A. Brandes.' *Verhandelingen van Het Bataviaasch Genootschap Der Kunsten En Wetenschappen*, 1913. https://archive.org/details/verhandelingenv601913bata/page/n7/mode/2up.

Kulke, Hermann, and K.W. Taylor. 'Epigraphical References to the City and the State in Early Indonesia, with an Introduction by K. W. Taylor.' *Indonesia* 52 (October 1991): 1–22. https://hdl.handle. net/1813/53959.

Kumar, Ann, John H. McGlynn, Mastini Hardjoprakoso, Perpustakaan Nasional, and Lontar Foundation, eds. *Illuminations: The Writing Traditions of Indonesia ; Featuring Manuscripts from the National Library of Indonesia.* 1. ed. New York, NY: Weatherhill, 1996.

Kusuma, Oktafia, Nanda Nichita, Dhiemas Victoriawan, and Ahmad Naufal Azizi. 'GAYATRI: Mistress behind Political Concept of Monarchy Throne for Democratic People in Majapahit Kingdom.' *6th International Conference on Trends in Social Sciences and Humanities,* September 20, 2019. https://doi.org/10.17758/ERPUB. EA1216217.

Lewis, Mark Edward. *China between Empires: The Northern and Southern Dynasties.* 1. Harvard Univ. Press paperback ed. History of Imperial China. Cambridge, Mass: The Belknap Press of Harvard Univ. Press, 2011.

———. *China's Cosmopolitan Empire: The Tang Dynasty.* 1. Harvard Univ. Press paperback ed. History of Imperial China. Cambridge, Mass.: The Belknap Press of Harvard Univ. Press, 2012.

Leyden, Dr. John. *Malay Annals.* London: Longman, Hurst, Rees, Ormf, and Brown, 1821. http://www.sabrizain.org/malaya/library/ leydenannals3.pdf.

Liebner, Host Hubertus. 'The Siren of Cirebon. A Tenth-Century Trading Vessel Lost in the Java Sea.' University of Leeds, 2014.

Linde, Herald van der. *Jakarta: History of a Misunderstood City.* Singapore: Marshall Cavendish, 2020.

Linehan, W. 'The Kings of 14th Century Singapore.' *Journal of the Malaysian Branch of the Royal Asiatic Society* 42, no. 1 (215) (1969): 53–62.

Liu, Xinru. *Ancient India and Ancient China: Trade and Religious Exchanges AD1-600.* Delhi: Oxford University Press, 1988.

Ludovico di Varthema, and John Winter Jones. *The Travels of Ludovico Di Varthema in Egypt, Syria, Arabia Deserta and Arabia Felix, in Persia, India, and Ethiopia, A.D. 1503 to 1508.* Edited by George Percy Badger. The Hakluyt Society, 1863. https://archive.org/ details/travelsofludovic00vartrich/page/n12/mode/1up?q=java.

Ma Huan, and JVG Mills. *The Overall Survey of the Ocean's Shores.* Cambridge: Published for the Hakluyt Society at the University press, 1433.

Malawani, Mukhamad Ngainul, Franck Lavigne, Wayan Jarrah Sastrawan, Jamaluddin, Ahmad Sirulhaq, and Danang Sri Hadmoko. 'The 1257 CE Cataclysmic Eruption of Samalas Volcano

(Indonesia) Revealed by Indigenous Written Sources: Forgotten Kingdoms, Emergency Response, and Societal Recovery.' *Journal of Volcanology and Geothermal Research* 432 (December 1, 2022): 107688. https://doi.org/10.1016/j.jvolgeores.2022.107688.

Manguin, Pierre-Yves. 'The Southeast Asian Ship: An Historical Approach.' *Journal of Southeast Asian Studies* 11, no. 2 (1980): 266–76.

———. 'Trading Ships of the South China Sea. Shipbuilding Techniques and Their Role in the History of the Development of Asian Trade Networks.' *Journal of the Economic and Social History of the Orient* 36, no. 3 (1993): 253–80. https://doi.org/10.2307/3632633.

Meij, Dick van der. 'Kakawin Sutasoma and Kakawin Nāgara Krtāgama.' *Bijdragen Tot de Taal-, Land- En Volkenkunde / Journal of the Humanities and Social Sciences of Southeast Asia* 167, no. 2–3 (2011): 322–32. https://doi.org/10.1163/22134379-90003596.

Meulen, W. J. van der. 'In Search of "Ho-Ling."' *Indonesia*, no. 23 (1977): 87–111. https://doi.org/10.2307/3350886.

———. 'Ptolemy's Geography of Mainland Southeast Asia and Borneo.' *Indonesia*, no. 19 (1975): 1–32. https://doi.org/10.2307/3350700.

Michell, George. *Hindu Art and Architecture*. World of Art. New York: Thames & Hudson, 2000.

———. *Late Temple Architecture of India, 15th to 19th Centuries: Continuities, Revivals, Appropriations, and Innovations*. First edition. New Delhi: Oxford University Press, 2015.

Miksic, John N. 'Recent Publications on Angkor.' Edited by Jacques Dumarçay, Pascal Royère, Michael Smithies, and M. Matsubara. *Journal of Southeast Asian Studies* 34, no. 1 (2003): 153–58.

Miksic, John N, and Sri Hardiati Soekatno Endang. *The Legacy of Majapahit*. Singapore: National Heritage Board, 1995.

Miksic, John N., and Southeast Asian Ceramic Society, eds. *Southeast Asian Ceramics: New Light on Old Pottery*. Singapore: Southeast Asian Ceramic Society: Editions Didier Millet, 2009.

Miksic, John N., and Anita Tranchini. *Borobudur: Golden Tales of the Buddhas*, 2017.

Milbrath, Susan. *Star Gods of the Maya: Astronomy in Art, Folklore, and Calendars*. 1st ed. The Linda Schele Series in Maya and Pre-Columbian Studies. Austin: University of Texas Press, 1999.

Minattur, Joseph. 'Gaja Mada's Pelapa.' *Journal of the Malaysian Branch of the Royal Asiatic Society* 39, no. 1 (209) (1966): 185–87.

Moens, J.L. 'Het Buddhisme Op Java En Sumatra in Zijn Laatste Bloeiperiode.' *Indische Taal, Land-En Volkenkunde*, no. 64 (1924): 521–79.

———. 'Wisnuwardhana, Vost van Singasari, En Zijn Madjapaitse

Santanapratisantana.' *Tijdschift van Het Bataviaasch Genootschap* 85 (1954): 365–436.

Monaguna, Peter Worsley, S. Supomo, Thomas M. Hunter, Margaret Fletcher, Monaguna, and Monaguna. *Mpu Monaguṇa's Sumanasāntaka: An Old Javanese Epic Poem, Its Indian Source and Balinese Illustrations*. Bibliotheca Indonesica / Koninklijk Instituut Voor Taal-, Land- En Volkenkunde, volume 36. Leiden: Brill, 2013.

Muller, H. R. A. *Javanese Terracottas: Terra Incognita*. Lochem: Tijdstroom, 1978.

Mulyadi, Dr. Ir. Lalu. *Makna Motif Relief Dan Arca Candi Surowono Dan Candi Tegowangi Situs Kerajaan Kadiri*. Malang: Dream Litera Buana, 2018.

Munandar, Agus Aris. *Ibukota Majapahit, Masa Kejayaan Dan Pencapaian*. Jakarta: Kommunitas Bambu, 2008.

———. 'Kedudukan Dan Peran Perempuan Dalam Masa Jawa Kuno: Era Majapahit.' *Jumantara* 6, no. 1 (2015). https://ejournal. perpusnas.go.id/jm/article/view/006001201501/328.

Munoz, Paul Michel. *Early Kingdoms: Indonesian Archipelago & the Malay Peninsula*, 2016.

Muusses, Martha Adraina. *Singhawikramawarddhana*. Weltevreden: Kolff en Co., 1923. https://resolver.kb.nl/resolve?urn=MM KB31:036577000:00001.

Naerssen, F. H. Van. 'De Saptopapatti Naar Aanleiding van Een Tekstverbetering in Den Nagarakrtagama.' *Bijdragen Tot de Taal- , Land- En Volkenkunde / Journal of the Humanities and Social Sciences of Southeast Asia* 90, no. 1 (1933): 239–58. https://doi. org/10.1163/22134379-90001416.

Nguyet, Tutet, Hugo E. Kreijger, Jan Fontein, Marijke Klokke, Nandana Chutiwongs, Pauline L Scheurleer, Jaap Polak, and John Guy. 'Arts of Asia: Majapahit, the Golden Age of Indonesia Late 13th-Early 16th Century.' *Arts of Asia*, December 2000.

Nicholl, Robert. 'Brunei Rediscovered: A Survey of Early Times.' *Journal of Southeast Asian Studies* 14, no. 1 (1983): 32–45.

Nihom, M. 'The Identification and Original Site of a Cult Statue on East Java: The Jaka Dolog.' *Journal of the American Oriental Society* 106, no. 3 (1986): 485–501. https://doi. org/10.2307/602107.

Nihom, Max. 'Ruler and Realm: The Division of Airlangga's Kingdom in the Fourteenth Century.' *Indonesia*, Cornell University Southeast Asia Program, 42, no. 1986–10 (1986): 70–100.

Noorduyn, J. 'Bujangga Manik's Journeys through Java: Topographical Data from an Old Sundanese Source.' *Bijdragen Tot de Taal-, Land- En Volkenkunde* 138, no. 4 (1982): 413–42.

————. 'Concerning the Reliability of Tome Pires' Data on Java.' *Bijdragen Tot de Taal-, Land- En Volkenkunde* 132, no. 4 (1976): 467–71.

————. 'Majapahit in the Fifteenth Century.' *Bijdragen Tot de Taal-, Land- En Volkenkunde* 134, no. 2/3 (1978): 207–74.

————. 'The Eastern Kings in Majapahit, with an Appendix by Brian E. Colles.' *Bijdragen Tot De Taal-, Land- En Volkenkunde Van Nederlandsch-Indië* 131, no. 4 (1975): 479–89.

————. 'The Names of Hayam Wuruk's Sisters.' *Bijdragen Tot de Taal-, Land- En Volkenkunde* 124, no. 4 (1968): 542–44.

Noorduyn, J., and A. Teeuw, eds. *Three Old Sundanese Poems.* Bibliotheca Indonesica 29. Leiden: KITLV Press, 2006.

'Notulen van de Algemeene En Bestuursvergaderingen van Het Bataviaasch Genootschap.' *Bataviaasch Genootschap van Kunsten En Wetenschappen* 10 (1872): 142–44.

O'Brien, Kate. *Sutasoma: The Ancient Tale of a Buddha-Prince from 14th Century Java by the Poet Mpu Tantular.* Bangkok, Thailand: Orchid Press, 2008.

Odorico, and Vincent Hunink. *Mijn reis naar het verre oosten: een verslag uit het begin van de veertiende eeuw.* Amsterdam: Athenaeum-Polak & Van Gennep, 2008.

Olson, Carl. *The Different Paths of Buddhism: A Narrative-Historical Introduction.* New Brunswick, N.J: Rutgers University Press, 2005.

Ooi, Keat Gin. *Southeast Asia: A Historical Encyclopedia, from Angkor Wat to East Timor.* Santa Barbara, Calif.: ABC-CLIO, 2004.

Oudheidkundige Dienst in Nederlandsch-Indie. 'Oorkonden van Trawoelan.' *Oudheidkundig Verslag 1918,* n.d., 109.

————. 'Oudheidkundig Verslag ..., 1913,' n.d., 45–50.

————. 'Oudheidkundig Verslag 1921,' n.d., 28–34.

————. 'Oudheidkundig Verslag 1928,' n.d., 32.

Park, Hyunhee. 'Open Space and Flexible Borders.' In *The Maritime Silk Road,* edited by Franck Billé, Sanjyot Mehendale, and James W. Lankton, 45–69. Global Connectivities, Regional Nodes, Localities. Amsterdam University Press, 2022. https://doi.org/10.2307/j.ctv2x00w7b.6.

Permata, Nabila Mega, Agus Aris Munandar, and Evan Gavriel Harazaki. 'Makna Atribut Istimewa Pada Arca Perwujudan Tokoh-Tokoh Perempuan Majapahit: Kajian Arkeologi Religi Hindu-Buddha.' *Heritage of Nusantara: International Journal of Religious Literature and Heritage* 11, no. 2 (December 13, 2022): 136–70. https://doi.org/10.31291/hn.v11i2.662.

Pigafetta, Antonio, approximately 1480-approximately 1534. *The Voyage of Magellan; the Journal of Antonio Pigafetta.* Englewood Cliffs, N.J.: Prentice-Hall, [1969], 1969. https://search.library.wisc.edu/catalog/999896097802121.

Pigaud, Theodore G. Th. *Javaanse Volksvertoningen*. Yogyakarta: Martinus Nijhoff, 1938.

Pigaud, Theodore G. Th., and H. J. De Graaf. 'The First Islamic States Of Java 15th And 16th Centuries.' In *Islamic States in Java 1500-1700*, 1–24. Eight Dutch Books and Articles by Dr. H.J. de Graaf. Brill, 1976. www.jstor.org/stable/10.1163/j.ctt1w8h12p.4.

Pigeaud, Theodore G. Th and Prapañca. *Java in the 14th Century: A Study in Cultural History : The Nāgara-Kĕrtāgama by Rakawi Prapañca of Majapahit, 1365 A.D.* Vol. I–IV. The Hague: Martinus Nijhoff, 1960. https://doi.org/10.1007/978-94-011-8772-5.

Pires, Tome. *The Suma Oriental of Tomé Pires : An Account of the East, from the Red Sea to Japan, Written in Malacca and India in 1512-1515 ; and, the Book of Francisco Rodrigues, Rutter of a Voyage in the Red Sea, Nautical Rules, Almanack and Maps, Written and Drawn in the East before 1515*, 1512. https://archive.org/details/McGillLibrary-136385-182/page/n327/mode/1up.

Poerbatjaraka, R.Ng. 'De Bijzetting van Kertanegara Te Toemapel.' *Oudheidkundig Verslag 1918*, 1918, 112–15.

———. 'De Dood van Raden Wijaya, Den Eerste Koning En Stichter van Majapahit.' *Tijdschift van Het Bataviaasch Genootschap*, no. 56 (1914): 143–48.

———. 'De Inskriptie van Het Mahaksobhya Beeld Te Simpang (Soerabaya).' *Bijdragen Tot de Taal-, Land- En Volkenkunde / Journal of the Humanities and Social Sciences of Southeast Asia* 78, no. 1 (1922): 426–62. https://doi.org/10.1163/22134379-90001594.

———. 'De Naam van Den Nagarakertagama.' *Tijdschift van Het Bataviaasch Genootschap*, no. 56 (1914): 194.

———. 'De Persoon van Prapanca.' *Oudheidkundig Verslag 1924*, 1924, 151–57.

———. 'Nirartha-Prakreta.' *Bijdragen Tot de Taal-, Land- En Volkenkunde / Journal of the Humanities and Social Sciences of Southeast Asia* 107, no. 2/3 (1951): 201–25.

———. *Niticastra; Oud-Javaansche Tekst Met Vertaling*. Bibliotheca Javanica 4. Bandung: Kon. Bataviaasch Genootschap van Kunsten en Wetenschappen, 1933.

———. 'Oorkonde van Kitarajasa Wit 1296 A. D. (Penanggoengan).' *Inscripties van Nederlandsch-Indie*, 1940, 33–50.

———. *Pandji-Verhalen Onderling Vergeleken*. Bandung: A.C. Nix, 1940.

———. 'Vier Oorkonden in Koper.' *Tijdschift van Het Bataviaasch Genootschap* 76, no. 1936 (1936): 373–90.

Poesponegoro, Marwati Djoened, ed. *Sejarah Nasional Indonesia*. Ed. pemutakhiran. Jakarta: Balai Pustaka, 2008.

Prabowo, A, A Tripena, A Sugandha, and A Riyadi. 'On The Javanese
   Ethnoastronomy: Time Dimension on the Calendrical Inscriptions
   on Majapahit Era until Now.' *Journal of Physics: Conference
   Series* 1179, no. 1 (n.d.): 12159. https://doi.org/10.1088/1742-
   6596/1179/1/012159.

Prapanca, Prof. Dr. H. Kern, and Dr. N.J. Krom. *Het Oud-Javaansche
   Lofdicht Nagarakertagama (1365 A.D.).* Weltevreden: Drukkerij
   Volkslectuur, 1922.

Prapanca, and S. O. Robson. *Deśawarṇana: Nāgarakṛtāgama.*
   Verhandelingen van Het Koninklijk Instituut Voor Taal-, Land- En
   Volkenkunde 169. Leiden: KITLV, 1995.

Pringle, Robert. *A Short History of Bali: Indonesia's Hindu Realm.*
   Short History of Asia Series. Crows Nest, N.S.W: Allen & Unwin,
   2004.

Proudfoot, Ian. 'In Search of Lost Time: Javanese and Balinese
   Understandings of the Indic Calendar.' *Bijdragen Tot de Taal-,
   Land- En Volkenkunde* 163, no. 1 (2007): 86–122.

Pullen, Lesley. 'Hindu Buddhist Java: Examining the Evolution of Dress
   on Sculpture.' 2019. https://www.academia.edu/40636805/Hindu_
   Buddhist_Java_Examining_the_Evolution_of_Dress_on_Sculpture.

———. *Patterned Splendour; Textile Presented on Javanese Metal and
   Stone Sculptures.* S.l.: ISEAS - Yusof Ishak Institute, 2021.

———. 'Worn Textiles of Singasari,' 2019. https://www.academia.
   edu/39824698/Worn_Textiles_of_Singhasari.

Raffles, Thomas Stamford. *The History of Java.* Vol. Vol II. London:
   Black, Parbury and Allen, 1817.

Raffles, T.S. *The History of Java: In Two Volumes.* 2 vols. The
   History of Java. J. Murray, 1830. https://books.google.com.hk/
   books?id=gJEC2q7DzpQC.

Ras, J. J. 'Geschiedschrijving En de Legitimiteit van Het Koningschap
   Op Java.' *Bijdragen Tot de Taal-, Land- En Volkenkunde* 150, no.
   3 (1994): 518–38.

Rassers, Dr W. H. *Inleiding Tot de Bestudeering van de Javaansche
   Kris.* Mededeeling van Der Koningklijk Nederlansche Akademie
   van Wetenschappen. Amsterdam: N.V Noord-Hollandsche
   Uitgeversmaatschappij, 1938.

———. 'Kabajan.' *Bijdragen Tot de Taal-, Land- En Volkenkunde /
   Journal of the Humanities and Social Sciences of Southeast Asia*
   100, no. 1 (1941): 377–404. https://doi.org/10.1163/22134379-
   90001278.

———. 'On the Javanese Kris.' *Bijdragen Tot de Taal-, Land- En
   Volkenkunde / Journal of the Humanities and Social Sciences
   of Southeast Asia* 99, no. 1 (1940): 501–82. https://doi.
   org/10.1163/22134379-90001300.

Reichle, Natasha. *Violence and Serenity: Late Buddhist Sculpture from*

Indonesia. Honolulu: University of Hawai'i Press, 2007.

Reid, Anthony. *A History of Southeast Asia: Critical Crossroads*. The Blackwell History of the World. Chichester, West Sussex: Wiley/Blackwell, 2015.

Rentse, Anker. 'Majapahit Amulets in Kelantan.' *Journal of the Malayan Branch of the Royal Asiatic Society* 14, no. 3 (126) (1936): 302–4.

Reynolds, Craig J. 'A New Look at Old Southeast Asia.' *The Journal of Asian Studies* 54, no. 2 (1995): 419–46. https://doi.org/10.2307/2058745.

Ricklefs, M. C. *A History of Modern Indonesia since c. 1200*. Basingstoke: Palgrave, 2001.

Ricklefs, M.C. 'Babad Sangkala and the Javanese Sense of History.' *Archipel*, 1998, 125–40.

Ringpapontsan, Tenzin Choepak. 'Conquering the Conqueror: Reassessing the Relationship between Qibilai Khan and 'Phags Pa Lama.' The Australian National University, n.d. https://openresearch-repository.anu.edu.au/bitstream/1885/114562/1/Ringpapontsang%20Thesis%202017.pdf.

Robson, S.O. 'Java at the Crossroads; Aspects of Javanese Cultural History in the 14th and 15th Centuries.' *Bijdragen Tot de Taal-, Land- En Volkenkunde / Journal of the Humanities and Social Sciences of Southeast Asia* 137, no. 2–3 (January 1, 1981): 259–92. https://doi.org/10.1163/22134379-90003500.

———. 'Notes on the Early Kidung Literature.' *Bijdragen Tot de Taal-, Land- En Volkenkunde* 135, no. 2/3 (1979): 300–322.

———. 'The Force of Destiny, or the Kidung Harsa-Wijaya Reread.' *Indonesia and the Malay World* 28, no. 82 (November 2000): 243–53. https://doi.org/10.1080/13639810020022724.

Robson, S.O., and Prateep Changchit. 'The Cave Scene: Or Bussaba Consults the Candle.' *Bijdragen Tot de Taal-, Land- En Volkenkunde* 155, no. 4 (1999): 579–95.

Rockhill, W.W. 'Notes on the Relations and Trade of China with the Eastern Archipelago and the Coast of the Indian Ocean During the Fourteenth Century.' *T'oung Pao* 15, 1914. https://archive.org/details/in.ernet.dli.2015.56081/page/n429/mode/1up.

Rossabi, Morris. *Khubilai Khan: His Life and Times*. Berkeley: Univ. of Calif. Press, 1988.

Rouffaer, G. 'Was Malaka Emporium Voor 1400 AD Genaamd Malajoer? En Waar Lag Woerawari, Ma-Hasin, Langka, Batoesawar?' *Bijdragen Tot de Taal-, Land- En Volkenkunde van Nederlandsch-Indië* 77, no. 1 (1921): 1–174.

Sambodo, G.A. 'Prasasti Waruṅgahan, Sebuah Data Baru Dari Masa Awal Majapahit.' *AMERTA* 36, no. 1 (2018): 23–36. https://doi.

org/10.24832/AMT.V36I1.438.

Santiko, Hariani. 'The Goddess Durgā in the East-Javanese Period.' *Asian Folklore Studies* 56, no. 2 (1997): 209–26. https://doi.org/10.2307/1178725.

SarDesai, Damodar Ramaji. *Southeast Asia: Past & Present*. 5. ed. Boulder, Colo.: Westview Press, 2003.

Sardjono, Sandra, and Christopher Buckley. 'A 700-Years Old Blue-and-White Batik from Indonesia' 2022 (August 11, 2022).

Sartono, S, and Bandono. 'The Destruction of Majapahit from the Perspctive of Geology.' In *The Legacy of Majapahit*. Singapore: National Heritage Board, 1995.

Sastrawan, Wayan Jarrah. 'How to Read a Chronicle: The Pararaton as a Conglomerate Text.' *Indonesia and the Malay World* 48, no. 140 (January 2, 2020): 2–23. https://doi.org/10.1080/13639811.2020.1701325.

———. 'Portents of Power: Natural Disasters throughout Indonesian History.' *Indonesia* 113, no. 1 (April 2022): 9–30. https://doi.org/10.1353/ind.2022.0001.

———. 'Raffles as a Historian of Java.' In *Raffles Revisited: Essays on Collecting and Colonialism in Java, Singapore, and Sumatra*, edited by Stephen A. Murphy, Leonard Y. Andaya, and Asian Civilisations Museum (Singapore), 180–93. Singapore: Asian Civilisations Museum, 2021.

———. 'The Precarious Past: Historical Practices in Indic Java.' The University of Sydney, 2021.

———. 'Was Majapahit Really an Empire?' *New Mandala*, January 9, 2020. https://www.newmandala.org/was-majapahit-really-an-empire/.

Scheurleer, Pauline L. 'The Well-Known Javanese Statue in The Tropenmuseum, Amsterdam, And Its Place in Javanese Sculpture.' *Artibus Asiae* 68, no. 2 (2008): 287–332.

Schrieke, B. *Indonesian Sociological Studies: Selected Writings of B. Schrieke*. Ruker and Realm in early Java. Vol. 2. 2 vols. The Hague and Bandung: W. van Hoeve Ltd, 1957.

Sedyawati, Edi. *Gaṇeśa Statuary of the Kaḍiri and Sinhasāri Periods: A Study of Art History*. Verhandelingen van Het Koninklijk Instituut Voor Taal-, Land- En Volkenkunde 160. Leiden: KITLV Press, 1994.

'Selden Map of China.' China, 1629 1620. https://digital.bodleian.ox.ac.uk/objects/58b9518f-d5ea-4cb3-aa15-f42640c50ef3/.

Shaw, Miranda Eberle. *Passionate Enlightenment: Women in Tantric Buddhism*. Princeton, N.J: Princeton University Press, 1994.

Sidomulyo, Hadi. 'From Kuṭa Rāja to Singhasāri: Towards a Revision of the Dynastic History of 13th Century Java.' *Archipel* 80, no. 1 (2010): 77–138. https://doi.org/10.3406/arch.2010.4177.

———. 'Gravestones and Candi Stones. Reflections on the Grave Complex of Troloyo.' *Bulletin de l'École Française d'Extrême-Orient*, 2012, 95–152.

———. 'Krtanagara and the Resurrection of Mpu Bharada.' *Indonesia and the Malay World* 39, no. 113 (March 2011): 123–42. https://doi.org/10.1080/13639811.2010.513882.

Silva Rego, A. da. *Documentação Para a História Das Missões Do Padroado Português Do Oriente: Índia*. Documentação Para a História Das Missões Do Padroado Português Do Oriente: Índia, 第 12 卷. Agência Geral das Colónias, Divisão de Publicações e Biblioteca, 1947. https://books.google.com.hk/books?id=I6jOdpuR57QC.

Sinclair, Iain. 'Vajramahākāla and the Śaivasaugata Rulers of Dharmāśraya and Siṅhasāri.' *Entangled Religions* 13, no. 7 (July 15, 2022). https://doi.org/10.46586/er.13.2022.9678.

Slametmuljana. *A Story of Majapahit*. Singapore University Press, 1976.

Slametmulyana. *Negarakretagama Dan Tafsir Sejarahnya*. Jakarta: Bhratara Karya Aksara, 1979.

Smart, Ninian. *The World's Religions*. 2nd ed. Cambridge; New York: Cambridge University Press, 1998.

Soedjatmoko, ed. *An Introduction to Indonesian Historiography*. 4th printing. Ithaca: Cornell Univ. Pr, 1980.

Soekmono, Ping Amranand, and Peter Schoppert, eds. *Borobudur: Prayer in Stone*. Paris: Ed. Millet, 1990.

Soekmono, R. *Chandi Borobudur: A Monument of Mankind*. Assen: Paris: Van Gorcum; The Unesco Press, 1976.

Soekmono, R. *Pengantar sejarah kebudayaan Indonesia 2*. Cet. ke-17. Yogyakarta: Penerbit Kanisius, 2002.

Soewito-Santoso. *Kresnayana; The Kresna Legend in Indonesia*. New Delhi: International Academy of Indian Culture, 1986.

ST. 'Jayanegara and de Vrouw van Tanca.' *Oudheidkundig Verslag 1924*, n.d., 146–52.

Stapel, F.W. *Geschiedenis van Nederlandsch Indië*. Vol. 1–5. 5 vols. Amsterdam: Joost van den Vondel, 1938.

Stein Callenfels, P.V. van. 'De Graftempel Te Bhayalango.' *Oudheidkundig Verslag 1916*, 1916, 150–57.

———. 'De Leeftijd Der Vosten van Tumapel.' *Oudheidkundig Verslag 1920*, n.d., 107–10.

———. 'Historische Gegevens Uit Balische Oorkonden.' *Oudheidkundig Verslag 1920*, no. 1920 (n.d.): 130–34.

———. 'Plaatsnamen in de Negarakertagama.' *Oudheidkundig Verslag 1917*, no. 1917 (n.d.): 61–64.

Stein Callenfels, P.V. van, and L. van Vuuren. 'Bijdrage Tot de Topografiie van Der Residentie Soerabaia in de 14de Eeuw.'

Tijdschrift van Het Aardrijkskundig Genootschp 41 (1924): 67–75.

Stephen, Michele. 'The Yogic Art of Dying, Kundalinī Yoga, and the Balinese Pitra Yadnya.' *Bijdragen Tot de Taal-, Land- En Volkenkunde / Journal of the Humanities and Social Sciences of Southeast Asia* 166, no. 4 (2010): 426–74. https://doi. org/10.1163/22134379-90003610.

Stephenson, Nina. 'The Past, Present, And Future of Javanese Batik: A Bibliographic Essay.' *Art Documentation: Journal of the Art Libraries Society of North America* 12, no. 3 (1993): 107–13.

Stutterheim, W.F. 'Een Bijzettingsbeeld van Koning Krtanagara in Berlijn?' *Tijdschift Voor Indische Taal-,Land-En Volkenkunde* 72 (1932): 715–26.

———. *Het Hinduisme in Den Archipel.* Vol. 2. Leerboek Der Indische Cultuurgeschiedenis. Groningen-Den Haag-Batavia: J.B. Wolters, 1932.

———. *Oudheden van Bali.* Vol. 1. Singaradja Bali: Kitya Liefrinck-van der Tuuk, 1929.

———. 'Oudheidkundige Aantekeeningen.' *Bijdragen Tot de Taal-, Land- En Volkenkunde / Journal of the Humanities and Social Sciences of Southeast Asia* 89, no. 1 (January 1, 1932): 97–116. https://doi.org/10.1163/22134379-90001431.

———. 'The Arrangement of the Rāma Reliefs of Candi Loro Jonggrang and the Course of the Sun.' In *In Praise of Prambanan*, edited by Roy E. Jordaan, 161–74. Brill, 1996. www.jstor.org/ stable/10.1163/j.ctt1w76w08.13.

Stutterheim, W.F., and R. Goris. *De Kraton van Majapahit.* Vol. 7. Brill, 1948. http://www.jstor.org/stable/10.1163/j.ctvbqs5m3.

Sun, Laichen. 'Imperial Idea Compromised: Northern and Southern Courts Across the New Frontier in the Early Yuan Era.' In *China's Encounters on the South and Southwest: Reforging the Fiery Frontier over Two Millennia*, edited by James Anderson and John K. Whitmore, 193–231. Handbook of Oriental Studies = Handbuch Der Orientalistik. Section 3, Southeast Asia, volume 22. Leiden: Brill, 2014.

Supomo, S. 'Arjunawijaya: A Kakawin of Mpu Tantular,' 1971, 2v. https://doi.org/10.25911/5D70F429E36E5.

Surya, Reggie, and Felicia Tedjakusuma. 'Diversity of Sambals, Traditional Indonesian Chili Pastes.' *Journal of Ethnic Foods* 9, no. 1 (July 7, 2022): 25. https://doi.org/10.1186/s42779-022-00142-7.

Sutherland, Heather. 'Geography as Destiny?' In *A World of Water*, edited by Peter Boomgaard, 27–70. Rain, Rivers and Seas in Southeast Asian Histories. Brill, 2007. http://www.jstor.org/ stable/10.1163/j.ctt1w76vd0.5.

Suwignyo, Agus. 'Indonesian National History Textbooks after the New Order: What's New under the Sun?' *Bijdragen Tot de Taal,*

Land- En Volkenkunde / Journal of the Humanities and Social
Sciences of Southeast Asia 170, no. 1 (2014): 113–31. https://doi.
org/10.1163/22134379-17001008.

Tamalia, Alisjahbana. 'Prabowo Promises Top Priority for Protection of
Majapahit Heritage Site When He Becomes President of Indonesia.'
Independent Observer, November 23, 2018. https://observerid.
com/prabowo-promises-top-priority-for-protection-of-majapahit-
heritage-site-when-he-becomes-president-of-indonesia/.

Teeuw, A., and S. O. Robson, eds. *Bhomāntaka: The Death of Bhoma*.
Bibliotheca Indonesica 32. Leiden: KITLV Press, 2005.

Teeuw, A., and E.M. Uhlenbeck. 'Over de Interpretatie van de
Nagarakrtagama.' *Bijdragen Tot de Taal-, Land- En Volkenkunde
/ Journal of the Humanities and Social Sciences of Southeast
Asia* 114, no. 1–2 (January 1, 1958): 210–37. https://doi.
org/10.1163/22134379-90002276.

Telle, Kari. 'Spirited Warriors: Conspiracy and Protection on Lombok.'
In *Engaging the Spirit World: Popular Beliefs and Practices in
Modern Southeast Asia*, 5:42–61, 2011.

The Strait Times. '13th-Century Relics from Majapahit Kingdom Found
beneath Malacca River.' November 6, 2016, sec. Asia. https://www.
straitstimes.com/asia/se-asia/13th-century-relics-from-majapahit-
kingdom-found-beneath-malacca-river.

'Tijdschrift Voor Neerland's Indië Jrg 3, 1840 (2e Deel) [Volgno 6].
Geraadpleegd Op Delpher Op 26-12-2021, Https://Resolver.Kb.Nl/
Resolve?Urn=dts:2781006:Mpeg21:000,' n.d.

Toer, Pramoedja Ananta. 'My Apologies, in the Name of
Experience.' *Indonesia* 61 (April 1996): 1–14. https://hdl.handle.
net/1813/54076.

Trigangga. 'Tanggal Kematian Ken Angrok.' *Jurnal Musium Nasional
Prajnaparamita*, no. 2 (November 2014): 43–52.

Trigangga, Fifia Wardhani, and Desika Retno W. *Prasasti & Raja-Raja
Nusantara*. Jakarta: Museum Nasional Indonesia, 2015. https://
repositori.kemdikbud.go.id/24363/1/Prasasti%20dan%20raja-
raja%20nusantara.pdf.

Universitas Indonesia. *Laporan Penelitian Arkeologi Terpadu Indonesia
II (PATI II) 2012*. Depok, Jawa Barat: Fakultas Ilmu Pengetahuan
Budaya, Universitas Indonesia, 2008. https://direktorimajapahit.id/
halpustaka/8/1.

———, ed. *Laporan Penelitian Arkeologi Terpadu Indonesia II
(PATI II) 2012*. Depok, Jawa Barat: Fakultas Ilmu Pengetahuan
Budaya, Universitas Indonesia, 2013. https://direktorimajapahit.id/
halpustaka/8/1.

Valmiki, and R.T.H Griffith. *Ramayana*. Trübner & Co., 1870.

Van Setten van der Meer, N. C. *Sawah Cultivation in Ancient Java*,

Aspects of Development during the Indo-Javanese Period, 5th to 15th Century. Oriental Monograph Series, no. 22. Canberra: Faculty of Asian Studies, 1979.

Vanvugt, Ewald. *De schatten van Lombok: honderd jaar Nederlandse oorlogsbuit uit Indonesië.* Amsterdam: Mets, 1994.

Veerdonk, Jan van den. 'Curses in Javanese Royal Inscriptions from the Singhasari-Majapahit Period, AD 1222-1486.' *Bijdragen Tot de Taal-, Land- En Volkenkunde* 157, no. 1 (2001): 97–112.

Verbeek, Rogier D.M. 'De Oudheden van Majapahit in 1815 En 1887.' *Tijdschift Voor Indische Tall-,Land-En Volkenkunde* 33 (1890): 1–15.

Veth, P.J. *Java, Geographisch, Ethnologisch, Historisch.* Vol. 1–3. 3 vols. Haarlem: De Erven F. Bohn, N.V., 1878.

Vickers, Adrian C., Catrini Kubuontubuh, and Peter Carey. 'Majapahit and Panji Stories.' In *Majapahit: Inspiration for the World.*, 47–66. Jakarta: Arsari, 2014.

Vickers, Adrian C., and Yayasan Arsari Djojohadikusumo, eds. *Majapahit: Inspiration for the World.* First edition. Jakarta: Yayasan Arsari Djojohadikusumo, 2014.

Vyāsa, and H Verbruggen. *Mahābhārata.* Den Haag: Mirananda, 1991.

Wagner, Frits A. *The Art of Indonesia.* New York: Greystone Press, 1959.

Wallace, Alfed Russel. *The Malay Archipelago.* London: MacMillan, 1877.

Wei, Yang. 'Admiral Zheng He's Voyages to the "West Oceans."' *Maritime Asia* 16, no. 2 (Fall 2014).

Wessing, Robert. 'A Community of Spirits: People, Ancestors, and Nature Spirits in Java.' *Crossroads: An Interdisciplinary Journal of Southeast Asian Studies* 18, no. 1 (2006): 11–111.

———. 'A Princess from Sunda: Some Aspects of Nyai Roro Kidul.' *Asian Folklore Studies* 56, no. 2 (1997): 317–53. https://doi.org/10.2307/1178730.

———. 'Celebrations of Life: The "Gendhing Seblang" of Banyuwangi, East Java.' *Bulletin de l'École Française d'Extrême-Orient* 99 (2012): 155–225.

———. 'Dislodged Tales: Javanese Goddesses and Spirits on the Silver Screen.' *Bijdragen Tot de Taal-, Land- En Volkenkunde* 163, no. 4 (2007): 529–55.

———. 'Tarumanagara: What's in a Name?' *Journal of Southeast Asian Studies* 42, no. 2 (2011): 325–37.

———. 'Wearing the Cosmos: Symbolism in Batik Design.' *Crossroads: An Interdisciplinary Journal of Southeast Asian Studies* 2, no. 3 (1986): 40–82.

West, A.J. 'Bujangga Manik or, Java in the Fifteenth Century. An

Edition and Study of Oxford, Bodleian Library, MS Jav. b.3. (R).'
Leiden University, 2020.

———. 'Why Did People in Medieval Java Use so Many Different
Script Variants?' In *The Social and Cultural Contexts of Historic
Writing Practices*, edited by Philip J. Boyes, Philippa M. Steele, and
Natalia Elvira Astoreca, 185–208. Oxbow Books, 2021. https://doi.
org/10.2307/j.ctv2npq9fw.15.

Wicks, Robert Sigfrid. *Money, Markets, and Trade in Early Southeast
Asia: The Development of Indigenous Monetary Systems to A.D.
1400*. 2. ed. Studies on Southeast Asia. Ithaca, NY: SEAP, 1996.

Wieder, F.C. 'Kaartbeschijvingen.' In *Encyclopaedie van Nederlands-
Indie*. Vol. 2. 2. 1918, 1918.

Wijaya, Made. *Majapahit Style*. First edition. Sanur, Bali, Indonesia:
Wijaya Words, 2014.

Winstedt, R. O. 'Hikayat Hang Tuah.' *Journal of the Straits Branch of
the Royal Asiatic Society*, no. 83 (1921): 110–22.

Winter, Heinrich. 'Francisco Rodrigues' Atlas of ca. 1513.' *Imago
Mundi* 6 (1949): 20–26.

Wolters, O. W. *Early Indonesian Commerce: A Study of the Origins of
Srivijaya*. Ithaca, N.Y.: Cornell University Press, 1974.

———. 'Restudying Some Chinese Writings on Sriwijaya.' *Indonesia*,
no. 42 (1986): 1–41. https://doi.org/10.2307/3351186.

———. 'Studying Śrīvijaya.' *Journal of the Malaysian Branch of the
Royal Asiatic Society* 52, no. 2 (236) (1979): 1–32.

Worsley, Peter. 'Journeys, Palaces and Landscapes in the Javanese
Imaginary. Some Preliminary Comments Based on the Kakawin
Sumanasāntaka.' *Archipel* 83, no. 1 (2012): 147–71. https://doi.
org/10.3406/arch.2012.4342.

———. 'Southeast Asia in the 9th to 14th Centuries,' 335–68. ISEAS
Publishing, 1986. https://doi.org/10.1355/9789814377935-022.

Wright, Leigh. 'Brunei: An Historical Relic.' *Journal of the Hong Kong
Branch of the Royal Asiatic Society* 17 (1977): 12–29.

Yang, Shao-yun. *A Chinese Gazetteer of Foreign Lands A New
Translation of Part 1 of the Zhufan Zhi* 諸蕃志 *(1225)*. Denison
University, 2023. https://arcg.is/e15vm.

Zahorka, Herwig. *The Sunda Kingdoms of West Java - Glimpses of
History with Archaeological Artifacts and Contemporary Messages*.
Jakarta: Cipta Loka Caraka, 2007.

Zakharov, Anton O. 'The Sailendras Reconsidered.' *Nalanda-Sriwijaya
Centre Working Papers*, no. no.12 (August 2012): 1–38.

Zeeuw, Pieter de. '*De Expeditie Naar Lombok, 5 Juli-24 December
1894 ,1935*. Oosterbaan & Le Cointre, 1935. https://resolver.kb.nl/
resolve?urn=MMKB05:000037388:00005.